Horatio Alger, Jr.

RISEN FROM THE RANKS, OR HARRY WALTON'S SUCCESS

With Essays in Criticism

Annotated with Critical Introduction
by
Park, Ker-yong

Shinasa

CONTENTS

CRITICAL INTRODUCTION

THE TEXT OF *Risen from the Ranks*

Essays in Criticism

Critical Introduction

Horatio Alger, Jr.(1832~1899)의 작품세계와 생애

Horatio Alger, Jr (1832-1899)

I. 아메리칸 드림(American Dream)과 호라시오 엘저 스토리(Horatio Alger Story)

일반적으로 말해서, 아메리칸 드림은 미국이라는 나라가 살기 좋고 성공적인 삶을 제공한다는 꿈에 대한 미국인들의 믿음이고 미국의 믿음이다. 미국에서 살기 위해 세계 각지에서 이민 온 사람들에게 이 꿈은 자유와 평등한 권리를 뜻하기도 한다. 또한 아메리칸 드림은 미국의 관습과 전통으로서 미국에서 누구라도 열심히 일하고 규칙을 지킨다면, 물질적인 부와 사회적인 성공들로 보상을 받을 것이라는 정치적, 사회적, 경제적 사상이자 믿음이다. 대체로 이 꿈은 미국에서 동등한 기회와 자본주의 체제를 지지하며, 또한 일반적으로 자신의 부모들보다 더 성공적으로 될 수 있다는 생각도 담고 있다.

다시 말해서, 아메리칸 드림은 근면, 정직 그리고 결단력을 통해서 누구나 물질적이거나 정신적인 성공을 성취할 수 있다는 많은 미국인들이 믿는 종

종 프로테스탄트 노동윤리와 연관되어 있는 사상이다. 이 꿈은 많은 초기 정착자들이 품고 있었던 가치관이었고 그 이후의 세대들에게 전해져 오고 있는 믿음과 담론의 체계이다. 이 꿈의 실체와 그 수용과정은 끊임없이 거론되는 쟁점이며, 일부는 이 꿈의 실현가능성에 대한 지나친 낙관론을 비판하였고 이 꿈이 물질적 부만을 성공과 행복의 유일한 척도로 강조하는 쪽으로 기울어졌다고 그 문제점을 지적한다. 더 나아가서 이 꿈은 호라시오 엘저 스토리와 마찬가지로 개인의 자립을 지나치게 강조한 나머지 가난한 자들을 비난할 지경으로까지 보수적인 경향으로 흐를 수 있음도 문제시되고 있다.

역사적으로 볼 때, 아메리칸 드림은 정부형태와 경제면에서 구세계의 모델로부터 결별하면서 비롯되었다고 할 수 있다. 이러한 결별은 유럽에서는 전례 없는 자유, 특히 신분과 상관없는 극적인 사회적 수직 상승을 가능하게 하였다. 게다가 독립전쟁 시기부터 19세기 말까지 엄청난 미국의 물질적 자원들은 토지 소유의 가망성과 토지 또는 사업에 투자의 낙관적 전망도 제공하였다. 따라서 아메리칸 드림은 이미 18세기부터 이민의 가장 중요한 추진요소였다고 할 수 있다.

아일랜드의 감자기근, 스코틀랜드 고지대의 개간 그리고 유럽의 여러 지역에서 전제군주의 폭정과 나폴레옹 전쟁의 여파로부터 탈출하려는 가난에 쪼들린 서부 유럽사람들은 고국의 궁핍한 삶으로부터 벗어나기 위하여 미국에 왔다. 그들은 미국에 널리 존재한다고 들었던 물질적 안정과 헌법상의 자유의 보장에 대한 전망에 희망을 걸었던 것이다.

19세기 중엽부터 말까지 번창했으나 그 단순성과 낮은 예술성 때문에 미국문학사에서는 거의 거론되지 않았다가 최근 문화연구 특히 대중문화에 대한 연구가 활성화되면서 주목을 받게 된 싸구려소설(dime novel) 작가인 호라시오 엘저(Horatio Alger, Jr)는 아메리칸 드림을 이상화했던 소설들 즉 호라시오 앨저 스토리(Horatio Alger story)로 유명하다. 의지할 곳 없는 소년들의 출세기 또는 성공담에 관한 그의 소설들은 아메리칸 드림이 미국의 대중문화와 일상 담론에 깊이 뿌리내리는데 큰 역할을 하였다. 이제 그의 소설을 읽는 독자들은 거의 없다고 하더라도, 호라시오 엘저 스토리가 성공담을 뜻하는 일상적 표현으로 사용되고 있는 것은 사실이다.

그러나, 20세기에 아메리칸 드림은 도전을 받고 있다. 1929년부터 시작된 대공황과 30년대의 불황이 역경을 가져왔고, 대공황으로부터 직접 영향을 받은 사람들에게 아메리칸 드림과 호라시오 엘저 스토리는 거의 지난 날의 신화가 되었다. 마크 트웨인(Mark Twain, 1835-1910)과 드라이저(Theodore Dresier, 1971-1945)와 같은 미국의 작가들은 이 성공의 복음이 지나치게 1차원적인 현실 인식을 찬양하기 때문에 거부하였으며, 30년대에는 미국 전역에서 이 복음을 비판하였는데, 특히 웨스트(Nathanael West, 1903-1940)는 『에누리 없는 백만불』(*A Cool Million*, 1934)에서 호라시오 엘저 스토리를 매우 잔인할 정도로 패러디했다. 미국이 호라시오 엘저가 작품에서 강조했던 공화국이기는 하지만 인종차별과 성차별은 여전하였고, 매카시즘과 같은 반민주적 성향도 제거되지 않았기 때문에, 1960년대 히피 가치관을 지지한 새로운 젊은 세대는 아메리칸 드림과 같은 전통적인 가치관을 거부했다.

이 꿈이 가진 미래에 대한 희망적인 전망은 남아있지만, 아메리칸 드림이 여러 면에서 비판의 대상이 되고 있는 것 또한 사실이다. 우선 아메리칸 드림이 지나친 낙관주의와 단순한 현실인식으로 인해 대중을 호도하고 있다는 것이다. 즉, 결단력과 근면만 가지고는 누구나 출세하고 성공할 수 없다는 것이다. 아메리칸 드림의 개념은 또한 성공의 다른 요소들(교육수준의 영향력, 계층화된 사회에서 경제적 유동성의 희박성, 유전적 요소 등)을 무시한다. 특히, 정격유착과 비리가 심했던 도금시대(Gilded Age)인 19세기 후반에서는 누더기를 걸친 호라시오 엘저 스토리의 주인공인 개인주의자가 쉽게 성공할 수 있었는지는 모르지만, 거대한 주식회사, 소득세 그리고 정부의 규제가 있는 20세기에서는 넝마를 걸친 톰이나 구두닦이 딕이 출세하는 이야기는 낭만적인 과거의 추억에 불과하다.

II. 호라시오 엘저의 생애

호라시오 엘저는 130권이 넘는 청소년 소설을 썼던 19세기 후반에 활동했던 미국 작가다. 그의 작품 대부분은 '누더기 상태에서 부자로'(from rags to riches)의 성공담 또는 출세기로 평가되어 왔는데, 이 이야기들은 의지가지없는 가난한 소년들이 근면, 용기, 결단력 그리고 남에 대한 배려를 통하여 부와 성공이라는 아메리칸 드림을 성취할 수 있음을 보여준다. 그는 이제 미국의 문화적이고 사회적인 이상에 관한 역사에서 중요한 인물로 주목된다. 특히 1억부 넘게 팔린 그의 소설들은 공황기인 30년대에 보수적인 정치인들에 의해 대중적인 정치적 선전 도구로 사용되어서 '어려운 시절은 왔다가 가지만 미국은 흔들리지 않는다'는 믿음과 자립철학을 전파하면서 많이 거론되었다.

엘저의 소설은 대부분 거의 공식적으로 반복적인 주제와 플롯을 가지고 있음에도 인기가 있었다. 생존 시에 베스트셀러 작가로서 그의 작품은 인기면에서 마크 트웨인의 작품들과 경쟁할 정도였으며, 미국정신의 형성에 벤자민 프랭크린만큼 영향을 미쳤다고 한다. 또한 마크 트웨인이 19세기 후반부를 정치와 경제가 유착하고 부패한 도금시대(The Gilded Age)로 규정했음에도 불구하고 호라시오 엘저는 개인적 차원에서 사라져가는 산업화 이전 사회의 질서와 성공의 가능성을 꾸준히 설교하였다. 그러나 그가 미국 대중문화에 끼친 영향이 엄청남에도 불구하고 그의 작품은 낮은 예술성 때문에 미국문학사에서 거의 거론되고 있지 않다. 물론 그의 소설들은 확고하게 자리를 잡은 지배계급이 발휘하는 사회통제의 도구처럼 자주 사용되기도 하며, '유명 미국인들의 호라시오 엘저 협회'(Horatio Alger Association of Distinguished Americans)가 1947년에 '호라시오 엘저상'(the Horatio Alger Awards)을 제정하게까지 되었다. 이 상은 정치적 또는 종교적 보수주의와 경제적 정통성의 대의명분에 인정할만한 봉사를 한 사람에게 수여되는 상으로 미국 중등·고등교육기관연합회에서 후원을 하며, 그 수상자들 가운데에는 아이젠하워(Dwight Eisenhower) 대통령, 레이건(Ronald Reagan) 대통령, 그래함(Billy Graham) 목사, 배우 워싱턴(Denzel Washington), 연예인 윈프리(Oprah

Winfrey) 등이 있다. 또 이 협회는 23개주에서 주장학금과 국가 장학금도 1984년부터 수여해 오고 있다.

하버드 대학시절의 엘저(1852)

호라시오 엘저는 임종을 하면서 여동생에게 자신의 모든 편지와 일기 등의 모든 자료를 파기해달라고 부탁하였고 여동생이 이 유언을 받아들였기 때문에, 호라시오 엘저의 생애에 대해서는 그렇게 많이 알려져 있기 않다. 그의 첫 번째 전기는 1928년 허버트 메이즈(Herbert R. Mayes)에 의해 출판되었는데, 메이즈는 엘저에 관한 자료가 없다는 점을 핑계로 순전히 상상력과 추측에 의해 엘저의 전기를 소설처럼 써냈었다.

엘저는 매사추세츠(Massachusetts) 주 첼시(Chelsea)에서 유니테리언(Unitarian) 목사인 호라시오 엘저(Horatio Alger)와 올리브 페노(Olive Fenno) 사이에서 태어났다. 엘저는 10살이 될 때까지 집에서 아버지로부터 교육을 받았으며, 그 후에 매사추세츠주 말보로(Marlborough)에 있는 게이츠 아카데미(Gates Academy)에 입학하였다. 이 학교를 졸업한 1년 후 그는 16세에 하버드 대학교에 입학하였다. 대학 4년 동안 그는 시인이 되려는 꿈을 가지고 롱펠로우(Longfellow) 밑에서 공부를 하였다. 대학교를 졸업한 이후, 그는 교육과 글쓰기에 몰두하였지만 그렇게 성공적이지는 못하였다. 그래서 그는 목사가 될 목적으로 1857년에 하버드 신학대학에 입학하여 1860년까지 공부를 한 후에, 열 달 가량 유럽 여행을 하였다.

1864년 엘저는 케이프 코드(Cape Cod)에 있는 브루스터(Brewster)의 제일교구 유니테리언 교회(the First Parish Unitarian Church)의 목사로 취임하였지만, 1866년에 목사직을 사임하고 그의 아버지가 주임 목사로 있는 싸우스 노틱(South Natick)로 이주하였다. 엘저의 사망 후 교회 기록에 따르면, 그가 그

교구의 어린 소년들과 부적절한 관계를 가졌다는 혐의 때문에, 그는 사임을 하지 않을 수 없었다. 이 불미스러운 범죄에 대하여는 여러 문서들이 그 사실을 입증하고 있다.

1866년 엘저는 뉴욕시로 이사를 갔으며, 그곳에서 그는 싸구려 숙소에 방을 얻고 새 삶을 구상하기 시작했다. 그는 가난한 구두닦이, 신문팔이, 성냥팔이 등의 세계에 즉각 관심을 가지게 되었으며, 그래서 그는 그들과 시간을 같이 보내면서 '신문팔이 소년들의 하숙집'(the Newsboys' Lodging House)에서 숙식을 같이 하기도 하였다. 이 어린 소년들에 대한 그의 동정심과 그가 집에서 배웠던 도덕적 가치가 결합되어서 그의 첫 번째 인기 있는 작품인 『누더기를 입은 딕』(*Ragged Dick*, 1868)의 기초를 만들어냈다. 이 단행본이 연재물보다 더욱 인기를 끌게 되자, "누더기 상태에서 부자로"(the rise from rags to riches)의 주제를 가진 많은 소설들의 탄생을 가능하게 했다. 사실 이 주제는 엘저, 그리고 "호라시오 엘저 스토리"와 동의어가 되었으며, 그 성공의 공식은 행운, 용기 그리고 미덕에 기초를 두었다.

바꾸어 말하자면, 모든 엘저의 초기 소설들은 거의 천편일률적이다. 어린 소년이 근면과 양심적인 삶을 통해 가난에서 벗어나려고 애를 쓰는데, 이 때 그를 구하는 것은 필수적으로 행운이나 부자들의 도움(물론 어린 소년이 먼저 용감하거나 정직한 행동으로 부자들의 인정을 받는 과정이 필요하다)이다. 그리하여 소년은 누더기 상태에서 벗어나게 되는 것이다.

많은 작품을 집필했음에도 불구하고, 엘저는 결코 풍족한 삶을 누리지 못했다. 그에 대한 전설에 의하면, 그는 거의 모든 자신의 돈을 집 없는 소년들에게 주었으며, 어떤 경우에는 이 소년들로부터 사기를 당했다고도 한다. 그의 작품들은 이제는 현실성이 없어 보이는 낙관적인 건전함을 표현했지만, 그것들이 전하는 도덕적 메시지들은 미국의 꿈을 대중화하는데 중요한 요소였다.

III. 『개천에서 용났다: 해리 월튼 출세기』: 아메리칸 드림의 이상화

1874년 출판된 호라시오 엘저의 청소년 소설 『개천에서 용났다: 해리 월튼 출세기』(*Risen From The Ranks or Harry Walton's Sucess*)는 『성공담』(*Bound to Rise: Or, up the Ladder,* 1873)의 후속편이다. 16세인 해리 월튼은 뉴햄프셔주 빈농의 장남이었는데, 그의 아버지가 진 빚 때문에 해리는 가계 부담을 덜고 아버지 빚을 갚을 돈을 벌기 위해 세상에 나아가 일자리를 구하려고 집을 떠난다. 물론 그의 야망은 벤자민 프랭크린(Benjamin Franklin)의 전기를 읽고 결심하게 된 것으로서, 그도 프랭크린처럼 사회에서 존경받는 지위에 도달하고자 한다. 여기서 주목할 점은 해리가 자수성가한 인물로 벤자민 프랭크린을 꼽고 있다는 점과 그가 물질적 성공보다는 존경할만한 사회적 지위를 더 염두에 두고 있다는 점이다.

해리는 잠시 구둣방에 취직했다가 마술사 헨더슨(Professor Henderson)을 만나 그의 조수로서 일하면서 번 돈으로 아버지의 빚을 갚는데 이바지한다. 이제 해리는 자신이 꿈꾸어 왔던 출판업에 취직하기 위해 마술사와 작별하게 된다. 이 때, 마술사는 "요즘은 돈이 가장 큰 유혹이라서 정직이라는 것이 우리가 생각하는 것보다 훨씬 보기 드문 미덕"이라며 해리를 칭찬한다.

이렇게 마술사와 헤어지는 장면으로 시작되는 『개천에서 용났다: 해리 월튼 출세기』는 "개천에서 용났다"(*Risen From The Ranks*)는 영어 제목이 강조하듯이 해리 월튼의 성공담이다. 간단히 요약한다면, 이 작품은 16세의 해리가 작은 마을 신문사의 견습 식자공으로부터 시작해서 근면하고 성실하게 일해서 주변의 인정을 받고 도움을 받아서 19세의 나이에 그 신문사의 공동 소유주일 뿐만 아니라 영향력 있는 편집장의 자리에까지 출세하는 이야기이다.

여기서는 아메리칸 드림에 관한 엘저식의 공식처럼 전형적인 성취과정을 살펴보기 위하여 해리가 성공하고 출세하는 과정을 간단히 단계적으로 요약해보는 것이 필요하다. 우선 해리는 마술사 조수로서의 일자리를 정리하고 벤자민 프랭크린과 같은 인물이 되기 위해, 조그만 마을인 센트레빌에 있는 『센트레빌 가제트』(*Centreville Gazette*)라는 주간신문사에 견습 식자공으로 취직한다.

그는 이 신문사에 취직함과 동시에 유익한 친구를 우연히 사귀게 된다. 그는 근무 후 근처의 언덕에 올랐다가 우연히 그 곳의 사립 고등학교 학생인 오스카 빈센트(Oscar Vincent)를 만나 친구가 된다. 오스카는 첫 눈에 해리의 솔직함에 반해서 해리의 부족한 교육을 보충하는 역할을 한다.

영향력 있는 언론인이 되기에는 너무 무식하다고 생각하는 해리는 오스카를 통해 불어를 배우고, 책을 빌려 읽게 되며, 더 나아가서 프레스코드 고등학교 학생들의 토론 모임에 회원으로 참여하며 결국에는 그 학교의 재학생이 아니면서도 그 모임의 서기직을 거쳐 회장까지 맡게 된다. 또한 엘저의 공식에 따라서 학력 차이와 계급 차이를 뛰어 넘어서 해리를 돕는 오스카의 아버지도 신문사의 식자공에서부터 시작해서 지금은 보스턴의 유력한 신문사 편집장이 되었다는 사실도 밝혀진다.

한편 해리의 직장 선배인 퍼거슨(Ferguson)은 또 다른 면에서 해리의 후원자이다. 결혼을 하여 가정을 이룬 퍼거슨은 근검과 절약의 미덕을 강조하고 해리의 성실함을 높이 평가하면서 해리가 자신의 꿈을 이룰 것이라고 확신한다. 이렇게 엘저의 소설에는 주인공의 정신적, 물질적 후원자들이 많이 등장한다.

반면에 해리 주변에는 오스카나 퍼거슨과 같이 도움을 주는 친구나 직장 선배만 있는 것이 아니다. 해리의 돈을 훔쳤던 루크(Luke)와 해리의 직장 선배인 존 크랩(John Clapp)은 자신들의 직업에 불만을 품고 항상 해리에게 인쇄공은 벌이도 시원치 않고 좋지도 않은 일이라고 투덜댄다.

오스카의 학교 친구인 핏제랄드(Fitegerald Fletcher)도 해리의 직업을 천하게 여기고 그가 가난한 처지에 있는 것을 한껏 조롱한다. 그러나 이들 모두는 해리가 좌절할 정도로 타격을 주지 못하고 오히려 해리가 열심히 일하고 공부하는 계기를 마련해 줄 뿐이다.

이런 상황 속에서 해리는 계속 공부와 독서를 게을리 하지 않았으며, 보스톤에서 발간되는 문예지 『주간 스탠다드』(*Weekly Standard*)를 읽으며 편집인의 꿈을 키워간다. 더 나아가서 해리는 벤자민 프랭크린처럼 가명을 사용하여 '야망(Ambition)'이란 제목으로 글을 써서 주간지에 투고하여 실리게 된다. 이 때, 호라시오 엘저가 강조하는 점은 해리가 결코 천재가 아니라는 사실이다. 즉, 해리의 점진적인 성공은 그가 천재이기 때문이 아니라 그의 근면, 성실함의 결과라는 것이다. 아울러 그가 강조하는 성공은 이기심과 비리·부정의 늪을 피해야 가능하다는 것이다.

해리의 글이 유력한 잡지에 실린 다음 단계의 성공은 해리의 봉급이 오르고 또 그와 동시에 그가 견습공을 끝내고 정식 직공으로 승진하여 이 주간신문에 기사를 쓰게 되는 것이다.

해리의 출세는 이제 순풍에 돛을 단 듯이 점점 더 확실해지고, 그의 영향력도 커져간다. 해리는 보스턴의 오스카 집안에 초대를 받아 오스카 가족들과 친해진다. 그 여행길에 해리는 『주간 스탠다드』를 찾아가 원고를 프랭크린(Frank Lyn)이란 필명으로 투고하여 그 자리에서 원고를 게재하겠다는 약속까지 받아낸다. 더 나아가서 해리는 핏제랄드가 연정을 품고 있는 오스카의 여동생 모드(Maud)의 호감까지 받게 되는데, 그녀는 사람의 출신배경 따위는 중요하지 않다고 여길 정도로 사려가 깊다.

이제 해리는 『주간 스탠다드』의 원고료를 받는 기고가가 되었으며, 절제하고 저축하며 돈도 어느 정도 모으게 되었다. 이때 『센트레빌 가제트』의 편집장이자 소유주인 앤더슨(Anderson)이 요양차 서부에 있는 형의 집에 가는 일이 생기고, 해리는 앤더슨의 인정을 받아서 편집장 일을 임시로 대행하게 된다. 최선의 노력을 하면 성공할 것이라는 퍼거슨의 생각이 입증된 것이다.

이때, 해리는 편집장 대리 역할을 훌륭히 해내서 구독자들도 늘어나게 되었다. 이때 해리는 앤더슨씨로부터 이 주간지를 처분하려는데 인수할 생각이 없느냐는 제안을 받는다. 이제 해리와 퍼거슨은 마술사 헨더슨에게 돈을 일부 빌려서 『센트레빌 가제트』를 인수하여 공동소유자가 된 것이다. 이때 해리의 나이는 불과 19살이었다. 그리고 이들은 열심히 노력하여 그 빚도 12개월 만에 갚게 된다.

그 이후에 해리는 뉴햄프셔 주의회에 진출하고 결국에는 국회의원으로 당선되었으며, 오스카의 여동생 모드와 결혼도 하게 되었다. 그러나 작가가 다시 한 번 강조하듯이 해리는 결코 천재가 아니며 또 결코 부를 목적으로 삼지는 않았다. 그야말로, 근면과 성실 그리고 결단성에 의해 해리는 가난한 농부의 아들에서 국회의원 자리까지 출세한 것이다.

호라시오 엘저의 청소년 소설 대부분의 이미지는 그것들이 자본주의의 번영과 경제적 기회의 확산을 찬양하는 것으로 알려져 있다. 그래서 그의 비판가들이 호라시오 엘저가 미국의 청소년들에게 순전히 물질적인 이상만을 주입시킨 책임이 있다거나 또는 그가 기껏해야 극히 소수에게만 해당하는 성공 신화를 보편화 했다고 비난한다.

반면에 엘저의 소설에 대한 또 다른 해석은 그를 의도적인 시대착오주의자 또는 퇴행적이거나 시대역행적인 작가로 해석한다. 다시 말해서 그는 극적으로 변화하고 팽창하는 시대, 즉 도금시대에 사라져 가는 시대의 가치관을 다시 주장하는 낭만주의자라는 것이다. 그러나 이러한 해석들도 엘저의 소설들이 왜 여전히 미국의 대중문화에서 그리고 미 대통령의 취임사와 같은 정치 담론에서 지배적으로 사용되고 전유되고 있는가는 애써 외면하고 있는 것처럼 보인다.

엘저의 명성은 청소년들에게 교훈적 소설을 쓴 작가에서 진보적인 윤리주의자 그리고 정치적 이데올로그로 변화되었는데, 이러한 변화들은 그의 소설의 내용보다는 그의 작품을 읽는 시대적 정황과 맥락에 의해 결정되었다고 할 수 있다. 이러한 점은 엘저가 오해받은 정체성의 희생자임을 밝혀주지만, 동시에 그가 이렇게 이용될 소지를 가질 만큼 순진한 작가였다는 점도 증명해준다.

IV. 호라시오 엘저의 작품들

- *Voices of the Past* (1849)
- *Fair Harvard (book)* (1852)
- *A Welcome to May May* (1853)
- *Bertha's Christmas Vision. An Autumn Sheaf* (1856)
- *Nothing to Do: A Tilt at Our Best Society* (1857)
- *Nothing To Eat* (1857)
- *Frank's Campaign; or, What Boys can do on the Farm for the Camp* (1864)
- *Marie Bertrand* (1864)
- *Paul Prescott's Charge: A Story for Boys* (1865)
- *Charlie Codman's Cruise. A Story for Boys* (1866)
- *Helen Ford* (1866)
- *Timothy Crump's Ward; or, The New Years Loan, And What Became of It* (1866)
- *Fame and Fortune; or, The Progress of Richard Hunter* (1868)
- *John Maynard: A Ballad of Lake Erie January* (1868)
- *Luck And Pluck; or, John Oakley's Inheritance* (1869)
- *Mark the Match Boy; or, Richard Hunter's Ward* (1869)
- *Ragged Dick; or, Street Life in New York with the Bootblacks* (1868)
- *Struggling Upward; or, Luke Larkin's Luck* (1868)
- *Ralph Raymond's Heir; or, The Merchant's Crime* (1869)
- *Rough and Ready; or, Life Among the New York Newsboys* (1869)
- *Ben The Luggage Boy; or, Among the Wharves* (1870)
- *Rufus and Rose; or, The Fortunes of Rough and Ready* (1870)
- *Sink or Swim; or, Harry Raymond's Resolve* (1870)
- *Paul the Peddler; or the Fortunes of a Young Street Merchant* (1871)
- *Strong and Steady; or, Paddle Your Own Canoe* (1871)
- *Tattered Tom; or, The Story of a Street Arab* (1871)
- *Phil the Fiddler; or, The Story of a Young Street Musician* (1872)
- *Slow and Sure; The Story of Paul Hoffman the Young Street-Merchant* (1872)
- *Strive and Succeed; or, The Progress of Walter Conrad* (1872)
- *Bound to Rise; or, Up the Ladder* (1873)
- *Try and Trust; or, The Story of a Bound Boy* (1873)
- *Brave and Bold; or, The Fortunes of Robert Rushton* (1874)

- *Julius; or, The Street Boy out West* (1874)
- *Risen from the Ranks; or, Harry Walton's Success* (1874)
- *Grand'ther Baldwin's Thanksgiving* (1875)
- *Herbert Carter's Legacy; or, The Inventor's Son* (1875)
- *Jack's Ward; or, The Boy Guardian* (1875)
- *Seeking His Fortune, And Other Dialogues* (1875)
- *St. Nicholas (novel)* (1875)
- *The Young Outlaw; or, Adrift In The Streets* (1875)
- *Sam's Chance; and How He Improved It* (1876)
- *Shifting for Himself; or, Gilbert Greyson's Fortune's* (1876)
- *Life of Edwin Forrest (William Rounseville Alger)* (1877)
- *The New Schoolma'am; or, A Summer in North Sparta* (anonymous 1877)
- *Wait and Hope; or, Ben Bradford's Motto* (1877)
- *The Western Boy; or, The Road to Success* (1878)
- *The Young Adventurer; or, Tom's Trip Across the Plains* (1878)
- *The Telegraph Boy* (1879)
- *The Young Miner; or, Tom Nelson in California* (1879)
- *Tony the Hero* (1880)
- *The Young Explorer; or, Among the Sierras* (1880)
- *From Canal Boy to President; or, The Boyhood and Manhood of James A. Garfield* (1881)
- *Ben's Nugget; or, A Boy's Search for Fortune* (1882)
- *From Farm Boy to Senator: Being the History of the Boyhood and Manhood of Daniel Webster* (1882)
- *Abraham Lincoln: the Backwoods Boy; or, How A Young Rail-Splitter Became President* (1883)
- *The Train Boy* (1883)
- *The Young Circus Rider; or, The Mystery of Robert Rudd* (1883)
- *Dan, the Detective* (1884)
- *Do and Dare; or A Brave Boy's Fight for Fortune* (1884)
- *Hector's Inheritance; or, The Boys of Smith Institute* (1885)
- *Helping Himself; or, Grant Thornton's Ambition* (1886)
- *Frank Fowler, the Cash Boy* (1887)
- *Number 91; or, The Adventures of a New York Telegraph Boy* (1887)
- *The Store Boy; or, The Fortunes of Ben Barclay* (1887)

- *Bob Burton; or, The Young Ranchman of the Missouri* (1888)
- *The Errand Boy; or, How Phil Brent Won Success* (1888)
- *Tom Temple's Career* (1888)
- *Tom Thatcher's Fortune* (1888)
- *Tom Tracy* (1888)
- *The Young Acrobat of the Great North American Circus* (1888)
- *Luke Walton; or, The Chicago Newsboy* (1889)
- *The Erie Train Boy* (1890)
- *Five Hundred Dollars; or, Jacob Marlowe's Secret* (1890)
- *Mark Stanton* (1890)
- *Ned Newton; or, The Fortunes of a New York Bootblack* (1890)
- *A New York Boy* (1890)
- *The Odds Against Him; or, Carl Crawford's Experience* (1890)
- *Dean Dunham; or, The Waterford Mystery* (1891)
- *Digging for Gold. A Story of California* (1892)
- *The Young Boatman of Pine Point* (1892)
- *Cast Upon the Breakers* (1893)
- *Facing the World; or, The Haps and Mishaps of Harry Vane* (1893)
- *In a New World; or, Among the Gold-Fields of Australia* (1893)
- *Only an Irish Boy; Or, Andy Burke's Fortunes and Misfortunes* (1894)
- *Victor Vane, The Young Secretary* (1894)
- *The Disagreeable Woman; A Social Mystery* (1895)
- *Frank Hunter's Peril* (1896)
- *The Young Salesman* (1896)
- *Frank and Fearless; or, The Fortunes of Jasper Kent* (1897)
- *Walter Sherwood's Probation* (1897)
- *A Boy's Fortune; or, The Strange Adventures of Ben Baker* (1898)
- *The Young Bank Messenger* (1898)
- *Jed, The Poor House Boy* (1899)
- *Mark Mason's Victory; or, The Trials and Triumphs of a Telegraph Boy* (1899)
- *Rupert's Ambition (*1899)
- *Silas Snobden's Office Boy* (1899)
- *A Debt of Honor. The Story of Gerald Lane's Success in the Far West* (1900)
- *Falling in With Fortune; or, The Experiences of a Young Secretary* (1900)

- *Out for Business; or, Robert Frost's Strange Career* (1900)
- *Ben Bruce. Scenes in the Life of a Bowery Newsboy* (1901)
- *Lester's Luck* (1901)
- *Nelson the Newsboy; or, Afloat in New York* (1901)
- *Tom Brace: Who He Was and How He Fared* (1901)
- *Young Captain Jack; or, The Son of a Soldier* (1901)
- *Adrift in the City; or, Oliver Conrad's Plucky Fight* (1902)
- *Andy Grant's Pluck* (1902)
- *A Rolling Stone; or, The Adventures of a Wanderer* (1902)
- *Striving for Fortune; or, Walter Griffith's Trials and Successes* (1902)
- *Tom Turner's Legacy* (1902)
- *The World Before Him* (1902)
- *Bernard Brooks' Adventures. The Story of a Brave Boy's Trials* (1903)
- *Chester Rand; or, A New Path to Fortune* (1903)
- *Forging Ahead* (1903)
- *Adrift in New York; or, Tom and Florence Braving the World* (1904)
- *Finding a Fortune* (1904)
- *Jerry the Backwoods Boy; or, The Parkhurst Treasure* (1904)
- *Lost at Sea; or, Robert Roscoe's Strange Cruise* (1904)
- *From Farm to Fortune; or Nat Nason's Strange Experience* (1905)
- *Making His Mark* (1905)
- *Mark Manning's Mission. The Story of a Shoe Factory Boy* (1905)
- *The Young Book Agent; or, Frank Hardy's Road to Success* (1905)
- *Joe the Hotel Boy, or Winning Out by Pluck* (1906)
- *Randy of the River; or, The Adventures of a Young Deckhand* (1906)
- *The Young Musician; or, Fighting His Way* (1906)
- *Ben Logan's Triumph; or, The Boys of Boxwood Academy* (1908)
- *Wait and Win. The Story of Jack Drummond's Pluck* (1908)
- *Robert Coverdale's Struggle; or, On the Wave of Success* (1910)
- *Joe's Luck; or Always Wide Awake* (1913)
- *The Cousin's Conspiracy*
- *In Search of Treasure. The Story of Guy's Eventful Voyage*

V. 참고자료

Alger Jr., Horatio. *Risen From The Ranks or harry Walton's Success.* New York: Media Books, 1972.

Crowther, Jonathan ed. *Oxford Guide to British and American Culture.* Oxford: Oxford up, 1999

Duchak, Alicia. *A-Z of Modern America.* Lodon & New York: Routledge, 1999.

Elliott, Emory ed. *Columbia Literary History of The United States.* New York: Columbia up, 1998

Scharnhorst, Gary & Bales, jack. *The Lost Life of Horatio Alger, Jr.* Bloomington: Indiana up, 1985

Scruggs, Charles. "Framing the Margins" The Social Logic of Postmodern Culture." *African American Review* (Saint Louis Univ, St. Louis) 31:1 (Spring 1997): 130-132.

Yaffe, David. "Go West." *Partisan Review* (Boston Uiv., MA) 66:4 (Fall 1999): 670-674.

TEXT OF
RISEN FROM THE RANKS,
OR,
HARRY WALTON'S SUCCESS

RISEN FROM THE RANKS,
OR,
HARRY WALTON'S SUCCESS.

BY

HORATIO ALGER, JR.,

AUTHOR OF "RAGGED DICK," "TATTERED TOM," "LUCK AND PLUCK,"
"BRAVE AND BOLD" SERIES.

1874.

PREFACE

"Risen from the Ranks" contains the further History of Harry Walton, who was first introduced to the public in the pages of "Bound to Rise." Those who are interested in learning how far he made good the promise of his boyhood, may here find their curiosity gratified. For the benefit of those who may only read the present volume, a synopsis of Harry's previous life is given in the first chapter.

In describing Harry's rise from the ranks I have studiously avoided the extraordinary incidents and pieces of good luck, which the story writer has always at command, being desirous of presenting my hero's career as one which may be imitated by the thousands of boys similarly placed, who, like him, are anxious to rise from the ranks. It is my hope that this story, suggested in part by the career of an eminent American editor[1)], may afford encouragement to such boys, and teach them that "where there is a will there is always a way."

New York, October 1874.

1) 이 작품에서 직간접적으로 언급되는 Benjamin Franklin(1976~90)을 말한다.

CHAPTER I.

HARRY WALTON.

"I am sorry to part with you, Harry," said Professor Henderson. "You have been a very satisfactory and efficient assistant, and I shall miss you."

"Thank you, sir," said Harry. "I have tried to be faithful to your interests."

"You have been so," said the Professor emphatically. "I have had perfect confidence in you, and this has relieved me of a great deal of anxiety. It would have been very easy for one in your position to cheat me out of a considerable sum of money."

"It was no credit[1] to me to resist such a temptation as that," said Harry.

"I am glad to hear you say so, but it shows your inexperience nevertheless. Money is the great tempter nowadays. Consider how many defalcations and breaches of trust[2] we read of daily in confidential positions, and we are forced to conclude that honesty is a rarer virtue than we like to think it. I have every reason to believe that my assistant last winter purloined, at the least, a hundred dollars, but I was unable to prove it, and submitted to the loss. It may be the same next winter. Can't I induce you to change your resolution, and remain in my employ? I will advance your pay."

"Thank you, Professor Henderson," said Harry gratefully. "I appreciate your offer, even if I do not accept it. But I have made up mind to learn the printing business."

"You are to enter the office of the 'Centreville Gazette,' I believe.[3]"

"Yes, sir."

"How much pay will you get?"

"I shall receive my board the first month, and for the next six months have agreed to take two dollars a week and board."

---

1) credit : 명예, 명예가 되는 일. to one's credit: : ~에게 명예롭게도
2) breaches of trust : (법률) 신탁의무 위반, 배임.
3) I believe : 내가 알기로는

"That won't pay your expenses."

"It must," said Harry, firmly.

"You have laid up some money while with me, haven't you!"

"Yes, sir; I have fifty dollars in my pocket-book, besides having given eighty dollars at home."

"That is doing well, but you won't be able to lay up anything for the next year."

"Perhaps not in money, but I shall be gaining the knowledge of a good trade."

"And you like that better than remaining with me, and learning my business?"

"Yes, sir."

"Well, perhaps you are right. I don't fancy being a magician myself[4]; but I am too old to change. I like moving round, and I make a good living for my family. Besides I contribute to the innocent amusement of the public, and earn my money fairly."

"I agree with you, sir," said Harry. "I think yours is a useful employment, but it would not suit everybody. Ever since I read the life of Benjamin Franklin[5], I have wanted to learn to be a printer."

"It is an excellent business, no doubt, and if you have made up your mind I will not dissuade you. When you have a paper of your own, you can give your old friend, Professor Henderson, an occasional puff[6]."

"I shall be glad to do that," said Harry, smiling, "but I shall have to wait some time first."

"How old are you now?"

"Sixteen."

"Then you may qualify yourself for an editor in five or six years. I advise you to try it at any rate. The editor in America is a man of influence."

"I do look forward to it," said Harry, seriously. "I should not be satisfied to remain a journeyman[7] all my life, nor even the half of it."

"I sympathize with your ambition, Harry," said the Professor, earnestly,

---

4) found~ myself : (재귀용법) 나 자신을 ~라고 자부하다.
5) Benjamin Franklin (1706~90) : 미국의 자수성가한 유명한 외교관, 과학자, 출판인, 발명가
6) give~ a puff : ~을 선전하다, ~을 칭찬하다
7) journeyman : 도제로서의 수습기간을 끝낸 직공

"and I wish you the best success. Let me hear from you occasionally."

"I should be very glad to write you, sir."

"I see the stage is at the door, and I must bid you good-by. When you have a vacation, if you get a chance to come our way, Mrs. Henderson and myself will be glad to receive a visit from you. Good-by!" And with a hearty shake of the hand, Professor Henderson bade farewell to his late assistant.

Those who have read "Bound to Rise,"[8] and are thus familiar with Harry Walton's early history, will need no explanation of the preceding conversation. But for the benefit of new readers, I will recapitulate briefly the leading events in the history of the boy of sixteen who is to be our hero.

Harry Walton was the oldest son of a poor New Hampshire farmer, who found great difficulty in wresting from his few sterile acres a living for his family. Nearly a year before, he had lost his only cow by a prevalent disease, and being without money, was compelled to buy another of Squire Green, a rich but mean neighbor, on a six months' note, on very unfavorable terms. As it required great economy to make both ends meet, there seemed no possible chance of his being able to meet the note at maturity[9]. Beside, Mr. Walton was to forfeit ten dollars if he did not have the principal and interest[10] ready for Squire Green. The hard-hearted creditor was mean enough to take advantage of his poor neighbor's necessities, and there was not the slightest chance of his receding from his unreasonable demand. Under these circumstances Harry, the oldest boy, asked his father's permission to go out into the world and earn his own living. He hoped not only to do this, but to save something toward paying his father's note. His ambition had been kindled by reading the life of Benjamin Franklin, which had been awarded to him as a school prize. He did not expect to emulate Franklin, but he thought that by imitating him he might attain an honorable position in the community.

Harry's request was not at first favorably received. To send a boy out into the world to earn his own living is a hazardous experiment,

---

8) *"Bound to Rise"*의 후속편이 이 작품(*Risen from the ranks*)이다.

9) the note at maturity : 어음의 만기, 지불기일

10) principal and interest : 원금과 이자

and fathers are less sanguine than their sons. Their experience suggests difficulties and obstacles of which the inexperienced youth knows and possesses nothing. But in the present case Mr. Walton reflected that the little farming town in which he lived offered small inducements for a boy to remain there, unless he was content to be a farmer, and this required capital. His farm was too small for himself, and of course he could not give Harry a part when he came of age. On the whole, therefore, Harry's plan of becoming a mechanic seemed not so bad a one after all. So permission was accorded, and our hero, with his little bundle of clothes, left the paternal roof, and went out in quest of employment.

After some adventures Harry obtained employment in a shoe-shop as pegger. A few weeks sufficed to make him a good workman, and he was then able to earn three dollars a week and board. Out of this sum he hoped to save enough to pay the note held by Squire Green against his father, but there were two unforeseen obstacles. He had the misfortune to lose his pocket-book, which was picked up by an unprincipled young man, by name Luke Harrison, also a shoemaker, who was always in pecuniary difficulties[11], though he earned much higher wages than Harry. Luke was unable to resist the temptation, and appropriated the money to his own use. This Harry ascertained after a while, but thus far had succeeded in obtaining the restitution of but a small portion of his hard-earned savings. The second obstacle was a sudden depression in the shoe trade which threw him out of work. More than most occupations the shoe business is liable to these sudden fluctuations and suspensions[12], and the most industrious and ambitious workman is often compelled to spend in his enforced weeks of idleness all that he had been able to save when employed, and thus at the end of the year finds himself, through no fault of his own, no better off than at the beginning. Finding himself out of work, our hero visited other shoe establishments in the hope of employment. But his search was in vain. Chance in this emergency made him acquainted with Professor Henderson, a well-known magician and conjurer, whose custom it was to travel, through the fall and winter, from town to town, giving public exhibitions

11) in pecuniary difficulties : 금전상의 곤란에 처해있는
12) fluctuations and suspensions : (경기의) 동요와 부유

of his skill. He was in want of an assistant, to sell tickets and help him generally, and he offered the position to our hero, at a salary of five dollars a week. It is needless to say that the position was gladly accepted. It was not the business that Harry preferred, but he reasoned justly that it was honorable, and was far better than remaining idle. He found Professor Henderson as he called himself, a considerate and agreeable employer, and as may be inferred from the conversation with which this chapter begins, his services were very satisfactory. At the close of the six months, he had the satisfaction of paying the note[13] which his father had given, and so of disappointing the selfish schemes of the grasping creditor.

This was not all. He met with an adventure while travelling for the Professor, in which a highwayman who undertook to rob him, came off second best[14], and he was thus enabled to add fifty dollars to his savings. His financial condition at the opening of the present story has already been set forth.

Though I have necessarily omitted many interesting details, to be found in "Bound to Rise," I have given the reader all the information required to enable him to understand the narrative of Harry's subsequent fortunes.

---

13) the satisfaction of paying the note : 어음 지불의 이행
14) came off second best : 차선책으로 도망갈 수밖에 없었다.

CHAPTER II.

THE PRINTING OFFICE.

Jotham Anderson, editor and publisher of the "Centreville Gazette," was sitting at his desk penning an editorial paragraph, when the office door opened, and Harry Walton entered.

"Good-morning, Mr. Anderson," said our hero, removing his hat.

"Good-morning, my friend. I believe you have the advantage of me[1]," replied the editor.

Our hero was taken aback[2]. It didn't occur to him that the engagement was a far less important event to the publisher than to himself. He began to be afraid that the place had not been kept open for him.

"My name is Harry Walton," he explained. "I was travelling with Prof. Henderson last winter, and called here to get some bills printed."

"Oh yes, I remember you now. I agreed to take you into the office," said the editor, to Harry's great relief.

"Yes, sir."

"You haven't changed your mind, then?—You still want to be a printer?"

"Yes, sir."

"You have left the Professor, I suppose."

"I left him yesterday."

"What did he pay you?"

"Five dollars a week. He offered me six, if I would stay with him."

"Of course you know that I can't pay you any such wages at present."

"Yes, sir. You agreed to give me my board the first month, and two dollars a week for six months afterward."

"That is all you will be worth to me at first. It is a good deal less than you would earn with Professor Henderson."

"I know that, sir; but I am willing to come for that."

"Good. I see you are in earnest about printing, and that is a good

---

1) I believe you advantage of me : 누구시더라? (상대방은 알고 있는데, 이쪽은 상대방이 누구인지 모른다.)

2) ~was taken aback : 허를 찔리다, 깜짝 놀라다.

sign. I wanted you to understand just what you had to expect, so that you need not be disappointed."

"I sha'n't be disappointed, sir," said Harry confidently. "I have made up my mind to be a printer, and if you didn't receive me into your office, I would try to get in somewhere else."

"Then no more need be said. When do you want to begin?"

"I am ready any time."

"Where is your trunk?"

"At the tavern."

"You can have it brought over to my house whenever you please. The hotel-keeper will send it over for you. He is our expressman. Come into the house now, and I will introduce you to my wife."

The editor's home was just across the street from his printing office. Followed by Harry he crossed the street, opened the front door, and led the way into the sitting-room, where a pleasant-looking lady of middle age was seated.

"My dear," he said, "I bring you a new boarder."

She looked at Harry inquiringly.

"This young man," her husband explained, "is going into the office to learn printing. I have taken a contract to make a second Benjamin Franklin of him."[3)]

"Then you'll do more for him than you have been able to do for yourself," said Mrs. Anderson, smiling.

"You are inclined to be severe, Mrs. Anderson, but I fear you are correct. However, I can be like a guide-post, which points the way which it does not travel. Can you show Harry Walton—for that is his name—where you propose to put him?"

"I am afraid I must give you a room in the attic," said Mrs. Anderson. "Our house is small, and all the chambers on the second floor are occupied."

"I am not at all particular,"[4)] said Harry. "I have not been accustomed to elegant accommodations."

"If you will follow me upstairs, I will show you your room."

---

3) ~to make a second Benjamin Franklin of him : 그를 제 2의 벤자민 프랭크린으로 만들기로.
4) particular : 까다로운, 유별난

Pausing on the third landing, Mrs. Anderson found the door of a small but comfortable bed-room. There was no carpet on the floor, but it was painted yellow, and scrupulously clean. A bed, two chairs, a bureau and wash-stand completed the list of furniture.

"I shall like this room very well," said our hero.

"There is a closet," said the lady, pointing to a door in the corner. "It is large enough to contain your trunk, if you choose to put it in there. I hope you don't smoke."

"Oh, no, indeed," said Harry, laughing. "I haven't got so far along as that."[5)]

"Mr. Anderson's last apprentice—he is a journeyman now—was a smoker. He not only scented up the room, but as he was very careless about lights, I was continually alarmed lest he should set the house on fire. Finally, I got so nervous that I asked him to board somewhere else."

"Is he working for Mr. Anderson now?"

"Yes; you probably saw him in the office."

"I saw two young men at the case[6)]."

"The one I speak of is the youngest. His name is John Clapp."

"There is no danger of my smoking. I don't think it would do me any good. Besides, it is expensive, and I can't afford it."

"I see we think alike," said Mrs. Anderson, smiling. "I am sure we will get along well together."

"I shall try not to give you any trouble," said our hero, and his tone, which was evidently sincere, impressed Mrs. Anderson still more favorably.

"You won't find me very hard to suit, I hope. I suppose you will be here to supper?"

"If it will be quite convenient. My trunk is at the tavern, and I could stay there till morning, if you wished."

"Oh, no, come at once. Take possession of the room now, if you like, and leave an order to have your trunk brought here."

"Thank you. What is your hour for supper?"

"Half-past five."

---

5) get~ along : 나이를 먹다.

6) the case : (인쇄) 식자용 상자 (활자 케이스)

"Thank you. I will go over and speak to Mr. Anderson a minute."

The editor looked up as Harry reappeared.

"Well, have you settled arrangements with Mrs. Anderson?" he asked.

"Yes, sir, I believe so."

"I hope you like your room."

"It is very comfortable. It won't take me long to feel at home there."

"Did she ask you whether you smoked?"

"Yes, sir."

"I thought she would. That's where Clapp and she fell out."

Harry's attention was drawn to a thin, sallow young man of about twenty, who stood at a case on the opposite side of the room.

"Mrs. Anderson was afraid I would set the house on fire," said the young man thus referred to.

"Yes, she felt nervous about it. However, it is not surprising. An uncle of hers lost his house in that way. I suppose you don't smoke, Walton?"

"No, sir."

"Clapp smokes for his health. You see how stout and robust he is," said the editor, a little satirically.

"It doesn't do me any harm," said Clapp, a little testily.

"Oh, well, I don't interfere with you, though I think you would be better off if you should give up the habit. Ferguson don't smoke."

This was the other compositor, a man of thirty, whose case was not far distant from Clapp's.

"I can't afford it," said Ferguson; "nor could Clapp, if he had a wife and two young children to support."

"Smoking doesn't cost much," said the younger journeyman.

"So you think; but did you ever reckon it up?"

"No."

"Don't you keep any accounts?[7)]"

"No; I spend when I need to, and I can always tell how much I have left. What's the use of keeping accounts?"

"You can tell how you stand[8)]."

"I can tell that without taking so much trouble."

---

7) keep accounts : 장부를 적다.
8) stand : 생계를 유지하다.

"You see we must all agree to disagree," said Mr. Anderson. "I am afraid Clapp isn't going to be a second Benjamin Franklin."

"Who is?" asked Clapp.

"Our young friend here," said the editor.

"Oh, is he?" queried the other with a sneer. "It'll be a great honor I'm sure, to have him in the office."

"Come[9], no chaffing, Clapp," said Mr. Anderson.

Harry hastened to disclaim the charge, for Clapp's sneer affected him disagreeably.

"I admire Franklin," he said, "but there isn't much danger of my turning out a second edition of him.[10]"

"Professional already, I see, Walton," said the editor.

"When shall I go to work, Mr. Anderson?"

"Whenever you are ready."

"I am ready now."

"You are prompt."

"You won't be in such a hurry to go to work a week hence," said Clapp.

"I think I shall," said Harry. "I am anxious to learn as fast as possible."

"Oh, I forgot. You want to become a second Franklin."

"I sha'n't like him," thought our hero. "He seems to try to make himself disagreeable."

"Mr. Ferguson will give you some instruction, and set you to work," said his employer.

Harry was glad that it was from the older journeyman that he was to receive his first lesson, and not from the younger.

---

9) come : 자, 이봐.

10) a second edition of him : 벤자민 프랭크린의 2판, 즉 그를 꼭 빼닮은 사람.

CHAPTER III.

HARRY STUMBLES UPON AN ACQUAINTANCE.

After supper Harry went round to the tavern to see about his trunk. A group of young men were in the bar-room, some of whom looked up as he entered. Among these was Luke Harrison, who was surprised and by no means pleased to see his creditor. Harry recognized him at the same instant, and said, "How are you, Luke?"

"Is that you, Walton?" said Luke. "What brings you to Centreville? Professor Henderson isn't here, is he?"

"No; I have left him."

"Oh, you're out of a job, are you?" asked Luke, in a tone of satisfaction, for we are apt to dislike those whom we have injured, and for this reason he felt by no means friendly.

"No, I'm not," said Harry, quietly. "I've found work in Centreville."

"Gone back to pegging, have you? Whose shop are you in?"

"I am in a different business."

"You don't say![11] What is it?" asked Luke, with some curiosity.

"I'm in the office of the 'Centreville Gazette.' I'm going to learn the printing business."

"You are? Why[12], I've got a friend in the office,—John Clapp. He never told me about your being there."

"He didn't know I was coming. I only went to work this afternoon."

"So you are the printer's devil[13]?" said Luke, with a slight sneer.

"I believe so," answered our hero, quietly.

"Do you get good pay?"

"Not much at first. However, I can get along with what money I have, *and what is due me*."

Luke Harrison understood the last allusion, and turned away abruptly. He had no wish to pay up the money which he owed Harry, and for this reason was sorry to see him in the village. He feared, if the

---

11) you don't say! : you don't say that again! 너의 말대로다.

12) why : (새로운 사태를 발견하고 놀라서) 아니! 어마!

13) the printer's devil : 인쇄소의 견습.

conversation were continued, Harry would be asking for the money, and this would be disagreeable.

At this moment John Clapp entered the bar-room. He nodded slightly to Harry, but walked up to Luke, and greeted him cordially. There were many points of resemblance between them, and this drew them into habits of intimacy.

"Will you have something to drink, Harrison?" said Clapp.

"I don't mind if I do," answered Luke, with alacrity.

They walked up to the bar, and they were soon pledging each other in a fiery fluid[14)] which was not very likely to benefit either of them. Meanwhile Harry gave directions about his trunk, and left the room.

"So you've got a new 'devil' in your office," said Luke, after draining his glass.

"Yes. He came this afternoon. How did you hear?"

"He told me."

"Do you know him?" asked Clapp, in some surprise.

"Yes. I know him as well as I want to."

"What sort of a fellow is he?"

"Oh, he's a sneak—one of your pious chaps, that 'wants to be an angel, and with the angels stand.'"

"Then he's made a mistake in turning 'devil,'" said Clapp.

"Good for you!"[15)] said Luke, laughing. "You're unusually brilliant to-night, Clapp."

"So he's a saint, is he?"

"He set up for one[16)]; but I don't like his style myself. He's as mean as dirt. Why I knew him several months, and he never offered to treat in all that time. He's as much afraid of spending a cent as if it were a dollar."

"He won't have many dollars to spend just at present. He's working for his board."

"Oh, he's got money saved up," said Luke. "Fellows like him hang on to a cent when they get it. I once asked him to lend me a few dollars, just for a day or two, but he wouldn't do it. I hate such mean fellows."

---

14) fiery fluid : 독한 술

15) Good for you! : 좋았어! 됐다!

16) He set up for one : 그는 성자인 척한다.

"So do I. Will you have a cigar?"

"I'll treat this time," said Luke, who thought it polite to take his turn in treating once to his companion's four or five times.

"Thank you. From what you say, I am sorry Anderson has taken the fellow into the office."

"You needn't have much to say to him."

"I shan't trouble myself much about him. I didn't like his looks when I first set eyes on him. I suppose old Mother Anderson will like him. She couldn't abide my smoking, and he won't trouble her that way."

"So; he's too mean to buy the cigars."

"He said he couldn't afford it."

"That's what it comes to. By the way, Clapp, when shall we take another ride?"

"I can get away next Monday afternoon, at three."

"All right. I'll manage to get off at the same time. We'll go to Whiston and take supper at the hotel. It does a fellow good to get off now and then. It won't cost more than five dollars apiece altogether."

"We'll get the carriage charged. The fact is, I'm little low on funds."

"So am I, but it won't matter. Griffin will wait for his pay."

While Harry's character was being so unfavorably discussed, he was taking a walk by himself, observing with interest the main features of his new home. He had been here before with Professor Henderson, but had been too much occupied at that time to get a very clear idea of Centreville, nor had it then the interest for him which it had acquired since. He went upon a hill overlooking the village, and obtained an excellent view from its summit. It was a pleasant, well-built village of perhaps three thousand inhabitants, with outlying farms and farm-houses. Along the principal streets the dwellings and stores were closely built, so as to make it seem quite city-like. It was the shire town of the county[17], and being the largest place in the neighborhood, country people for miles around traded at its stores. Farmers' wives came to Centreville to make purchases, just as ladies living within a radius of thirty miles visit New York and Boston, for a similar purpose. Altogether, therefore, Centreville was quite a lively place, and a town of considerable local importance.

---

17) county : 군(주 다음가는 행정구역), shire도 county와 같은 뜻.

The fact that it had a weekly paper of its own, contributed to bring it into notice. Nor was that all. Situated on a little hillock was a building with a belfry, which might have been taken for a church but for a play-ground near by, which indicated that it had a different character. It was in fact the Prescott Academy,[18] so called from the name of its founder, who had endowed it with a fund of ten thousand dollars, besides erecting the building at his own expense on land bought for the purpose. This academy also had a local reputation, and its benefits were not confined to the children of Centreville. There were about twenty pupils from other towns who boarded with the Principal or elsewhere in the town, and made up the whole number of students in attendance—about eighty on an average.

Standing on the eminence referred to, Harry's attention was drawn to the Academy, and he could not help forming the wish that he, too, might share in its advantages.

"There is so much to learn, and I know so little," he thought.

But he did not brood over the poverty which prevented him from gratifying his desire. He knew it would do no good, and he also reflected that knowledge may be acquired in a printing office as well as within the walls of an academy or college.

"As soon as I get well settled," he said to himself, "I mean to get some books and study a little every day. That is the way Franklin did. I never can be an editor, that's certain, without knowing more than I do now. Before I am qualified to teach others, I must know something myself."

Looking at the village which lay below him, Harry was disposed to congratulate himself on his new residence.

"It looks like a pleasant place," he said to himself, "and when I get a little acquainted, I shall enjoy myself very well, I am sure. Of course I shall feel rather lonely just at first."

He was so engrossed by his thoughts that he did not take heed to[19] his steps, and was only reminded of his abstraction by his foot suddenly coming in contact with a boy who was lying under a tree, and pitching

18) Academy : 사립(중)고등학교
19) ~take heed to~ : ~에 주의를 돌리다.

headfirst over him.

"Holloa!" exclaimed the latter, "what are you about? You didn't take me for a foot-ball, did you?"

"I beg your pardon," said Harry, jumping up in some confusion. "I was so busy thinking that I didn't see you. I hope I didn't hurt you."

"Nothing serious. Didn't you hurt yourself?"

"I bumped my head a little, but it only struck the earth. If it had been a stone, it might have been different. I had no idea there was any one up here except myself."

"It was very kind of you to bow so low to a perfect stranger," said the other, his eyes twinkling humorously. "I suppose it would only be polite for me to follow your example."

"I'll excuse you," said Harry laughing.

"Thank you. That takes a great burden off my mind. I don't like to be outdone in politeness, but really I shouldn't like to tumble over you. My head may be softer than yours. There's one thing clear. We ought to know each other. As you've taken the trouble to come up here, and stumble over me, I really feel as if we ought to strike up a friendship.[20] What do you say?"

"With all my heart," said our hero.

20) ~strike up a friendship : 교제를 시작하다.

CHAPTER IV.

OSCAR VINCENT.

"Allow me to introduce myself," said the stranger boy. "My name is Oscar Vincent, from Boston, at present a student at the Prescott Academy, at your service."[1)]

As he spoke, he doffed his hat and bowed, showing a profusion of chestnut hair, a broad, open brow, and an attractive face, lighted up by a pleasant smile.

Harry felt drawn to him by a feeling which was not long in ripening into friendship.

Imitating the other's frankness, he also took off his hat and replied,—

"Let me introduce myself, in turn, as Harry Walton, junior apprentice in the office of the 'Centreville Gazette,' sometimes profanely called 'printer's devil.'"

"Good!"[2)] said Oscar, laughing. "How do you like the business?"

"I think I shall like it, but I have only just started in it. I went into the office for the first time to-day."

"I have an uncle who started as you are doing," said Oscar. "He is now chief editor of a daily paper in Boston."

"Is he?" said Harry, with interest. "Did he find it hard to rise?"

"He is a hard worker. I have heard him say that he used to sit up late of nights during his apprenticeship, studying and improving himself."

"That is what I mean to do," said Harry.

"I don't think he was as lazy as his nephew," said Oscar. "I am afraid if I had been in his place I should have remained in it."

"Are you lazy?" asked Harry, smiling at the other's frankness.

"A little so; that is, I don't improve my opportunities as I might. Father wants to make a lawyer of me so he has put me here, and I am preparing for Harvard."

"I envy you," said Harry. "There is nothing I should like so much

---

1) at your service : I am at your service. 무슨 일이든 시켜주세요. (솔직하고 친절한 답변)
2) Good! : 만족, 찬성, 놀람을 나타내는 표현.

as entering college."

"I daresay I shall like it tolerably well," said Oscar; "but I don't *hanker* after it, as the boy said after swallowing a dose of castor oil. I'll tell you what I should like better—"

"What?" asked Harry, as the other paused.

"I should like to enter the Naval Academy, and qualify myself for the naval service. I always liked the sea."

"Doesn't your father approve of your doing this?"

"He wouldn't mind my entering the navy as an officer, but he is not willing to have me enter the merchant service."

"Then why doesn't he send you to the Naval Academy?[3)]"

"Because I can't enter without receiving the appointment from a member of Congress. Our member[4)] can only appoint one, and there is no vacancy. So, as I can't go where I want to, I am preparing for Harvard."

"Are you studying Latin and Greek?"

"Yes."

"Have you studied them long?"

"About two years. I was looking over my Greek lesson when you playfully tumbled over me."

"Will you let me look at your book? I never saw a Greek book."

"I sometimes wish I never had," said Oscar; "but that's when I am lazy."

Harry opened the book—a Greek reader—in the middle of an extract from Xenophon, and looked with some awe at the unintelligible letters.

"Can you read it? Can you understand what it means?" he asked, looking up from the book.

"So-so.[5)]"

"You must know a great deal."

Oscar laughed.

"I wonder what Dr. Burton would say if he heard you," he said.

"Who is he?"

"Principal of our Academy. He gave me a blowing up[6)] for my ignorance

---

3) the Naval Academy : 해군사관학교
4) member : 국회의원
5) so~ so : 그저 그래.
6) blow up : 야단치다.

to-day, because I missed an irregular Greek verb. I'm not exactly a dunce, but I don't think I shall ever be a Greek professor."

"If you speak of yourself that way, what will you think of me? I don't know a word of Latin, of Greek, or any language except my own."

"Because you have had no chance to learn. There's one language I know more about than Latin or Greek."

"English?"

"I mean French; I spent a year at a French boarding-school, three years since."

"What! Have you been in France?"

"Yes; an uncle of mine—in fact, the editor—was going over, and urged father to send me. I learned considerable French, but not much else. I can speak and understand it pretty well."

"How I wish I had had your advantages," said Harry. "How did you like your French schoolmates?"

"They wouldn't come near me at first. Because I was an American they thought I carried a revolver and a dirk-knife, and was dangerous. That is their idea of American boys. When they found I was tame, and carried no deadly weapons, they ventured to speak with me, and after that we got along pretty well."

"How soon do you expect to go to college?"

"A year from next summer. I suppose I shall be ready by that time. You are going to stay in town, I suppose?"

"Yes, if I keep my place."

"Oh, you'll do that. Then we can see something of each other. You must come up to my room, and see me. Come almost any evening."

"I should like to. Do you live in Dr. Barton's family?"

"No, I hope not."

"Why not?"

"Oh, the Doctor has a way of looking after the fellows that room[7] in the house, and of keeping them at work all the time. That wouldn't suit me. I board at Mrs. Greyson's, at the south-east corner of the church common[8]. Have you got anything to do this evening?"

---

7) room : 기숙(하숙)하다.

8) common : 공유지

"Nothing in particular."

"Then come round and take a look at my den[9], or sanctum[10] I ought to call it; as I am talking to a member of the editorial profession."

"Not quite yet," said Harry, smiling.

"Oh, well that'll come in due time. Will you come?"

"Sha'n't I be disturbing you?"

"Not a bit. My Greek lesson is about finished, and that's all I've got to do this evening. Come round, and we will sit over the fire, and chat like old friends."

"Thank you, Oscar," said Harry, irresistibly attracted by his bright and lively acquaintance, "I shall enjoy calling. I have made no acquaintances yet, and I feel lonely."

"I have got over that," said Oscar. "I am used to being away from home and don't mind it."

The two boys walked together to Oscar's boarding-place. It was a large house, of considerable pretension[11] for a village, and Oscar's room was large and handsomely furnished. But what attracted Harry's attention was not the furniture, but a collection of over a hundred books, ranged on shelves at one end of the room. In his father's house it had always been so difficult to obtain the necessaries of life that books had necessarily been regarded as superfluities[12], and beyond a dozen volumes which Harry had read and re-read, he was compelled to depend on such as he could borrow. Here again his privileges were scanty, for most of the neighbors were as poorly supplied as his father.

"What a fine library you have, Oscar!" he exclaimed.

"I have a few books," said Oscar. "My father filled a couple of boxes, and sent me. He has a large library."

"This seems a large library to me," said Harry. "My father likes reading, but he is poor, and cannot afford to buy books."

He said that in a matter-of-fact tone, without the least attempt to conceal what many boys would have been tempted to hide. Oscar noted this, and liked his new friend the better for it.

---

9) den : 누추한 집
10) sanctum : 서재, 개인 방
11) pretension : 자부 즉, 상당히 자랑거리가 될 만한 건물
12) superfluities : 사치품

"Yes," he said, "books cost money, and one hasn't always the money to spare."

"Have you read all these books?"

"Not more than half of them. I like reading better than studying, I am afraid. I am reading the Waverley novels[13] now. Have you read any of them?"

"No; I never saw any of them before."

"If you see anything you would like to read, I will lend it to you with pleasure," said Oscar, noticing the interest with which Harry regarded the books.

"Will you?" said Harry, eagerly. "I can't tell you how much obliged I am. I will take good care of it."

"Oh, I am sure of that. Here, try Ivanhoe[14]. I've just read it, and it's tip-top."

"Thank you; I will take it on your recommendation. What a nice room you have!"

"Yes, it's pretty comfortable. Father told me to fix it up to suit me. He said he wouldn't mind the expense if I would only study."

"I should think anybody might study in such a room as this, and with such a fine collection of books."

"I'm rather lazy sometimes," said Oscar, "but I shall turn over a new leaf[15] some of these days, and astonish everybody. To-night, as I have no studying to do, I'll tell you what we'll do. Did you ever pop corn?"

"Sometimes."

"I've got some corn here, and Ma'am Greyson has a popper. Stay here alone a minute, and I'll run down and get it."

Oscar ran down stairs, and speedily returned with a corn-popper.

"Now we'll have a jolly time," said he. "Draw up that arm-chair, and make yourself at home. If Xenophon, or Virgil[16], or any of those Greek and Latin chaps call, we'll tell 'em we are transacting important

---

13) the Waverley novels : 영국의 소설가 sir Walter Scott(1771~1832)가 익명으로 발표했던 일련의 역사소설들

14) Ivanhoe : sir Walter Scott의 소설(1819)이며 그 주인공 이름이기도 하다.

15) turn over a new leaf : 마음을 고쳐먹고 새로 시작하다.

16) Xenophon, Virgil : Xenophon(C.430~C.354 B.C) 그리스 역사가, Virgil(70~19 B.C) 로마의 시인

business and can't be disturbed. What do you say?"

"They won't be apt to call on me," said Harry. I haven't the pleasure of knowing them."

"It isn't always a pleasure, I can assure you, Harry. Pass over the corn-popper."

CHAPTER V.

A YOUNG F. F. B.

As the two boys sat in front of the fire, popping and eating the corn, and chatting of one thing and another, their acquaintance improved rapidly. Harry learned that Oscar's father was a Boston merchant, in the Calcutta trade, with a counting-room on Long Wharf. Oscar was a year older than himself, and the oldest child. He had a sister of thirteen, named Florence, and a younger brother, Charlie, now ten. They lived on Beacon Street, opposite the Common. Though Harry had never lived in Boston, he knew that this was a fashionable street, and he had no difficulty in inferring that Mr. Vincent was a rich man. He felt what a wide gulf there was socially between himself and Oscar; one the son of a very poor country farmer, the other the son of a merchant prince[1]. But nothing in Oscar's manner indicated the faintest feeling of superiority, and this pleased Harry. I may as well say, however, that our hero was not one to show any foolish subserviency to a richer boy; he thought mainly of Oscar's superiority in knowledge; and although the latter was far ahead of Harry on this score[2], he was not one to boast of it.

Harry, in return for Oscar's confidence, acquainted him with his own adventures since he had started out to earn his own living. Oscar was most interested in his apprenticeship to the ventriloquist.

"It must have been jolly fun," he said. "I shouldn't mind travelling round with him myself. Can you perform any tricks?"

"A few," said Harry.

"Show me some, that's a good fellow."

"If you won't show others. Professor Henderson wouldn't like to have his tricks generally known. I could show more if I had the articles he uses. But I can do some without."

"Go ahead, Professor. I'm all attention."

Not having served an apprenticeship to a magician, as Harry did, I will not undertake to describe the few simple tricks which he had picked

---

1) a merchant prince : 거상, 호상

2) on this score : 이 점에 관하여

up, and now exhibited for the entertainment of his companion. It is enough to say that they were quite satisfactory, and that Oscar professed his intention to puzzle his Boston friends with them, when his vacation arrived.

About half-past eight, a knock was heard at the door.

"Come in!" called out Oscar.

The door was opened, and a boy about his own age entered. His name was Fitzgerald Fletcher. He was also a Boston boy, and the son of a retail merchant, doing business on Washington street. His father lived handsomely, and was supposed to be rich. At any rate Fitzgerald supposed him to be so, and was very proud of the fact. He generally let any new acquaintances understand very speedily that his father was a man of property, and that his family moved in the first circles of Boston Society. He cultivated the acquaintance of those boys who belonged to rich families, and did not fail to show the superiority which he felt to those of less abundant means. For example, he liked to be considered intimate with Oscar, as the social position of Mr. Vincent was higher than that of his own family. It gave him an excuse also for calling on Oscar in Boston. He had tried to ingratiate himself also with[3] Oscar's sister Florence, but had only disgusted her with his airs, so that he could not flatter himself with his success in this direction. Oscar had very little liking for him, but as school-fellows they often met, and Fitzgerald often called upon him. On such occasions he treated him politely enough, for it was not in his nature to be rude without cause.

Fitz was elaborately dressed, feeling that handsome clothes would help convey the impression of wealth, which he was anxious to establish. In particular he paid attention to his neckties, of which he boasted a greater variety than any of his school-mates. It was not a lofty ambition, but, such as it was[4], he was able to gratify it.

"How are you, Fitz?" said Oscar, when he saw who was his visitor. "Draw up a chair to the fire, and make yourself comfortable."

"Thank you, Oscar," said Fitzgerald, leisurely drawing off a pair of kid[5] gloves; "I thought I would drop in and see you."

---

3) ingratiate oneself with~ : ~의 비위를 맞추다. ~에게 알랑거리다.

4) such as it was : 그렇기는 하지만, 이런 정도이지만

5) kid : 염소 새끼 가죽

"All right! Will you have some popped corn?"

"No, thank you," answered Fitzgerald, shrugging his shoulders. "I don't fancy[6] the article."

"Don't you? Then you don't know what's good."

"Fancy passing round popped corn at a party in Boston," said the other. "How people would stare!"

"Would they? I don't know about that. I think some would be more sensible and eat. But, I beg your pardon, I haven't introduced you to my friend, Harry Walton. Harry, this is a classmate of mine. Fitzgerald Fletcher, Esq[7]., of Boston."

Fitzgerald did not appear to perceive that the title Esq. was sportively added to his name. He took it seriously, and was pleased with it, as a recognition of his social superiority. He bowed ceremoniously to our hero, and said, formally, "I am pleased to make your acquaintance, Mr. Walton."

"Thank you, Mr. Fletcher," replied Harry, bowing in turn.

"I wonder who he is," thought Fitzgerald.

He had no idea of the true position of our young hero, or he would not have wasted so much politeness upon him. The fact was, that Harry was well dressed, having on the suit which had been given him by a friend from the city. It was therefore fashionably cut, and had been so well kept as still to be in very good condition. It occurred to Fitz—to give him the short name he received from his school-fellows—that it might be a Boston friend of Oscar's, just entering the Academy. This might account for his not having met him before. Perhaps he was from an aristocratic Boston family. His intimacy with Oscar rendered it probable, and it might be well to cultivate his acquaintance. On this hint he spoke.

"Are you about to enter the Academy, Mr. Walton?"

"No; I should like to do so, but cannot."

"You are one of Oscar's friends from the city, I suppose, then?"

"Oh no; I am living in Centreville."

"Who can he be?" thought Fitz. With considerable less cordiality in

6) fancy : like

7) Esq : esquire의 준말로 Mr.나 Dr. 대신 성명 끝에 붙이는 경칭

his manner, he continued, impelled by curiosity,—

"I don't think I have met you before."

"No: I have only just come to the village."

Oscar understood thoroughly the bewilderment of his visitor, and enjoyed it. He knew the weakness of Fitz, and he could imagine how his feelings would change when he ascertained the real position of Harry.

"My friend," he explained, "is connected with the 'Centreville Gazette.'"

"In what capacity[8]?" asked Fitz, in surprise.

"He is profanely termed the 'printer's devil.' Isn't that so, Harry?"

"I believe you are right," said our hero, smiling. He had a suspicion that this relation would shock his new acquaintance.

"Indeed!" ejaculated Fitz, pursing up his lips, and, I was about to say, turning up his nose[9], but nature had saved him the little trouble of doing that.

"What in the world brings him here, then?" he thought; but there was no need of saying it, for both Oscar and Harry read it in his manner. "Strange that Oscar Vincent, from one of the first families of Boston, should demean himself by keeping company with a low printer boy!"

"Harry and I have had a jolly time popping corn this evening!" said Oscar, choosing to ignore his school-mate's changed manner.

"Indeed! I can't see what fun there is in it."

"Oh, you've got no taste. Has he, Harry?"

"His taste differs from ours," said our hero, politely.

"I should think so," remarked Fitz, with significant emphasis. "Was that all you had to amuse yourself?"

In using the singular pronoun[10], he expressly ignored the presence of the young printer.

"No, that wasn't all. My friend Harry has been amusing me with some tricks which he learned while he was travelling round with Professor Henderson, the ventriloquist and magician."

"Really, he is quite accomplished," said Fitz, with a covert sneer. "Pretty company Oscar has taken up with!" he thought. "How long were you in the circus business?" he asked, turning to Harry.

---

8) capacity : 지위, 자격, 관계

9) turn up one's nose (at) : ~을 비웃다. 경멸하다. 콧방귀 뀌다.

10) In using the singular pronoun : 즉 Oscar(you)에게만 말하면서

"I never was in the circus business."

"Excuse me. I should say, travelling about with the ventriloquist."

"About three months. I was with him when he performed here last winter."

"Ah! indeed. I didn't go. My father doesn't approve of my attending such common performances. I only attend first-class theatres, and the Italian opera."

"That's foolish," said Oscar. "You miss a good deal of fun, then. I went to Professor Henderson's entertainment, and I now remember seeing you there, Harry. You took money at the door, didn't you?"

"Yes."

"Now I understand what made your face seem so familiar to me, when I saw it this afternoon. By the way, I have never been into a printing office. If I come round to yours, will you show me round?"

"I should be very glad to, Oscar, but perhaps you had better wait till I have been there a little while, and learned the ropes[11]. I know very little about it yet."

"Won't you come too, Fitz?" asked Oscar.

"You must really excuse me," drawled Fitz. "I have heard that a printing office is a very dirty place. I should be afraid of soiling my clothes."

"Especially that stunning cravat."

"Do you like it? I flatter myself it's something a little extra[12]," said Fitz, who was always gratified by a compliment to his cravats.

"Then you won't go?"

"I haven't the slightest curiosity about such a place, I assure you."

"Then I shall have to go alone. Let me know when you are ready to receive me, Harry."

"I won't forget, Oscar."

"I wonder he allows such a low fellow to call him by his first name," thought Fitz. "Really, he has no proper[13] pride."

"Well," he said, rising, "I must be going."

"What's your hurry, Fitz?"

"I've got to write a letter home this evening. Besides, I haven't

---

11) ropes : 요령, 비결
12) extra : 특별한 것
13) proper : 품위 있는, 예절에 맞는

finished my Greek. Good-evening, Oscar."

"Good-evening, Fitz."

"Good-evening, Mr. Fletcher," said Harry.

"Evening!" ejaculated Fitz, briefly; and without a look at the low "printer-boy," he closed the door and went down stairs.

CHAPTER VI.

OSCAR BECOMES A PROFESSOR

"I am afraid your friend won't thank you for introducing me to him," said Harry, after Fitz had left the room.

"Fitz is a snob," said Oscar. "He makes himself ridiculous by putting on airs[1], and assuming to be more than he is. His father is in a good business, and may be rich—I don't know about that—but that isn't much to boast of."

"I don't think we shall be very intimate," said Harry, smiling. "Evidently a printer's apprentice is something very low in his eyes."

"When you are an influential editor he will be willing to recognize you. Let that stimulate your ambition."

"It isn't easy for a half-educated boy to rise to such a position. I feel that I know very little."

"If I can help you any, Harry, I shall be very glad to do it. I'm not much of a scholar[2], but I can help you a little. For instance, if you wanted to learn French, I could hear your lessons, and correct your exercises."

"Will you?" said Harry, eagerly. "There is nothing I should like better."

"Then I'll tell you what I'll do. You shall buy a French grammar[3], and come to my room two evenings a week, and recite what you get time to study at home."

"Won't it give you a great deal of trouble, Oscar?"

"Not a bit of it; I shall rather like it. Until you can buy a grammar, I will lend you mine. I'll set you a lesson out of it now."

He took from the book-shelves a French grammar, and inviting Harry to sit down beside him, gave him some necessary explanations as to the pronunciation of words according to the first lesson.

"It seems easy," said Harry. "I can take more than that."

---

1) put on air : 거드름 피우다.
2) not much of a scholar : 대단한 학생은 아니지만
3) grammar : 문법책, 입문서, 안내서

"It is the easiest of the modern languages, to us at least, on account of its having so many words similar to ours."

"What evening shall I come, Oscar?"

"Tuesday and Friday will suit me as well as any. And remember, Harry, I mean to be very strict in discipline. And, by the way, how will it do to call myself Professor?"

"I'll call you Professor if you want me to."

"We'll leave all high titles to Fitz, and I won't use the rod any oftener than it is absolutely necessary."

"All right, Professor Vincent," said Harry laughing, "I'll endeavor to behave with propriety."

"I wonder what they would say at home," said Oscar, "if they knew I had taken up the profession of teacher. Strange as it may seem to you, Harry, I have the reputation in the home-circle of being decidedly lazy. How do you account for it?"

"Great men are seldom appreciated[4]."

"You hit the nail on the head[5] that time—glad I am not the nail, by the way. Henceforth I will submit with resignation to injustice and misconstruction, since I am only meeting with the common fate of great men."

"What time is it, Oscar?"

"Nearly ten."

"Then I will bid you good-night," and Harry rose to go. "I can't tell how much I am obliged to you for your kind offer."

"Just postpone thanks till you find out whether I am a good teacher or not."

"I am sure of that."

"I am not so sure, but I will do what I can for you. Good-night. I'll expect you Friday evening. I shall see Fitz to-morrow. Shall I give him your love?"

"Never mind!" said Harry, smiling. "I'm afraid it wouldn't be appreciated."

"Perhaps not."

---

4) ~appreciated 다음에 at home 또는 at homeland를 넣으면 좋다. 위대한 사람은 가정(고향, 조국)에서 진가를 인정받지 못한다.

5) hit the nail on the head : 요점을 찌르다, 적절한 말을 하다.

As Harry left his lively companion, he felt that he had been most fortunate in securing his friendship—not only that he found him very agreeable and attractive, but he was likely to be of great use to him in promoting his plans of self-education. He had too much good sense not to perceive[6] that the only chance he had of rising to an influential position lay in qualifying himself for it, by enlarging his limited knowledge and improving his mind.

"I have made a good beginning," he thought. "After I have learned something of French, I will take up Latin, and I think Oscar will be willing to help me in that too."

The next morning he commenced work in the printing office. With a few hints from Ferguson, he soon comprehended what he had to do, and made very rapid progress.

"You're getting on fast, Harry," said Ferguson approvingly.

"I like it," said our hero. "I am glad I decided to be a printer."

"I wish I wasn't one," grumbled Clapp, the younger journeyman.

"Don't you like it?"

"Not much. It's hard work and poor pay. I just wish I was in my brother's shoes[7]. He is a bookkeeper in Boston, with a salary of twelve hundred a year, while I am plodding along[8] on fifteen dollars week."

"You may do better some day," said Ferguson.

"Don't see any chance of it."

"If I were in your place, I would save up part of my salary, and by and by[9] have an office, and perhaps a paper of my own."

"Why don't you do it, then?" sneered Clapp.

"Because I have a family to support from my earnings—you have only yourself."

"It doesn't help me any; I can't save anything out of fifteen dollars a week."

"You mean you won't," said Ferguson quietly.

"No I don't. I mean I can't."

"How do you expect I get along, then? I have a wife and two children

---

6) too~ not to~ : 너무 ~해서 ~하지 않을 수 없다. (꼭 한다)

7) in one's shoes : ~의 입장이 되어

8) plod along : 무거운 발걸음으로 걷다.

9) by and by : 곧, 머지않아

to support, and only get two dollars a week more than you."

"Perhaps you get into debt."

"No; I owe no man a dollar," said Ferguson emphatically. "That isn't all. I save two dollars a week; so that I actually support four on fifteen dollars a week—your salary. What do you say to that?"

"I don't want to be mean," said Clapp.

"Nor I. I mean to live comfortably, but of course I have to be economical."

"Oh, hang economy[10]!" said Clapp impatiently. "The old man used to lecture me about economy till I got sick of hearing the word."

"It is a good thing, for all that," persisted Ferguson. "You'll think so some day, even if you don't now."

"I guess you mean to run opposition to young Franklin, over there," sneered Clapp, indicating Harry, who had listened to the discussion with not a little interest.

"I think he and I will agree together pretty well," said Ferguson, smiling. "Franklin's a good man to imitate."

"If there are going to be two Franklins in the office, it will be time for me to clear out," returned Clapp.

"You can do better."

"How is that?"[11]

"Become Franklin No. 3."

"You don't catch me imitating any old fogy[12] like that. As far as I know anything about him, he was a mean, stingy old curmudgeon[13]!" exclaimed Clapp with irritation.

"That's rather strong language, Clapp," said Mr. Anderson, looking up from his desk with a smile. "It doesn't correspond with the general estimate of Franklin's character."

"I don't care," said Clapp doggedly, "I wouldn't be like Franklin if I could. I have too much self-respect."

Ferguson laughed, and Harry wanted to, but feared he should offend the younger journeyman, who evidently had worked himself into a bad

---

10) hang economy : 망할 놈의 절약
11) how is that? : 어떻게 하라구?
12) fogy : 구식사람
13) curmudgeon : 심술궂은 구두쇠

humor.[14)]

"I don't think you're in any danger," said Ferguson, who did not mind his fellow-workman's little ebullitions[15)] of temper.

Clapp scowled, but did not deign to reply[16)], partly, perhaps, because he knew that there was nothing to say.

From the outset Ferguson took a fancy to the young apprentice.

"He's got good, solid ideas," said he to Mr. Anderson, when Harry was absent. "He isn't so thoughtless as most boys of his age. He looks ahead."

"I think you are right in your judgment of him," said Mr. Anderson.

"He promises to be a faithful workman."

"He promises more than that," said Ferguson. "Mark my words[17)], Mr. Anderson; that boy is going to make his mark[18)] some day."

"It is a little too soon to say that, isn't it?"

"No; I judge from what I see. He is industrious and ambitious, and is bound to succeed. The world will hear of him yet[19)]."

Mr. Anderson smiled. He liked what he had seen of his new apprentice, but he thought Ferguson altogether too sanguine.

"He's a good, faithful boy," he admitted, "but it takes more than that to rise to distinction. If all the smart boys turned out smart men, they'd be a drug in the market[20)]."

But Ferguson held to his own opinion, notwithstanding. Time will show which was right.

The next day Ferguson said, "Harry, come round to my house, and take tea to-night. I've spoken to my wife about you, and she wants to see you."

"Thank you, Mr. Ferguson," said Harry. "I shall be very glad to come."

"I'll wait till you are ready, and you can walk along with me."

---

14) into a bad humor : 기분 나쁘게
15) ebullition : 복받침
16) did not design to reply : (자존심을 버리고) 대답을 하지 않다.
17) mark my words : 내 말을 들어요.
18) make one's mark : 이름을 떨치다
19) yet : (미래 시제에서)머지않아, 앞으로
20) a drug in the market : 남아돌아 팔리지 않는 상품

"All right; I will be ready in five minutes."

They set out together for Ferguson's modest home, which was about half a mile distant. As they passed up the village street Harry's attention was drawn to two boys who were approaching them. One he recognized at once as Fitzgerald Fletcher. He had an even more stunning necktie than when Harry first met him, and sported[21] a jaunty little cane, which he swung in his neatly gloved hand.

"I wonder if he'll notice me," thought Harry. "At any rate, I won't be wanting in politeness."

"Good-afternoon, Mr. Fletcher," he said, as they met.

Fitzgerald stared at him superciliously[22], and made the slightest possible nod.

"Who is that?" asked Ferguson.

"It is a boy who has great contempt for printers' devils and low apprentices," answered Harry. "I was introduced to him two evenings ago, but he evidently doesn't care about keeping up the acquaintance."

"Who is that, Fitz?" asked his companion in turn.

"It's a low fellow—a printer's devil," answered Fitz, shortly[23].

"How do you happen to know him?"

"Oscar Vincent introduced him to me. Oscar's a queer fellow. He belongs to one of the first families in Boston—one of my set[24], you know, and yet he actually invited that boy to his room."

"He's rather a good-looking boy—the printer."

"Think so?" drawled Fitz. "He's low—all apprentices are. I mean to keep him at a distance."

---

21) sport : 자랑해 보이다, 뽐내다.
22) superciliously : 오만하게
23) shortly : 무뚝뚝하게
24) set : 한패, 동아리

CHAPTER VII.

A PLEASANT EVENING.

"This is my house," said Ferguson, pausing at the gate.

Harry looked at it with interest.

It was a cottage, containing four rooms, and a kitchen in the ell part. There was a plot of about a quarter of an acre connected with it. Everything about it was neat, though very unpretentious.

"It isn't a palace," said Ferguson, "but," he added cheerfully, "it's a happy home, and from all I've read, that is more than can be said of some palaces. Step right in and make yourself at home."

They entered a tiny entry, and Mrs. Ferguson opened the door of the sitting-room. She was a pleasant-looking woman, and her face wore a smile of welcome.

"Hannah," said Ferguson, "this is our new apprentice, Harry Walton."

"I am glad to see you," she said, offering her hand. "My husband has spoken of you. You are quite welcome, if you can put up with humble fare[1])."

"That is what I have always been accustomed to," said Harry, beginning to feel quite at home.

"Where are the children, Hannah?"

Two children, a boy and a girl, of six and four years respectively, bounded into the room and answered for themselves. They looked shyly at Harry, but before many minutes their shyness had worn off[2]), and the little girl was sitting on his knee, while the boy stood beside him. Harry was fond of children, and readily adapted himself to his young acquaintances.

Supper was soon ready—a plain meal, but one that Harry enjoyed. He could not help comparing Ferguson's plain, but pleasant home, with Clapp's mode of life.

The latter spent on himself as much as sufficed his fellow-workman to support a wife and two children, yet it was easy to see which found

---

1) fare : food

2) worn off : 차츰 없어지다.

the best enjoyment in life.

"How do you like your new business?" asked Mrs. Ferguson, as she handed Harry a cup of tea.

"I like all but the name," said our hero, smiling.

"I wonder how the name came to be applied to a printer's apprentice any more than to any other apprentice," said Mrs. Ferguson.

"I never heard," said her husband. "It seems to me to be a libel[3) upon our trade. But there is one comfort. If you stick to the business, you'll outgrow[4) the name."

"That is lucky; I shouldn't like to be called the wife of a ——. I won't pronounce the word lest the children should catch it."

"What is it, mother?" asked Willie, with his mouth full.

"It isn't necessary for you to know, my boy."

"Do you know Mr. Clapp?" asked Harry.

"I have seen him, but never spoke with him."

"I never asked him round to tea," said Ferguson.

"I don't think he would enjoy it any better than I. His tastes are very different from mine, and his views of life are equally different."

"I should think so," said Harry.

"Now I think you and I would agree very well. Clapp dislikes the business, and only sticks to it because he must get his living in some way. As for me, if I had a sum of money, say five thousand dollars, I would still remain a printer, but in that case I would probably buy out[5) a paper, or start one, and be a publisher, as well as a printer."

"That's just what I should like," said Harry.

"Who knows but we may be able to go into partnership some day, and carry out our plan."

"I would like it," said Harry; "but I am afraid it will be a good while before we can raise the five thousand dollars."

"We don't need as much. Mr. Anderson started on a capital of a thousand dollars, and now he is in comfortable circumstances."

"Then there's hopes for us."

"At any rate I cherish hopes of doing better some day. I shouldn't

---

3) a libel : 비방, 불명예가 되는 것
4) outgrow : 벗어나다.
5) buy out : 권리를 사다.

like always to be a journeyman. I manage to save up a hundred dollars a year. How much have we in the savings bank, Hannah?"

"Between four and five hundred dollars, with interest."

"It has taken me four years to save it up. In five more, if nothing happens, I should be worth a thousand dollars. Journeymen printers don't get rich very fast."

"I hope to have saved up something myself, in five years," said Harry.

"Then our plan may come to pass, after all. You shall be editor, and I publisher."

"I should think you would prefer to be an editor," said his wife.

"I am diffident of[6] my powers in the line of composition," said Ferguson. "I shouldn't be afraid to undertake local items, but when it comes to an elaborate editorial[7], I should rather leave it in other hands."

"I always liked writing," said Harry. "Of course I have only had a school-boy's practice, but I mean to practise more in my leisure hours."

"Suppose you write a poem for the 'Gazette,' Walton."

Harry smiled.

"I am not ambitious enough for that," he replied. "I will try plain prose."

"Do so," said Ferguson, earnestly. "Our plan may come to something after all, if we wait patiently. It will do no harm to prepare yourself as well as you can. After a while you might write something for the 'Gazette.' I think Mr. Anderson would put it in."

"Shall I sign it P. D.?" asked Harry.

"P. D. stands for Doctor of Philosophy."

"I don't aspire to such a learned title. P. D. also stands for Printer's Devil."

"I see. Well, joking aside[8], I advise you to improve yourself in writing."

"I will. That is the way Franklin did."

"I remember. He wrote an article, and slipped it under the door of the printing office, not caring to have it known that he was the author."

"Shall I give you a piece of pie, Mr. Walton?" said Mrs. Ferguson.

---

6) I am diffident of : 나는 ~에 자신이 없다.

7) editorial : 사설

8) joking aside : 농담은 그만두고 (차치하고)

"Thank you.".

"Me too," said Willie, extending his plate.

"Willie is always fond of pie," said his father, "In a printing office *pi*[9] is not such a favorite."

When supper was over, Mr. Ferguson showed Harry a small collection of books, about twenty-five in number, neatly arranged on shelves.

"It isn't much of a library," he said, "but a few books are better than none. I should like to buy as many every year; but books are expensive, and the outlay would make too great an inroad upon[10] my small surplus."

"I always thought I should like a library," said Harry, "but my father is very poor, and has fewer books than you. As for me, I have but one book besides the school-books I studied, and that I gained as a school prize—The Life of Franklin."

"If one has few books he is apt to prize them more," said Ferguson, "and is apt to profit by them more."

"Have you read the History of China?" asked Harry, who had been looking over his friend's books.

"No; I have never seen it."

"Why[11], there it is," said our hero, "In two volumes."

"Take it down," said Ferguson, laughing.

Harry did so, and to his surprise it opened in his hands, and revealed a checker-board[12].

"You see appearances are deceitful. Can you play checkers?"

"I never tried."

"You will easily learn. Shall I teach you the game?"

"I wish you would."

They sat down; and Harry soon became interested in the game, which requires a certain degree of thought and foresight.

"You will make a good player after a while," said his companion. "You must come in often and play with me."

"Thank you, I should like to do so. It may not be often, for I am

---

9) pi : 뒤죽박죽이 된 활자

10) make an inroad upon~ : ~을 잠식하다.

11) why : (새로운 사태를 발견하고 놀라서) 이런!, 어마!

12) a checker-board : 서양 장기판

taking lessons in French, and I want to get on[13] as fast as possible."

"I did not know there was any one in the village who gave lessons in French."

"Oh, he's not a professional teacher. Oscar Vincent, one of the Academy boys, is teaching me. I am to take two lessons a week, on Tuesday and Friday evenings."

"Indeed, that is a good arrangement. How did it come about?"

Harry related the particulars[14] of his meeting with Oscar.

"He's a capital[15] fellow," he concluded. "Very different from another boy I met in his room. I pointed him out to you in the street. Oscar seems to be rich, but he doesn't put on any airs, and he treated me very kindly."

"That is to his credit[16]. It's the sham aristocrats that put on most airs. I believe you will make somebody[17], Walton. You have lost no time in getting to work."

"I have no time to lose. I wish I was in Oscar's place. He is preparing for Harvard, and has nothing to do but to learn."

"I heard a lecturer once who said that the printing office is the poor man's college, and he gave a great many instances of printers who had risen high in the world, particularly in our own country."

"Well, that is encouraging. I should like to have heard the lecture."

"I begin to think, Harry, that I should have done well to follow your example. When I was in your position, I might have studied too, but I didn't realize the importance as I do now. I read some useful books, to be sure, but that isn't like studying."

"It isn't too late now."

Ferguson shook his head.

"Now I have a wife and children," he said. "I am away from them during the day, and the evening I like to pass socially with them."

"Perhaps you would like to be divorced," said his wife, smiling. "Then you would get time for study."

---

13) get on : 앞으로 나아가다, 진척하다.
14) particulars : 상세, 명세, 세부사항들
15) capital : 으뜸가는, 뛰어난
16) to one's credit : ~에게 명예롭게도
17) somebody : 어엿한 인물, 대단한 인물

"I doubt if that would make me as happy, Hannah. I am not ready to part with you just yet. But our young friend here is not quite old enough to be married, and there is nothing to prevent his pursuing his studies. So, Harry, go on, and prepare yourself for your editorial duties."

Harry smiled thoughtfully. For the first time he had formed definite plans for his future. Why should not Ferguson's plans be realized?

"If I live long enough," he said to himself, "I will be an editor, and exert some influence in the world."

At ten o'clock he bade good-night to Mr. and Mrs. Ferguson, feeling that he had passed a pleasant and what might prove a profitable[18] evening.

18) profitable : 유익한, 도움이 되는

CHAPTER VIII.

FLETCHER's VIEWS ON SOCIAL POSITION.

"You are getting on finely, Harry," said Oscar Vincent, a fortnight later. "You do credit to my teaching. As you have been over all the regular verbs now, I will give you a lesson in translating."

"I shall find that interesting," said Harry, with satisfaction.

"Here is a French Reader," said Oscar, taking one down from the shelves. "It has a dictionary at the end. I won't give you a lesson. You may take as much as you have time for, and at the same time three or four of the irregular verbs. You are going about[1] three times as fast as I did when I commenced French."

"Perhaps I have a better teacher than you had," said Harry, smiling.

"I shouldn't wonder," said Oscar. "That explains it to my satisfaction. Well, now the lesson is over, sit down and we'll have a chat. Oh, by the way, there's one thing I want to speak to you about. We've got a debating society[2] at our school. It is called 'The Clionian[3] Society.' Most of the students belong to it. How would you like to join?"

"I should like it very much. Do you think they would admit me?"

"I don't see why not. I'll propose you at the next meeting, Thursday evening. Then the nomination will lie over[4] a week, and be acted upon[5] at the next meeting."

"I wish you would. I never belonged to a debating society, but I should like to learn to speak."

"It's nothing when you're used to it. It's only the first time you know, that troubles you. By Jove![6] I remember how my knees trembled when I first got up and said Mr. President. I felt as if all eyes were upon me, and I wanted to sink through the floor. Now I can get up and chatter

---

1) be going about : 열심히 하다.
2) debating society : 토론 모임, 토론회.
3) Clio : 역사의 여신
4) lie over : 연기되다.
5) be acted upon : 결정되다, 판결을 내리다.
6) by Jove! : 맹세코!, 천만에!

with the best of them[7]. I don't mean that I can make an eloquent speech or anything of that kind, but I can talk at a minute's notice on almost any subject."

"I wish I could."

"Oh, you can, after you've tried a few times. Well, then, it's settled. I'll propose you at the next meeting."

"How lucky I am to have fallen in with you[8], Oscar."

"I know what you mean. I'm your guide, philosopher, and friend, and all that sort of thing. I hope you'll have proper veneration for me.

It's rather a new character for me. Would you believe it, Harry,— at home I am regarded as a rattle-brained[9] chap, instead of the dignified Professor that you know me to be. Isn't it a shame?"

"Great men are seldom appreciated at home, Oscar."

"I know that. I shall have to get a certificate from you, certifying to my being a steady and erudite[10] young man."

"I'll give it with the greatest pleasure."

"Holloa[11], there's a knock. Come in!" shouted Oscar.

The door opened, and Fitzgerald Fletcher entered the room.

"How are you, Fitz?" said Oscar. "Sit down and make yourself comfortable. You know my friend, Harry Walton, I believe[12]?"

"I believe I had the honor to meet him here one evening," said Fitzgerald stiffly, slightly emphasizing the word "honor."

"I hope you are well, Mr. Fletcher," said Harry, more amused than disturbed by the manner of the aristocratic visitor.

"Thank you, my health is good," said Fitzgerald with equal stiffness, and forthwith[13] turned to Oscar, not deigning to devote any more attention to Harry.

Our hero had intended to remain a short time longer, but, under the circumstances, as Oscar's attention would be occupied by Fletcher, with

---

7) with the best of them : 누구 못지않게
8) fall in with : ~과 우연히 마주치다, ~과 친구가 되다.
9) rattle-brained: rattle-headed, 머리가 빈.
10) erudite : 학식이 있는, learned, scholarly
11) holloa : hallo, 이봐, 이런 (남의 주의를 끌거나, 놀라움을 나타내는 소리)
12) I believe : 내가 알기로는
13) forthwith : immediately

whom he was not on intimate terms, he thought he might spend the evening more profitably at home in study.

"If you'll excuse me, Oscar," he said, rising, "I will leave you now, as I have something to do this evening."

"If you insist upon it, Harry, I will excuse you. Come round Friday evening."

"Thank you."

"Do you have to work at the printing office in the evening?" Fletcher deigned to inquire.

"No; I have some studying to do."

"Reading and spelling, I suppose," sneered Fletcher.

"I am studying French."

"Indeed!" returned Fletcher, rather surprised. "How can you study it without a teacher?"

"I have a teacher."

"Who is it?"

"Professor Vincent," said Harry, smiling.

"You didn't know that I had developed into a French Professor, did you, Fitz? Well, it's so, and whether it's the superior teaching or not, I can't say, but my scholar is getting on famously."

"It must be a great bore to teach," said Fletcher.

"Not at all. I like it."

"Every one to his taste[14]," said Fitzgerald unpleasantly.

"Good-night, Oscar. Good-night, Mr. Fletcher," said Harry, and made his exit.

"You're a strange fellow, Oscar," said Fletcher, after Harry's departure.

"Very likely, but what particular strangeness do you refer to now?"

"No one but you would think of giving lessons to a printer's devil."

"I don't know about that."

"No one, I mean, that holds your position in society."

"I don't know that I hold any particular position in society."

"Your family live on Beacon Street, and move in the first circles. I am sure my mother would be disgusted if I should demean myself[15]

---

14) Every one to his taste : 입맛대로지, 취향대로지. to one's taste (기호에 맞도록)
15) demean oneself : (품위, 인격을) 떨어뜨리다.

so far as to give lessons to any vulgar apprentice."

"I don't propose to give lessons to any vulgar apprentice."

"You know whom I mean. This Walton is only a printer's devil."

"I don't know that that is any objection to him. It isn't morally wrong to be a printer's devil, is it?"

"What a queer fellow you are, Oscar. Of course I don't mean that. I daresay he's well enough in his place, though he seems to be very forward[16] and presuming[17], but you know that he's not your equal."

"He is not my equal in knowledge, but I shouldn't be surprised if he would be some time. You'd be astonished to see how fast he gets on."

"I daresay. But I mean in social position."

"It seems to me you can't think of anything but social position."

"Well, it's worth thinking about."

"No doubt, as far as it is deserved. But when it is founded on nothing but money, I wouldn't give much for it."

"Of course we all know that the higher classes are more refined—"

"Than printers' devils and vulgar apprentices, I suppose," put in Oscar, laughing,

"Yes."

"Well, if refinement consists in wearing kid gloves and stunning neckties, I suppose the higher classes, as you call them, are more refined."

"Do you mean me?" demanded Fletcher, who was noted for the character of his neckties.

"Well, I can't say I don't. I suppose you regard yourself as a representative of the higher classes, don't you?"

"To be sure I do," said Fletcher, complacently.

"So I supposed. Then you see I had a right to refer to you. Now listen to my prediction. Twenty-five years from now, the boy whom you look down upon as a vulgar apprentice will occupy a high position, and you will be glad to number[18] him among your acquaintances."

"Speak for yourself[19], Oscar," said Fletcher, scornfully.

---

16) forward : 주제넘은, 건방진.
17) presuming : 주제넘은, 뻔뻔스러운
18) number : ~과 동일한 것으로 보다.
19) speak for yourself : 너나 그래라!

"I speak for both of us."

"Then I say I hope I can command better associates than this friend of yours."

"You may, but I doubt it."

"You seem to be carried away[20] by him," said Fitzgerald, pettishly. "I don't see anything very wonderful about him, except dirty hands."

"Then you have seen more than I have."

"Of course a fellow who meddles with printer's ink must have dirty hands. Faugh![21]" said Fletcher, turning up his nose.

At the same time he regarded complacently his own fingers, which he carefully kept aloof from anything that would soil or mar their aristocratic whiteness.

"The fact is, Fitz," said Oscar, argumentatively, "our upper ten[22], as we call them, spring from just such beginnings as my friend Harry Walton. My own father commenced life in a printing office. But, as you say, he occupies a high position at present."

"Really!" said Fletcher, a little taken aback[23], for he knew that Vincent's father ranked higher than his own.

"I daresay your own ancestors were not always patricians[24]."

Fletcher winced. He knew well enough that his father commenced life as a boy in a country grocery, but in the mutations of fortune had risen to be the proprietor of a large dry-goods store on Washington Street. None of the family cared to look back to the beginning of his career. They overlooked the fact that it was creditable to him to have risen from the ranks[25], though the rise was only in wealth, for Mr. Fletcher was a purse-proud parvenu[26], who owed all the consideration[27] he enjoyed to his commercial position. Fitz liked to have it understood that he was of patrician lineage, and carefully ignored the little grocery, and certain country relations who occasionally paid a visit to their wealthy

---

20) be carried away : (비유적) 넋을 잃게 되다.
21) Faugh! : (혐오, 경멸을 나타내는) 피이, 쳇!
22) the upper ten : upper class, 상류계급, 귀족계급
23) be taken aback : 깜짝 놀라다, 허를 찔리다.
24) patrician : (고대 로마의) 귀족
25) rise from the ranks : 병졸에서 장교가 되다. 낮은 신분에서 출세하다.
26) parvenu : 벼락부자, 갑자기 출세한 사람
27) consideration : 존중, 존경

relatives, in spite of the rather frigid welcome they received.

"Oh, I suppose there are exceptions," Fletcher admitted reluctantly. "Your father was smart."

"So is Harry Walton. I know what he is aiming at, and I predict that he will be an influential editor some day."

"Have you got your Greek lesson?" asked Fletcher, abruptly, who did not relish the course the conversation had taken.

"Yes."

"Then I want you to translate a passage for me. I couldn't make it out.[28)]"

"All right."

Half an hour later Fletcher left Vincent's room.

"What a snob[29)] he is!" thought Oscar.

And Oscar was right.

---

28) make~ out : 작성하다.
29) snob : 속물, 지위 · 재산 숭배자, 윗사람에게 아첨하고 아랫사람에게 뽐내는 사람.

CHAPTER IX.

THE CLIONIAN SOCIETY.

On Thursday evening the main school of the Academy building was lighted up, and groups of boys, varying in age from thirteen to nineteen, were standing in different parts of the room. These were members of the Clionian Society, whose weekly meeting was about to take place.

At eight o'clock precisely the President took his place at the teacher's desk, with the Secretary at his side, and rapped for order[1]. The presiding officer was Alfred DeWitt, a member of the Senior Class, and now nearly ready for college. The Secretary was a member of the same class, by name George Sanborn.

"The Secretary will read the minutes[2] of the last meeting," said the President, when order had been obtained.

George Sanborn rose and read his report, which was accepted.

"Are any committees prepared to report?" asked the President.

The Finance Committee reported through its chairman, recommending that the fee for admission be established at one dollar, and that each member be assessed[3] twenty-five cents monthly.

"Mr. President," said Fitzgerald Fletcher, rising to his feet, "I would like to say a word in reference to this report."

"Mr. Fletcher has the floor.[4]"

"Then, Mr. President, I wish to say that I disagree with the Report of the Committee. I think a dollar is altogether too small. It ought to be at least three dollars, and I myself should prefer five dollars. Again, sir, the Committee has recommended for the monthly assessment the ridiculously small sum of twenty-five cents. I think it ought to be a dollar."

"Mr. President, I should like to ask the gentleman his reason," said Henry Fairbanks, Chairman of the Finance Committee. "Why should

---

1) rap for order : call to order, 회의를 시작하다, 개회를 선언하다. (조용히 합시다 하면서)
2) the minutes : 의사록, 회의록.
3) be assessed : 할당하다, 부과하다.
4) have (get) the floor : 발언권을 얻다.

we tax the members to such an extent, when the sums reported are sufficient to defray[5)] the ordinary expenses of the Society, and to leave a small surplus besides?"

"Mr. President," returned Fletcher, "I will answer the gentleman. We don't want to throw open the Society to every one that can raise a dollar. We want to have an exclusive[6)] society."

"Mr. President," said Oscar Vincent, rising, "I should like to ask the gentleman for how many he is speaking. He certainly is not speaking for me. I don't want the Society to be exclusive. There are not many who can afford to pay the exorbitant sums which he desires fixed for admission fee and for monthly assessments, and I for one[7)] am not willing to exclude any good fellow who desires to become one of us, but does not boast as heavy a purse as the gentleman who has just spoken."

These remarks of Oscar were greeted with applause, general enough to show that the opinions of nearly all were with him.

"Mr. President," said Henry Fairbanks, "though I am opposed to the gentleman's suggestion, (does he offer it as an amendment[8)]?) I have no possible objection to his individually paying the increased rates which he recommends, and I am sure the Treasurer will gladly receive them."

Laughter and applause greeted this hit[9)], and Fletcher once more arose, somewhat vexed at the reception of his suggestion.

"I don't choose—" he commenced.

"The gentleman will address the chair[10)]," interrupted the President.

"Mr. President, I don't choose to pay more than the other members, though I can do it without inconvenience. But, as I said, I don't believe in being too democratic. I am not in favor of admitting anybody and everybody into the Society."

"Mr. President," said James Hooper, "I congratulate the gentleman on the flourishing state of his finances. For my own part, I am not ashamed to say that I cannot afford to pay a dollar a month assessment,

---

5) defray : 지불하다, 부담하다
6) exclusive : 특정계급의 사람들을 대상으로 하는, 배타적인.
7) for one : 한 개인으로서는
8) amendment : 수정안, 개정안
9) this hit : 일격, 핵심을 찌르는 말
10) address the chair : 발언권을 요청하다.

and, were it required, I should be obliged to offer my resignation."

"So much the better," thought Fitzgerald, for, as Hooper was poor, and went coarsely clothed, he looked down upon him. Fortunately for himself he did not give utterance to his thought.

"Does Mr. Fletcher put his recommendation into the form of an amendment?" asked the President.

"I do."

"Be kind enough to state it, then."

Fletcher did so, but as no one seconded it[11], no action was of course taken[12].

"Nominations for membership are now in order[13]," said the President.

"I should like to propose my friend Henry Walton."

"Who is Henry Walton?" asked a member.

"Mr. President, may I answer the gentleman?" asked Fitzgerald Fletcher, rising to his feet.

"As the nominee is not to be voted upon this evening, it is not in order."

"Mr. President," said Oscar, "I should be glad to have the gentleman report his information."

"Mr. Fletcher may speak if he desires it, but as the name will be referred to[14] the Committee on Nominations, it is hardly necessary."

"Mr. President, I merely wish to inform the Society, that Mr. Walton occupies the dignified position of printer's devil in the office of the 'Centreville Gazette.'"

"Mr. President," said Oscar, "may I ask the indulgence of the Society long enough to say that I am quite aware of the fact. I will add that Mr. Walton is a young man of excellent abilities, and I am confident will prove an accession to[15] the Society."

"I cannot permit further remarks on a matter which will come in due course before the Committee on Nominations," said the President.

"The next business in order is the debate."

---

11) seconded it : 수정안에 재청하다.
12) action was taken : 의결 · 결정하다.
13) be in order : (회의 절차에 따라) 규칙대로, ~차례입니다.
14) be referred to : ~에 회부되다.
15) an accession to : ~에 동의, 승낙, 가입

Of the debate, and the further proceedings, I shall not speak, as they are of no special interest. But after the meeting was over, groups of members discussed matters which had come up during the evening. Fletcher approached Oscar Vincent, and said, "I can't see, Oscar, why you are trying to get that printer's devil into our Society."

"Because he's a good fellow, and smart enough to do us credit."

"If there were any bootblacks[16] in Centreville I suppose you'd be proposing them?" said Fletcher with a sneer.

"I might, if they were as smart as my friend Walton."

"You are not very particular about your friends," said Fletcher in the same tone.

"I don't ask them to open their pocket-books, and show me how much money they have."

"I prefer to associate with gentlemen."

"So do I."

"Yet you associate with that printer's devil."

"I consider him a gentleman."

Fletcher laughed scornfully.

"You have strange ideas of a gentleman," he said.

"I hold the same," said James Hooper, who had come up in time to hear the last portion of the conversation. "I don't think a full purse is the only or the chief qualification of a gentleman. If labor is to be a disqualification, then I must resign all claims to be considered a gentleman, as I worked on a farm for two years before coming to school, and in that way earned the money to pay my expenses here."

Fletcher turned up his nose, but did not reply. Hooper was a good scholar and influential in the Society, but in Fletcher's eyes he was unworthy of consideration.

"Look here, Fletcher,—what makes you so confoundedly[17] exclusive in your ideas?" asked Henry Fairbanks.

"Because I respect myself," said Fletcher in rather a surly[18] tone.

"Then you have one admirer," said Fairbanks.

"What do you mean by that?" asked Fletcher, suspiciously.

---

16) bootblack : 구두닦이
17) confoundedly : 지독하게, 어리둥절하게
18) surly : 퉁명스럽게

"Nothing out of the way. I believe in self-respect, but I don't see how it[19] is going to be endangered by the admission of Oscar's friend to the Society."

"Am I expected to associate on equal terms with a printer's devil?"

"I can't answer for you. As for me, if he is a good fellow, I shall welcome him to our ranks. Some of our most eminent men have been apprenticed to the trade of printer. I believe, after all, it is the name that has prejudiced you."

"No it isn't. I have seen him."

"Henry Walton?"

"Yes."

"Where?"

"In Oscar's room."

"Well?"

"I don't like his appearance."

"What's the matter with his appearance?" asked Oscar.

"He looks low."

"That's where I must decidedly contradict you, Fitz, and I shall appeal confidently to the members of the Society when they come to know him, as they soon will, for I am sure no one else shares your ridiculous prejudices. Harry Walton, in my opinion, is a true gentleman, without reference to his purse, and he is bound to rise hereafter, take my word[20] for it."

"There's plenty of room for him to rise," said Fletcher with a sneer.

"That is true not only of him, but of all of us, I take it."

"Do you refer to me?"

"Oh no," said Oscar with sarcasm. "I am quite aware that you are at the pinnacle of eminence, even if you do flunk[21] in Greek occasionally."

Fitzgerald had failed in the Greek recitation during the day, and that in school parlance is sometimes termed a "flunk." He bit his lip in mortification at this reference, and walked away, leaving Oscar master of the situation.

---

19) it : self-respect
20) take one's word : ~말을 믿다.
21) flunk : 실패 · 낙제하다.

"You had the best of him[22] there, Vincent," said George Sanborn. "He has gone off in disgust."

"I like to see Fletcher taken down," said Henry Fairbanks. "I never saw a fellow put on so many airs. He is altogether too aristocratic to associate with ordinary people."

"Yes," said Oscar, "he has a foolish pride, which I hope he will some time get rid of."

"He ought to have been born in England, and not in a republic[23]."

"If he had been born in England, he would have been unhappy unless he had belonged to the nobility," said Alfred DeWitt.

"Look here, boys," said Tom Carver, "what do you say to mortifying Fitz's pride?"

"Have you got a plan in view, Tom? If so, out with it[24]."

"Yes: you know the pedler that comes into town about once a month to buy up rags, and sell his tinwares."

"I have seen him. Well, what of him?"

"He is coming early next week. Some of us will see him privately, and post him up as to[25] Fitz's relations and position, and hire him to come up to school, and inquire for Fitz, representing himself as his cousin. Of course Fitz will deny it indignantly, but he will persist and show that he knows all about the family."

"Good! Splendid!" exclaimed the boys laughing. "Won't Fitz be raving[26]?"

"There's no doubt about that. Well, boys, I'll arrange it all, if you'll authorize[27] me."

"Go ahead, Tom. You can draw upon us for the necessary funds."

Fletcher had retired to his room, angry at the opposition his proposal had received, and without any warning of the humiliation which awaited him.

---

22) have (get) the best of~ : ~를 이기다, ~를 능가하다.
23) a republic : 공화국인 미국
24) out with it : 이야기해봐, 꺼내봐.
25) post~ up as to : ~가 ~라는 소문을 퍼뜨리다.
26) rave : scream
27) authorize : 권한을 주다, 위임하다.

CHAPTER X.

THE TIN-PEDLER.

Those of my readers who live in large cities are probably not familiar with the travelling tin-pedler[1], who makes his appearance at frequent intervals in the country towns and villages of New England. His stock of tinware embraces a large variety of articles for culinary purposes, ranging from milk-pans to nutmeg-graters. These are contained in a wagon of large capacity, in shape like a box, on which he sits enthroned a merchant prince. Unlike most traders, he receives little money, most of his transactions being in the form of a barter, whereby he exchanges his merchandise for rags, white and colored, which have accumulated in the household, and are gladly traded off[2] for bright tinware. Behind the cart usually depend two immense bags, one for white, the other for colored rags, which, in time, are sold to paper manufacturers. It may be that the very paper on which this description is printed, was manufactured from rags so collected.

Abner Bickford was the proprietor of such an establishment as I have described. No one, at first sight, would have hesitated to class him as a Yankee. He was long in the limbs, and long in the face, with a shrewd twinkle in the eye, a long nose, and the expression of a man who respected himself and feared nobody. He was unpolished, in his manners, and knew little of books, but he belonged to the same resolute and hardy[3] type of men who in years past sprang to arms, and fought bravely for an idea. He was strong in his manhood, and would have stood unabashed before a king. Such was the man who was to mortify the pride of Fitzgerald Fletcher.

Tom Carver watched for his arrival in Centreville, and walking up to his cart, accosted him.

"Good-morning, Mr. Bickford."

"Good-mornin', young man. You've got the advantage of me. I never

---

1) tin-pedler(peddler) : 고물상, 행상 (고물과 물건을 교환하는)
2) trade off : 교환하다.
3) hardy : 건장한, 튼튼한

saw you before as I know of."

"I am Tom Carver, at your service."

"Glad to know you. Where do you live? Maybe your wife would like some tinware this mornin'?" said Abner, relaxing his gaunt features into a smile.

"She didn't say anything about it when I came out," said Tom, entering into the joke.

"Maybe you'd like a tin-dipper for your youngest boy?"

"Maybe I would, if you've got any to give away[4])."

"I see you've cut your eye-teeth[5]). Is there anything else I can do for you? I'm in for a trade."

"I don't know, unless I sell myself for rags."

"Anything for a trade. I'll give you two cents a pound."

"That's too cheap. I came to ask your help in a trick we boys want to play on one of our number."

"Sho! you don't say so. That aint exactly in my line[6])."

"I'll tell you all about it. There's a chap at our school—the Academy, you know—who's awfully stuck up. He's all the time bragging about belonging to a first family in Boston, and turning up his nose at poorer boys. We want to mortify him."

"Just so!" said Abner, nodding. "Drive ahead[7])!"

"Well, we thought if you'd call at the school and ask after him, and pretend he was a cousin of yours, and all that, it would make him mad."

"Oh, I see," said Abner, nodding, "he wouldn't like to own a tin-pedler for his cousin."

"No," said Tom; "he wants us to think all his relations are rich. I wouldn't mind at all myself," he added, it suddenly occurring to him that Abner's feelings might be hurt.

"Good!" said Abner, "I see you aint one of the stuck-up[8]) kind. I've got some relations in Boston myself, that are rich and stuck up. I never go near 'em. What's the name of this chap you're talkin' about?"

---

4) give away : 거저 주다.
5) cut one's eye-teeth : 철이 들다.
6) in (out of) one's line : 성미에 맞아 (안 맞아)
7) Drive ahead : go ahead
8) stuck-up : 거만한, 건방진

"Fletcher—Fitzgerald Fletcher."

"Fletcher!" repeated Abner. "Whew[9]! well, that's a joke!"

"What's a joke?" asked Tom, rather surprised.

"Why, he *is* my relation—a sort of second cousin. Why, my mother and his father are own[10] cousins. So, don't you see we're second cousins?"

"That's splendid!" exclaimed Tom. "I can hardly believe it."

"It's so. My mother's name was Fletcher—Roxanna Fletcher—afore she married. Jim Fletcher—this boy's father—used to work in my grandfather's store, up to Hampton, but he got kinder discontented, and went off to Boston, where he's been lucky, and they do say he's mighty rich now. I never go nigh him, 'cause I know he looks down on his country cousins, and I don't believe in pokin' my nose in[11] where I aint wanted."

"Then you are really and truly Fitz's cousin?"

"If that's the boy's name. Seems to me it's a kinder queer one. I s'pose it's a fust-claas name. Sounds rather stuck up."

"Won't the boys roar when they hear about it! Are you willing to enter into our plan?"

"Well," said Abner, "I'll do it. I can't abide folks that's stuck up. I'd rather own a cousin like you."

"Thank you, Mr. Bickford."

"When do you want me to come round?"

"How long do you stay in town?"

"Well, I expect to stop overnight at the tavern; I can't get through in one day."

"Then come round to the Academy to-morrow morning, about half-past eight. School don't begin till nine, but the boys will be playing ball alongside. Then we'll give you an introduction to your cousin."

"That'll suit me well enough. I'll come."

Tom Carver returned in triumph, and communicated to the other boys the arrangement he had made with Mr. Bickford, and his unexpected discovery of the genuine relationship that existed between Fitz and the

---

9) whew: 놀라움, 실망, 안도의 표현

10) own : 피를 나눈, 직접적인

11) poke one's nose in~ : ~(쓸데없이) 참견하다.

tin-pedler. His communication was listened to with great delight, and no little[12] hilarity, and the boys discussed the probable effect of the projected meeting.

"Fitz will be perfectly raving," said Henry Fairbanks. "There's nothing that will take down his pride so much."

"He'll deny the relationship, probably," said Oscar.

"How can he?"

"He'll do it. See if he don't. It would be death to all his aristocratic claims to admit it."

"Suppose it were yourself, Oscar?"

"I'd say, 'How are you, cousin? How's the business?'" answered Oscar, promptly.

"I believe you would, Oscar. There's nothing of the snob about you."

"I hope not."

"Yet your family stands as high as Fletcher's."

"That's a point I leave to others to discuss," said Oscar. "My father is universally respected, I am sure, but he rose from the ranks. He was once a printer's devil, like my friend Harry Walton. Wouldn't it be ridiculous in me to turn up my nose at Walton, just because he stands now where my father did thirty years ago? It would be the same thing as sneering at father."

"Give us your hand, Oscar," said Henry Fairbanks. "You've got no nonsense about you—I like you."

"I'm not sure whether your compliment is deserved, Henry," said Oscar, "but if I have any nonsense it isn't of that kind."

"Do you believe Fitz has any suspicion that he has a cousin in the tin business?"

"No; I don't believe he has. He must know he has poor relations, living in the country, but he probably thinks as little as possible about them. As long as they don't intrude themselves upon his greatness, I suppose he is satisfied."

"And as long as no one suspects that he has any connection with such plebeians."

"Of course."

---

12) no little : not a little, much

"What sort of a man is this tin-pedler, Tom?" asked Oscar.

"He's a pretty sharp fellow—not educated, or polished, you know, but he seems to have some sensible ideas. He said he had never seen the Fletchers; because he didn't want to poke his nose in where he wasn't wanted. He showed his good sense also by saying that he had rather have me for a cousin than Fitz."

"That isn't a very high compliment—I'd say the same myself."

"Thank you, Oscar. Your compliment exalts me. You won't mind my strutting[13] a little."

And Tom humorously threw back his head, and strutted about with mock[14] pride.

"To be sure," said Oscar, "you don't belong to one of the first families of Boston, like our friend, Fitz."

"No, I belong to one of the second families. You can't blame me, for I can't help it."

"No, I won't blame you, but of course I consider you low."

"I am afraid, Tom, I haven't got any cousins in the tin trade, like Fitz."

"Poor Fitz! he little dreams of his impending trial. If he did, I am afraid he wouldn't sleep a wink[15] to-night."

"I wish I thought as much of myself as Fitz does," said Henry Fairbanks. "You can see by his dignified pace, and the way he tosses his head, how well satisfied he is with being Fitzgerald Fletcher, Esq."

"I'll bet five cents he won't strut round so much to-morrow afternoon," said Tom, "after his interview with his new cousin. But hush, boys! Not a word more of this. There's Fitz coming up the hill. I wouldn't have him suspect what's going on, or he might defeat our plans by staying away."

---

13) strut: 점잔빼며 걷다.
14) mock : 흉내, 모조품, 가짜
15) do not sleep a wink : 한 숨도 못자다.

CHAPTER XI.

FITZ AND HIS COUSIN.

The next morning at eight the boys began to gather in the field beside the Seminary. They began to play ball, but took little interest in the game, compared with the "tragedy in real life," as Tom jocosely called it, which was expected soon to come off[1].

Fitz appeared upon the scene early. In fact one of the boys called for him, and induced him to come round to school earlier than usual. Significant glances were exchanged when he made his appearance, but Fitz suspected nothing, and was quite unaware that he was attracting more attention than usual.

Punctually at half-past eight, Abner Bickford with his tin-cart appeared in the street, and with a twitch of the rein began to ascend the Academy Hill.

"Look there," said Tom Carver, "the tin-pedler's coming up the hill. Wonder if he expects to sell any of his wares to us boys. Do you know him, Fitz?"

"I!" answered Fitzgerald with a scornful look, "what should I know of a tin-pedler?"

Tom's mouth twitched, and his eyes danced with the anticipation of fun.

By this time Mr. Bickford had brought his horse to a halt, and jumping from his box, approached the group of boys, who suspended their game.

"We don't want any tinware," said one of the boys, who was not in the secret.

"Want to know! Perhaps you haven't got tin enough to pay for it. Never mind, I'll buy you for old rags, at two cents a pound."

"He has you there, Harvey," said Tom Carver. "Can I do anything for you, sir?"

"Is your name Fletcher?" asked Abner, not appearing to recognize Tom.

"Why, he wants you, Fitz!" said Harvey, in surprise.

---

1) come off: 일어나다, 발생하다.

"This gentleman's name is Fletcher," said Tom, placing his hand on the shoulder of the astonished Fitzgerald.

"Not Fitz Fletcher?" said Abner, interrogatively.

"My name is Fitzgerald Fletcher," said the young Bostonian, haughtily, "but I am at a loss to understand why you should desire to see me."

Abner advanced with hand extended, his face lighted up with an expansive grin.

"Why, Cousin Fitz," he said heartily, "do you mean to say you don't know me?"

"Sir," said Fitzgerald, drawing back, "you are entirely mistaken in the person. I don't know you."

"I guess it's you that are mistaken, Fitz," said the pedler, familiarly; "why, don't you remember Cousin Abner, that used to trot you on his knee when you was a baby? Give us your hand, in memory of old times."

"You must be crazy," said Fitzgerald, his cheeks red with indignation, and all the more exasperated because he saw significant smiles on the faces of his school-companions.

"I s'pose you was too young to remember me," said Abner. "I haint[2] seen you for ten years."

"Sir," said Fitz, wrathfully, "you are trying to impose upon[3] me. I am a native of Boston."

"Of course you be," said the imperturbable pedler. "Cousin Jim—that's your father—went to Boston when he was a boy, and they do say he's worked his way up to be a mighty rich man. Your father is rich, aint he?"

"My father is wealthy, and always was," said Fitzgerald.

"No he wasn't, Cousin Fitz," said Abner. "When he was a boy, he used to work in grandfather's store up to Hampton; but he got sort of discontented and went to Boston. Did you ever hear him tell of his cousin Roxanna? That's my mother."

"I see that you mean to insult me, fellow," said Fitz, pale with passion. "I don't know what your object is, in pretending that I am your relation.

2) haint : have (has) not

3) impose upon~ : ~을 속이다.

If you want any pecuniary help—"

"Hear the boy talk![4]" said the pedler, bursting into a horse laugh. "Abner Bickford don't want no pecuniary help, as you call it. My tin-cart'll keep me, I guess."

"You needn't claim relationship with me," said Fitzgerald, scornfully; "I haven't any low relations."

"That's so," said Abner, emphatically; "but I aint sure whether I can say that for myself."

"Do you mean to insult me?"

"How can I? I was talkin' of my relations. You say you aint one of 'em."

"I am not."

"Then you needn't go for to put on the coat. But you're out of your reckoning[5], I guess. I remember your mother very well. She was Susan Baker."

"Is that true, Fitz?"

"Ye—es," answered Fitz, reluctantly.

"I told you so," said the pedler, triumphantly.

"Perhaps he is your cousin, after all," said Henry Fairbanks.

"I tell you he isn't," said Fletcher, impetuously.

"How should he know your mother's name, then, Fitz?" asked Tom.

"Some of you fellows told him," said Fitzgerald.

"I can say, for one, that I never knew it," said Tom.

"Nor I."

"Nor I."

"We used to call her Sukey Baker," said Abner. "She used to go to the deestrict school along of Mother. They was in the same class. I haven't seen your mother since you was a baby. How many children has she got?"[6]

"I must decline answering your impertinent questions." said Fitzgerald, desperately. He began to entertain[7], for the first time, the horrible suspicion that the pedler's story might be true—that he might after all be his

---

4) Hear the boy talk! : 말하는 것 보게!

5) out of one's reckoning : 판단을 그르치다.

6) 이 대사에서 보이는 문법적 오류는 교육받지 못했음을 보여주는 것들임.

7) entertain : ~을 생각하다.

cousin. But he resolved that he never would admit it— NEVER! Where would be his pretentious claims to aristocracy—where his pride—if this humiliating discovery were made? Judging of his school-fellows and himself, he feared that they would look down upon him.

"You seem kind o' riled to find that I am your cousin," said Abner. "Now, Fitz, that's foolish. I aint rich, to be sure, but I'm respectable. I don't drink nor chew, and I've got five hundred dollars laid away[8] in the bank."

"You're welcome to[9] your five hundred dollars," said Fitz, in what was meant to be a tone of withering sarcasm.

"Am I? Well, I'd orter be, considerin' I earned it by hard work. Seems to me you've got high notions, Fitz. Your mother was kind of flighty, and I've heard mine say Cousin Jim—that's your father—was mighty sot up[10] by gettin' rich. But seems to me you ought not to deny your own flesh and blood."

"I don't know who you refer to, sir."

"Why, you don't seem to want to own me as your cousin."

"Of course not. You're only a common tin-pedler."

"Well, I know I'm a tin-pedler, but that don't change my bein' your cousin."

"I wish my father was here to expose your falsehood."

"Hold on there![11]" said Abner. "You're goin' a leetle too far[12]. I don't let no man, nor boy neither, charge me with lyin', if he is my cousin, I don't stand that, nohow."

There was something in Abner's tone which convinced Fitzgerald that he was in earnest, and that he himself must take care not to go too far.

"I don't wish to have anything more to say to you," said Fitz.

"I say, boys," said Abner, turning to the crowd who had now formed a circle around the cousins, "I leave it to you if it aint mean for Fitz to treat me in that way. If he was to come to my house, that aint the

---

8) lay away : 저축하다.
9) You are welcome to~ : 네가 ~하던 알바 아니다.
10) sot up : 술에 빠지다.
11) Hold on there! : 그만 두게!
12) go too far : 지나치다, 극단에 흐르다.

way I'd treat him."

"Come, Fitz," said Tom, "you are not behaving right. I would not treat my cousin that way."

"He isn't my cousin, and you know it," said Fitz, stamping with rage.

"I wish I wasn't," said Abner. "If I could have my pick, I'd rather have him," indicating Tom. "But blood can't be wiped out. We're cousins, even if we don't like it."

"Are you quite sure you are right about this relationship?" asked Henry Fairbanks, gravely. "Fitz, here, says he belongs to one of the first families of Boston."

"Well, I belong to one of the first families of Hampton," said Abner, with a grin. "Nobody don't look down on me, I guess."

"You hear that, Fitz," said Oscar. "Be sensible, and shake hands with your cousin."

"Yes, shake hands with your cousin!" echoed the boys.

"You all seem to want to insult me," said Fitz, sullenly.

"Not I," said Oscar, "and I'll prove it—will you shake hands with me, sir?"

"That I will," said Abner, heartily. "I can see that you're a young gentleman, and I wish I could say as much[13] for my cousin, Fitz."

Oscar's example was followed by the rest of the boys, who advanced in turn, and shook hands with the tin-pedler.

"Now Fitz, it's your turn," said Tom.

"I decline," said Fitz, holding his hands behind his back.

"How much he looks like his marm did when she was young," said Abner. "Well, boys, I can't stop no longer. I didn't think Cousin Fitz would be so stuck up, just because his father's made some money. Good-mornin'!"

"Three cheers for Fitz's cousin!" shouted Tom.

They were given with a will, and Mr. Bickford made acknowledgment by a nod and a grin.

"Remember me to your mother when you write, Cousin Fitz," he said at parting.

Fitz was too angry to reply. He walked off sullenly, deeply mortified

---

13) as much : 그 만큼, 같게.

and humiliated, and for weeks afterward nothing would more surely throw him into a rage than any allusion to his cousin the tin-pedler. One good effect, however, followed. He did not venture to allude to the social position of his family in presence of his school-mates, and found it politic[14] to lay aside some of his airs of superiority.

---

14) politic : 현명한

Chapter XII.

HARRY JOINS THE CLIONIAN SOCIETY.

A week later Harry Walton received the following note:—

"Centreville, May 16th, 18—,

"Dear Sir: At the last meeting of the Clionian Society you were elected a member. The next meeting will be held on Thursday evening, in the Academy building.

"Yours truly,

"GEORGE SANBORN,

"Secretary. "MR. HARRY WALTON."

Our hero read this letter with satisfaction. It would be pleasant for him to become acquainted with the Academy students, but he thought most of the advantages which his membership would afford him in the way of writing and speaking. He had never attempted to debate, and dreaded attempting it for the first time; but he knew that nothing desirable would be accomplished without effort, and he was willing to make that effort.

"What have you there, Walton?" asked Clapp, noticing the letter which he held in his hand.

"You can read it if you like," said Harry.

"Humph!" said Clapp; "so you are getting in with[1] the Academy boys?"

"Why shouldn't he?" said Ferguson.

"Oh, they're a stuck-up set."

"I don't find them so—that is[2], with one exception," said Harry.

"They are mostly the sones of rich men, and look down on those who have to work for a living."

Clapp was of a jealous and envious disposition, and he was always fancying slights where they were not intended.

1) get in with~ : ~와 친해지다.

2) that is : that is to say, 즉, 말하자면

"If I thought so," said Harry, "I would not join the Society, but as they have elected me, I shall become a member, and see how things turn out."

"It is a good plan, Harry," said Ferguson. "It will be a great advantage to you."

"I wish I had a chance to attend the Academy for a couple of years," said our hero, thoughtfully.

"I don't," said Clapp. "What's the good of studying Latin and Greek, and all that rigmarole[3]? It won't bring you money, will it?"

"Yes," said Ferguson. "Education will make a man more competent to earn money, at any rate in many cases. I have a cousin, who used to go to school with me, but his father was able to send him to college. He is now a lawyer in Boston, making four or five times my income. But it isn't for the money alone that an education is worth having. There is a pleasure in being educated."

"So I think," said Harry.

"I don't see it," said Clapp. "I wouldn't be a bookworm for anybody. There's Walton learning French. What good is it ever going to do him?"

"I can tell you better by and by, when I know a little more," said Harry. "I am only a beginner now."

"Dr. Franklin would never have become distinguished if he had been satisfied with what he knew as an apprentice," said Ferguson.

"Oh, if you're going to bring up Franklin again, I've got through," said Clapp with a sneer. "I forgot that Walton was trying to be a second Franklin."

"I don't see much chance of it," said Harry, good-humoredly. "I should like to be if I could."

Clapp seemed to be in an ill-humor, and the conversation was not continued. He had been up late the night before with Luke Harrison, and both had drank more than was good for them. In consequence, Clapp had a severe headache, and this did not improve his temper.

"Come round Thursday evening, Harry," said Oscar Vincent, "and go to the Society with me. I will introduce you to the fellows. It will

3) rigmarole : 시시한 긴 이야기

be less awkward, you know."

"Thank you, Oscar. I shall be glad to accept your escort."

When Thursday evening came, Oscar and Harry entered the Society hall arm in arm. Oscar led his companion up to the Secretary and introduced him.

"I am glad to see you, Mr. Walton," said he. "Will you sign your name to the Constitution[4]? That is all the formality[5] we require."

"Except a slight pecuniary disbursement," added Oscar.

"How much is the entrance fee?" asked Harry.

"One dollar. You will pay that to the Treasurer."

Oscar next introduced our hero to the President, and some of the leading members, all of whom welcomed him cordially.

"Good-evening, Mr. Fletcher," said Harry, observing that young gentleman near him.

"Good-evening, sir," said Fletcher stiffly, and turned on his heel[6] without offering his hand.

"Fletcher don't feel well," whispered Oscar. "He had a visit from a poor relation the other day—a tin-pedler—and it gave such a shock to his sensitive system[7] that he hasn't recovered from it yet."

"I didn't imagine Mr. Fletcher had such a plebeian relative," said Harry.

"Nor did any of us. The interview was rich. It amused us all, but what was sport[8] to us was death to poor Fitz. You have only to make the most distant allusion to a tin-pedler in his hearing, and he will become furious."

"Then I will be careful."

"Oh, it won't do any harm. The fact was, the boy was getting too overbearing, and putting on altogether too many airs. The lesson will do him good, or ought to."

Here the Society was called to order, and Oscar and Harry took their seats.

---

4) the Constitution : (모임의) 정관
5) formality : 절차
6) turn on one's heel : 돌아서다.
7) system : 몸, 전신
8) sport : 웃음거리.

The exercises proceeded in regular order until the President announced a declamation[9] by Fitzgerald Fletcher.

"Mr. President," said Fletcher, rising, "I must ask to be excused. I have not had time to prepare a declamation."

"Mr. President," said Tom Carver, "under the circumstances I hope you will excuse Mr. Fletcher, as during the last week he has had an addition to his family."

There was a chorus of laughter, loud and long, at this sally. All were amused except Fletcher himself, who looked flushed and provoked.

"Mr. Fletcher is excused," said the President, unable to refrain from smiling. "Will any member volunteer to speak in his place? It will be a pity to have our exercises incomplete."

Fletcher was angry, and wanted to be revenged on somebody. A bright idea came to him. He would place the "printer's devil," whose admission to the Society he resented, in an awkward position. He rose with a malicious smile upon his face.

"Mr. President," he said, "doubtless Mr. Walton, the new member who has done us the *honor_* to join our society, will be willing to supply my place[10]."

"We shall certainly be glad to hear a declamation from Mr. Walton, though it is hardly fair to call upon him at such short notice[11]."

"Can't you speak something, Harry?" whispered Oscar. "Don't do it, unless you are sure you can get through[12]."

Harry started in surprise when his name was first mentioned, but he quickly resolved to accept his duty. He had a high reputation at home for speaking, and he had recently learned a spirited poem, familiar, no doubt, to many of my young readers, called "Shamus O'Brien." It is the story of an Irish volunteer, who was arrested for participating in the Irish rebellion of '98, and is by turns spirited and pathetic. Harry had rehearsed it to himself only the night before, and he had confidence in a strong and retentive memory. At the President's invitation he rose to his feet, and said, "Mr. President, I will do as well as I can, but

---

9) declamation : 낭독, 낭송.

10) supply one's place : ~를 대신하다, 보충하다.

11) at (on) short notice : 급히, 곧바로

12) get through : 끝내다, 성취하다.

I hope the members of the Society will make allowance for me[13], as I have had no time for special preparation."

All eyes were fixed with interest upon our hero, as he advanced to the platform, and, bowing composedly, commenced his declamation. It was not long before that interest increased, as Harry proceeded in his recitation. He lost all diffidence, forgot the audience, and entered thoroughly into the spirit of the piece. Especially when, in the trial scene, Shamus is called upon to plead[14] guilty or not guilty, Harry surpassed himself, and spoke with a spirit and fire which brought down the house. This is the passage:—

"My lord, if you ask me, if in my life-time
I thought any treason, or did any crime,
That should call to my cheek, as I stand alone here,
The hot blush of shame, or the coldness of fear,
Though I stood by the grave to receive my death-blow,
Before God and the world I would answer you, no!
But if you would ask me, as I think it like,
If in the rebellion I carried a pike,
An' fought for ould Ireland from the first to the close,
An' shed the heart's blood of her bitterest foes,
I answer you, *yes*; and I tell you again,
Though I stand here to perish, it's my glory that then
In her cause I was willing my veins should run dhry,
An' that now for her sake I am ready to die."

After the applause had subsided, Harry proceeded, and at the conclusion of the declamation, when he bowed modestly and left the platform, the hall fairly shook with the stamping, in which all joined except Fletcher, who sat scowling with dissatisfaction at a result so different from his hopes. He had expected to bring discomfiture to our hero. Instead, he had given him an opportunity to achieve a memorable triumph.

---

13) make allowance for~ : ~를 관대히 보아주다.
14) plead : 변론하다, 주장하다.

"You did yourself credit, old boy![15]" said Oscar, seizing and wringing the hand of Harry, as the latter resumed his seat. "Why, you ought to go on the stage!"

"Thank you," said Harry; "I am glad I got through well."

"Isn't Fitz mad, though? He thought you'd break down. Look at him!"

Harry looked over to Fletcher, who, with a sour expression, was sitting upright, and looking straight before him.

"He don't look happy, does he?" whispered Oscar, comically.

Harry came near laughing aloud, but luckily for Fletcher's peace of mind, succeeded in restraining himself.

"He won't call you up again in a hurry; see if he does," continued Oscar.

"I am sure we have all been gratified by Mr. Walton's spirited declamation," said the President, rising. "We congratulate ourselves upon adding so fine a speaker to our society, and hope often to have the pleasure of hearing him declaim."

There was a fresh outbreak of applause, after which the other exercises followed. When the meeting was over the members of the Society crowded around Harry, and congratulated him on his success. These congratulations he received so modestly, as to confirm the favorable impression he had made by his declamation.

"By Jove![16] old fellow," said Oscar, as they were walking home, "I am beginning to be proud of you. You are doing great credit to your teacher."

"Thank you, Professor," said Harry. "Don't compliment me too much, or I may become vain[17], and put on airs."

"If you do, I'll get Fitz to call, and remind you that you are only a printer's devil, after all."

---

15) old boy! " 여보게! 친구!
16) By Jove! : 반드시, 맹세코.
17) vain : 우쭐대는, 허영심이 강한

CHAPTER XIII.

VACATION BEGINS AT THE ACADEMY.

Not long after his election as a member of the Clionian Society, the summer term of the Prescott Academy closed. The examination took place about the tenth of June, and a vacation followed, lasting till the first day of September. Of course, the Clionian Society, which was composed of Academy students, suspended its meetings for the same length of time. Indeed, the last meeting for the season took place during the first week in June, as the evenings were too short and too warm, and the weather was not favorable to oratory. At the last meeting, an election was held of officers to serve for the following term. The same President and Vice-President were chosen; but as the Secretary declined to serve another term, Harry Walton, considerably to his surprise, found himself elected in his place.

Fitzgerald Fletcher did not vote for him. Indeed, he expressed it as his opinion that it was a shame to elect a "printer's devil" Secretary of the Society.

"Why is it?" said Oscar. "Printing is a department of literature, and the Clionian is a literary society, isn't it?"

"Of course it is a literary society, but a printer's devil is not literary."

"He's as literary as a tin-pedler," said Tom Carver, maliciously.

Fletcher turned red, but managed to say, "And what does that prove?"

"We don't object to you because you are connected with the tin business."

"Do you mean to insult me?" demanded Fletcher, angrily. "What have I to do with the tin business?"

"Oh, I beg pardon, it's your cousin that's in it."

"I deny the relationship," said Fletcher, "and I will thank you not to refer again to that vulgar[1] pedler."

"Really, Fitz, you speak rather roughly, considering he's your cousin. But as to Harry Walton, he's a fine fellow, and he has an excellent handwriting, and I was very glad to vote for him."

---

1) vulgar : 천박한, 상스러운.

Fitzgerald walked away, not a little[2] disgusted, as well at the allusion to the tin-pedler, as at the success of Harry Walton in obtaining an office to which he had himself secretly aspired. He had fancied that it would sound well to put "Secretary of the Clionian Society" after his name, and would give him increased consequence[3] at home. As to the tin-pedler, it would have relieved his mind to hear that Mr. Bickford had been carried off[4] suddenly by an apoplectic fit, and notwithstanding the tie of kindred, he would not have taken the trouble to put on mourning[5] in his honor.

Harry Walton sat in Oscar Vincent's room, on the last evening of the term. He had just finished reciting the last French lesson in which he would have Oscar's assistance for some time to come.

"You have made excellent progress," said Oscar. "It is only two months since you began French, and now you take a long lesson in translation."

"That is because I have so good a teacher. But do you think I can get along without help during the summer?"

"No doubt of it. You may find some difficulties, but those you can mark, and I will explain when I come back. Or I'll tell you what is still better. Write to me, and I'll answer. Shall I write in French?"

"I wish you would, Oscar."

"Then I will. I'm rather lazy with the pen, but I can find time for you. Besides, it will be a good way for me to keep up my French."

"Shall you be in Boston all summer, Oscar?"

"No; our family has a summer residence at Nahant, a sea-shore place twelve miles from Boston. Then I hope father will let me travel about a little on my own account[6]. I want to go to Saratoga and Lake George."

"That would be splendid."

"I wish you could go with me, Harry."

"Thank you, Oscar, but perhaps you can secure Fletcher's company. That will be much better than that of a 'printer's devil' like myself."

"It may show bad taste, but I should prefer your company, notwith-

---

2) not a little : 크게, 적지 않게.
3) consequence : (지위, 입장 등의) 중요함, 저명함.
4) be carried off : ~의 생명을 빼앗다, 죽다.
5) put on (go into, take to) mourning : 상복을 입다.
6) on one's own account : ~의 비용으로

standing your low employment."

"Thank you, Oscar. I am much obliged."

"Fitz has been hinting to me how nice it would be for us to go off somewhere together, but I don't see it in that light. I asked him why he didn't secure board with his cousin, the tin-pedler, but that made him angry, and he walked away in disgust. But I can't help pitying you a little, Harry."

"Why? On account of my occupation?"

"Partly. All these warm summer days, you have got to be working at the case, while I can lounge in the shade, or travel for pleasure. Sha'n't you have a vacation?"

"I don't expect any. I don't think I could well be spared[7]. However, I don't mind it. I hope to do good deal of studying while you are gone."

"And I sha'n't do any."

"Neither would I, perhaps, in your position. But there's a good deal of difference between us. You are a Latin and Greek scholar, and can talk French, while I am at the bottom of the ladder. I have no time to lose."

"You have begun to mount the ladder, Harry. Don't be discouraged. You can climb up."

"But I must work for it. I haven't got high enough up to stop and rest. But there is one question I want to ask you, before you go."

"What is it?"

"What French book would you recommend after I have finished this Reader? I am nearly through now."

"Telemaque will be a good book to take next. It is easy and interesting. Have you got a French dictionary?"

"No; but I can buy one."

"You can use mine while I am gone. You may as well have it as not. I have no copy of Telemaque, but I will send you one from Boston."

"Agreed, provided you will let me pay you for it."

"So I would, if I had to buy one. But I have got an old copy, not very ornamental, but complete. I will send it through the mail."

"Thank you, Oscar. How kind you are!"

---

7) be spared : do without, 짬을 내다.

"Don't flatter me, Harry. The favors you refer to are but trifles. I will ask a favor of you in return."

"I wish you would."

"Then help me pack my trunk. There's nothing I detest so much. Generally I tumble things in helter-skelter[8)], and get a good scolding from mother for doing it, when she inspects my trunk."

"I'll save you the trouble[9)], then. Bring what you want to carry home, and pile it on the floor, and I'll do the packing."

"A thousand thanks, as the French say. It takes a load off my mind. By the way, here's a lot of my photographs. Would you like one to remember your professor by?"

"Very much, Oscar."

"Then take your choice. They don't do justice to my beauty[10)], which is of a stunning description, as you are aware, nor do they convey an idea of the lofty intellect which sits enthroned behind my classic brow; but such as they are, you are welcome to one."

"Any one would think, to hear you, that you had no end of self-conceit, Oscar," said Harry, laughing.

"How do you know that I haven't? Most people think they are beautiful. A photographer told my sister that he was once visited by a frightfully homely man from the country, who wanted his 'picter took.' When the result was placed before him, he seemed dissatisfied. 'Don't you think it like?' said the artist.— 'Well, ye-es,' he answered slowly, 'but it hasn't got my sweet expression about the mouth!'"

"Very good," said Harry, laughing; "that's what's the matter with your picture."

"Precisely. I am glad your artistic eye detects what is wanting. But, hold! there's a knock. It's Fitz, I'll bet a hat."

"Come in!" he cried, and Fletcher walked in.

"Good-evening, Fletcher," said Oscar. "You see I'm packing, or rather Walton is packing. He's a capital[11)] packer."

"Indeed!" sneered Fletcher. "I was not aware that Mr. Walton was

8) in helter-skelter : 당황하여, 허둥지둥하여
9) save~ the trouble : ~의 수고를 덜다.
10) do justice to~ : ~을 올바로 평가하다, ~을 정당하게 다루다.
11) capital : principal, 으뜸가는

in that line of business. What are his terms[12)]?"

"I refer you to him."

"What do you charge for packing trunks, Mr. Walton?"

"I think fifty cents would be about right," answered Harry, with perfect gravity. "Can you give me a job, Mr. Fletcher?"

"I might, if I had known it in time, though I am particular who handles my things."

"Walton is careful, and I can vouch for[13)] his honesty," said Oscar, carrying out the joke. "His wages in the printing office are not large, and he would be glad to make a little extra money."

"It must be very inconvenient to be poor," said Fletcher, with a supercilious[14)] glance at our hero, who was kneeling before Oscar's trunk.

"It is," answered Harry, quietly, "but as long as work is to be had I shall not complain."

"To be sure!" said Fletcher. "My father is wealthy, and I shall not have to work."

"Suppose he should fail?" suggested Oscar.

"That is a very improbable supposition," said Fletcher, loftily.

"But not impossible?"

"Nothing is impossible."

"Of course. I say, Fitz, if such a thing should happen, you've got something to fall back upon[15)]."

"To what do you refer?"

"Mr. Bickford could give you an interest in the tin business."

"Good-evening!" said Fletcher, not relishing[16)] the allusion.

"Good-evening! Of course I shall see you in the city."

"I suppose I ought not to tease Fitz," said Oscar, after his visitor had departed, "but I enjoy seeing how disgusted he looks."

In due time the trunk was packed, and Harry, not without regret, took leave of[17)] his friend for the summer.

---

12) terms: condition
13) vouch for : 보증하다, 단언하다.
14) supercilious : naughty
15) fall back upon : 의지하다.
16) relish : enjoy
17) take leave of~ : ~와 작별하다.

CHAPTER XIV.

HARRY BECOMES AN AUTHOR.

The closing of the Academy made quite a difference in the life of Centreville. The number of boarding scholars was about thirty, and these, though few in number, were often seen in the street and at the postoffice, and their withdrawal left a vacancy. Harry Walton felt quite lonely at first; but there is no cure for loneliness like occupation, and he had plenty of that. The greater part of the day was spent in the printing office, while his evenings and early mornings were occupied in study and reading. He had become very much interested in French, in which he found himself advancing rapidly. Occasionally he took tea at Mr. Ferguson's, and this he always enjoyed; for, as I have already said, he and Ferguson held very similar views on many important subjects. One evening, at the house of the latter, he saw a file of weekly papers, which proved, on examination, to be back numbers of the "Weekly Standard," a literary paper issued in Boston.

"I take the paper for my family," said Ferguson. "It contains quite a variety of reading matter, stories, sketches[1] and essays."

"It seems quite interesting," said Harry.

"Yes, it is. I will lend you some of the back numbers, if you like."

"I would like it. My father never took a literary paper; his means were so limited that he could not afford it."

"I think it is a good investment. There are few papers from which you cannot obtain in a year more than the worth of the subscription[2]. Besides, if you are going to be an editor, it will be useful for you to become familiar with the manner in which such papers are conducted."

When Harry went home he took a dozen copies of the paper, and sat up late reading them. While thus engaged an idea struck him. It was this: Could not he write something which would be accepted for publication in the "Standard"? It was his great ambition to learn to write for the press[3], and he felt that he was old enough to commence.

---

1) sketch : 소품, 단편, 짤막한 글.

2) subscription : (예약) 구독료

"If I don't succeed the first time, I can try again," he reflected.

The more he thought of it, the more he liked the plan. It is very possible that he was influenced by the example of Franklin, who, while yet a boy in his teens, contributed articles to his brother's paper though at the time the authorship was not suspected. Finally he decided to commence writing as soon as he could think of a suitable subject. This he found was not easy. He could think of plenty of subjects of which he was not qualified to write, or in which he felt little interest; but he rightly decided that he could succeed better with something that had a bearing[4] upon his own experience or hopes for the future.

Finally he decided to write on Ambition.

I do not propose to introduce Harry's essay in these pages, but will give a general idea of it, as tending to show his views of life.

He began by defining ambition as a desire for superiority, by which most men were more or less affected, though it manifested itself in very different ways, according to the character of him with whom it was found. Here I will quote a passage, as a specimen of Harry's style and mode of expression.

"There are some who denounce ambition as wholly bad and to be avoided by all; but I think we ought to make a distinction between true and false ambition. The desire of superiority is an honorable motive, if it leads to honorable exertion. I will mention Napoleon as an illustration of false ambition, which is selfish in itself, and has brought misery and ruin, to prosperous nations. Again, there are some who are ambitious to dress better than their neighbors, and their principal thoughts are centred upon the tie of their cravat, or the cut[5] of their coat, if young men; or upon the richness and style of their dresses, if they belong to the other sex. Beau Brummel[6] is a noted instance of this kind of ambition. It is said that fully half of his time was devoted to his toilet[7], and the other half to displaying it in the streets, or in society. Now this is a very low form of ambition, and it is wrong to indulge it, because it

3) the press : 정기간행물, 신문
4) a bearing : relation, reference
5) cut : 재단, 마름질
6) Beau Brummel : 19세기 초 영국 멋쟁이.
7) one's toilet : ~의 화장, 몸단장

is a waste of time which could be much better employed."

Harry now proceeded to describe what he regarded as a true and praiseworthy ambition. He defined it as a desire to excel in what would be of service to the human race, and he instanced his old Franklin, who, induced by an honorable ambition, worked his way up to a high civil station, as well as a commanding position in the scientific world. He mentioned Columbus as ambitious to extend the limits of geographical knowledge, and made a brief reference to the difficulties and discouragements over which he triumphed on the way to success. He closed by an appeal to boys and young men to direct their ambition into worthy channels, so that even if they could not leave behind a great name, they might at least lead useful lives, and in dying have the satisfaction of thinking that they done some service to the race.

This will give a very fair idea of Harry's essay. There was nothing remarkable about it, and no striking originality in the ideas, but it was very creditably expressed for a boy of his years, and did even more credit to his good judgment, since it was an unfolding of the principles by which he meant to guide his own life.

It must not be supposed that our hero was a genius, and that he wrote his essay without difficulty. It occupied him two evenings to write it, and he employed the third in revising and copying it. It covered about five pages of manuscript, and, according to his estimate, would fill about two-thirds of a long column in the "Standard."

After preparing it, the next thing was to find a *nom de plume*[8)], for he shrank from signing his own name. After long consideration, he at last decided upon Franklin, and this was the name he signed to his maiden[9)] contribution to the press.

He carried it to the post-office one afternoon, after his work in the printing office was over, and dropped it unobserved into the letter-box. He did not want the postmaster to learn his secret, as he would have done had he received it directly from him, and noted the address on the envelope.

For the rest of the week, Harry went about his work weighed down

---

8) nom de plume : name of feather (pen), 필명.
9) maiden : 처음의, 처녀~의

with his important secret—a secret which he had not even shared with Ferguson. If the essay was declined, as he thought it might very possibly be, he did not want any one to know it. If it were accepted, and printed, it would be time enough then to make it known. But there were few minutes in which his mind was not on his literary venture. His pre-occupation was observed by his fellow-workmen in the office, and he was rallied[10] upon it, good-naturedly, by Ferguson, but in a different spirit by Clapp.

"It seems to me you are unusually silent, Harry," said Ferguson. "You're not in love, are you?"

"Not that I know of," said Harry, smiling. "It's rather too early yet."

"I've known boys of your age to fancy themselves in love."

"He is more likely thinking up some great discovery," said Clapp, sneering. "You know he's a second Franklin."

"Thank you for the compliment," said our hero, good-humoredly, "but I don't deserve it. I don't expect to make any great discovery at present."

"I suppose you expect to set the river on fire[11], some day," said Clapp, sarcastically.

"I am afraid it wouldn't do much good to try," said Harry, who was too sensible to take offence. "It isn't so easily done."

"I suppose some day we shall be proud of having been in the same office with so great a man," pursued Clapp.

"Really, Clapp, you're rather hard[12] on our young friend," said Ferguson. "He doesn't put on any airs of superiority, or pretend to anything uncommon."

"He's very kind—such an intellect as he's got, too!" said Clapp.

"I'm glad you found it out," said Harry. "I haven't a very high idea of my intellect yet. I wish I had more reason to do so."

Finding that he had failed in his attempt to provoke Harry by his ridicule, Clapp desisted, but he disliked him none the less.

The fact was, that Clapp was getting into a bad way. He had no high aim in life, and cared chiefly for the pleasure of the present moment. He had found Luke Harrison a congenial companion, and they had been

---

10) rally : barter
11) set the river (Thames) on fire : 세상을 깜짝 놀라게 하다.
12) hard : 무정한, 냉혹한

associated in more than one excess. The morning previous, Clapp had entered the printing office so evidently under the influence of liquor[13], that he had been sharply reprimanded by Mr. Anderson.

"I don't choose to interfere with your mode of life, unwise and ruinous as I may consider it," he said, "as long as it does not interfere with your discharge of duty. But to-day you are clearly incapacitated for labor, and I have a right to complain. If it happens again, I shall be obliged to look for another journeyman."

Clapp did not care to leave his place just at present, for he had no money saved up, and was even somewhat in debt, and it might be some time before he got another place. So he rather sullenly agreed to be more careful in future, and did not go to work till the afternoon. But though circumstances compelled him to submit, it put him in bad humor, and made him more disposed to sneer than ever. He had an unreasoning[14] prejudice against Harry, which was stimulated by Luke Harrison, who had this very sufficient reason for hating our hero, that he had succeeded in injuring him. As an old proverb has it "We are slow to forgive those whom we have injured."

---

13) under the influence of liquor : 술 취한 상태로

14) unreasoning : 이치에 맞지 않는

CHAPTER XV.

A LITERARY DEBUT.

Harry waited eagerly for the next issue of the "Weekly Standard." It was received by Mr. Anderson in exchange for the "Centreville Gazette," and usually came to hand on Saturday morning. Harry was likely to obtain the first chance of examining the paper, as he was ordinarily sent to the post-office on the arrival of the morning mail.

His hands trembled as he unfolded the paper and hurriedly scanned the contents. But he looked in vain for his essay on Ambition. There was not even a reference to it. He was disappointed, but he soon became hopeful again.

"I couldn't expect it to appear so soon," he reflected. "These city weeklies have to be printed some days in advance.[1] It may appear yet."

So he was left in suspense another week, hopeful and doubtful by turns of the success of his first offering for the press. He was rallied from time to time on his silence in the office, but he continued to keep his secret. If his contribution was slighted, no one should know it but himself.

At last another Saturday morning came around and again he set out for the post-office. Again he opened the paper with trembling fingers, and eagerly scanned the well-filled columns. This time his search was rewarded. There, on the first column of the last page, in all the glory of print[2], was his treasured essay!

A flash of pleasure tinged his cheek, and his heart beat rapidly, as he read his first printed production. It is a great event in the life of a literary novice, when he first sees himself. Even Byron[3] says,—

"'Tis pleasant, sure, to see one's self in print."

To our young hero the essay read remarkably well—better than he had expected; but then, very likely he was prejudiced in its favor. He

---

1) in advance : before, 미리.
2) print : 인쇄물, 간행물.
3) Byron : 영국 시인(1778~ 1824)

read it through three times on his way back to the printing office, and each time felt better satisfied.

"I wonder if any of the readers will think it was written by a boy?" thought Harry. Probably many did so suspect, for, as I have said, though the thoughts were good and sensible, the article was only moderately well expressed. A practised critic would readily have detected marks of immaturity, although it was a very creditable production for a boy of sixteen.

"Shall I tell Ferguson?" thought Harry.

On the whole he concluded to remain silent just at present. He knew Ferguson took the paper, and waited to see if he would make any remark about it.

"I should like to hear him speak of it, without knowing that I was the writer," thought our hero.

Just before he reached the office, he discovered with satisfaction the following editorial reference to his article:—

"We print in another column an essay on 'ambition' by a new contributor. It contains some good ideas, and we especially commend it to the perusal[4] of our young readers. We hope to hear from 'Franklin' again."

"That's good," thought Harry. "I am glad the editor likes it. I shall write again as soon as possible."

"What makes you look so bright, Harry?" asked Ferguson, as he re-entered the office. "Has any one left you a fortune[5]?"

"Not that I know of," said Harry. "Do I look happier than usual?"

"So it seems to me."

Harry was spared answering this question, for Clapp struck in, grumbling, as usual: "I wish somebody'd leave me a fortune. You wouldn't see me here long."

"What would you do?" asked his fellow-workman.

"Cut work to begin with. I'd go to Europe and have a jolly time."

"You can do that without a fortune."

"I should like to know how?"

---

4) perusal : reading, 정독.

5) leave~ a fortune : ~에게 재산을 남기다.

"Be economical, and you can save enough in three years to pay for a short trip. Bayard Taylor was gone two years, and only spent five hundred dollars."

"Oh, hang economy[6)]!" drawled Clapp. "It don't suit me. I should like to know how a feller's going to economize on fifteen dollars a week."

"I could."

"Oh, no doubt," sneered Clapp, "but a man can't starve."

"Come round and take supper with me, some night," said Ferguson, good-humoredly, "and you can judge for yourself whether I believe in starving."

Clapp didn't reply to this invitation. He would not have enjoyed a quiet evening with his fellow-workman. An evening at billiards or cards, accompanied by bets on the games, would have been much more to his mind[7)].

"Who is Bayard Taylor, that made such a cheap tour in Europe?" asked Harry, soon afterward.

"A young journalist who had a great desire to travel. He has lately published an account of his tour. I don't buy many books, but I bought that. Would you like to read it?"

"Very much."

"You can have it any time."

"Thank you."

On Monday, a very agreeable surprise awaited Harry.

"I am out of copy[8)]," he said, going up to Mr. Anderson's table.

"Here's a selection for the first page," said Mr. Anderson. "Cut it in two, and give part of it to Clapp."

Could Harry believe his eyes! It was his own article on ambition, and it was to be reproduced in the "Gazette." Next to the delight of seeing one's self in print for the first time, is the delight of seeing that first article copied. It is a mark of appreciation which cannot be mistaken.

Still Harry said nothing, but, with a manner as unconcerned as possible, handed the lower half of the essay to Clapp to set up. The signature

---

6) hang economy! : 빌어먹을 절약!
7) to one's mind : ~의 마음에 들어, 기분에 맞아.
8) copy : 원고, 기사거리.

"Franklin" had been cut off, and the name of the paper from which the essay had been cut was substituted.

"Wouldn't Clapp feel disgusted," thought Harry, "if he knew that he was setting up an article of mine. I believe he would have a fit[9])."

He was too considerate to expose his fellow-workman to such a contingency, and went about his work in silence.

That evening he wrote to the publisher of the "Standard," inclosing[10]) the price of two copies of the last number, which he desired should be sent to him by mail. He wished to keep one himself, and the other he intended to forward to his father, who, he knew, would sympathize with him in his success as well as his aspirations. He accompanied the paper by a letter in which he said,—

"I want to improve in writing as much as, I can. I want to be something more than a printer, sometime. I shall try to qualify myself for an editor; for an editor can exert a good deal of influence in the community. I hope you will approve my plans."

In due time Harry received the following reply:—

"My dear son:—I am indeed pleased and proud to hear of your success, not that it is a great matter in itself, but because I think it shows that you are in earnest in your determination to win an honorable position by honorable labor. I am sorry that my narrow means have not permitted me to give you those advantages which wealthy fathers can bestow upon their sons. I should like to have sent you to college and given you an opportunity afterward of studying for a profession. I think your natural abilities would have justified such an outlay[11]). But, alas! poverty has always held me back. It shuts out you, as it has shut out me, from the chance of culture. Your college, my boy, must be the printing office. If you make the best of that, you will find that it is no mean instructor. Not Franklin alone, but many of our most eminent and influential men have graduated from it.

"You will be glad to hear that we are all well. I have sold the cow which I bought of Squire Green, and got another in her place that proves to be much better. We all send much love, and your mother wishes

---

9) a fit : 발작, 경련.
10) inclose : enclose, 동봉하다.
11) outlay : 지출(액).

me to say that she misses you very much, as indeed we all do. But we know that you are better off in Centreville than you would be at home, and that helps to make us contented. Don't forget to write every week.

"Your affectionate father,

"HIRAM WALTON.

"P. S[12].—If you print any more articles, we shall be interested to read them."

Harry read this letter with eager interest. He felt glad that his father was pleased with him, and it stimulated him to increased exertions.

"Poor father!" he said to himself. "He has led a hard life, cultivating that rocky little farm. It has been hard work and poor pay with him. I hope there is something better in store[13] for him. If I ever get rich, or even well off, I will take care that he has an easier time."

After the next issue of the "Gazette" had appeared, Harry informed Ferguson in confidence[14] that he was the author of the article on Ambition.

"I congratulate you, Harry," said his friend. "It is an excellent essay, well thought out, and well expressed. I don't wonder, now you tell me of it. It sounds like you. Without knowing the authorship, I asked Clapp his opinion of it."

"What did he say?"

"Are you sure it won't hurt your feelings?"

"It may; but I shall get over it. Go ahead."

"He said it was rubbish."

Harry laughed.

"He would be confirmed in his decision, if he knew that I wrote it," he said.

"No doubt. But don't let that discourage you. Keep on writing by all means, and you'll become an editor in time."

---

12) P.S. : Postscript, 추신.
13) in store : 비축하여.
14) in confidence : 비밀로.

CHAPTER XVI.

FERDINAND B. KENSINGTON.

It has already been mentioned that John Clapp and Luke Harrison were intimate. Though their occupations differed, one being a printer and the other a shoemaker, they had similar tastes, and took similar views of life. Both were discontented with the lot[1] which Fortune had assigned them. To work at the case, or the shoe-bench, seemed equally irksome, and they often lamented to each other the hard necessity which compelled them to it. Suppose we listen to their conversation, as they walked up the village street, one evening about this time, smoking cigars.

"I say[2], Luke," said John Clapp, "I've got tired of this kind of life. Here I've been in the office a year, and I'm not a cent richer than when I entered it, besides working like a dog all the while."

"Just my case," said Luke. "I've been shoe-makin' ever since I was fourteen, and I'll be blest if I can show five dollars, to save my life."

"What's worse," said Clapp, "there isn't any prospect of anything better in my case. What's a feller to do on fifteen dollars a week?"

"Won't old Anderson raise your wages?"

"Not he! He thinks I ought to get rich on what he pays me now," and Clapp laughed scornfully. "If I were like Ferguson, I might. He never spends a cent without taking twenty-four hours to think it over beforehand."

My readers, who are familiar with Mr. Ferguson's views and ways of life, will at once see that this was unjust, but justice cannot be expected from an angry and discontented man.

"Just so," said Luke. "If a feller was to live on bread and water, and get along with one suit of clothes a year, he might save something, but that aint *my* style."

"Nor mine."

"It's strange how lucky some men are," said Luke. "They get rich without tryin'. I never was lucky. I bought a ticket in a lottery once,

---

1) the lot : destiny

2) I say : 어이, 이봐

but of course I didn't draw anything. Just my luck[3]!"

"So did I," said Clapp, "but I fared no better. It seemed as if Fortune had a spite against me. Here I am twenty-five years old, and all I'm worth is two dollars and a half, and I owe more than that to the tailor."

"You're as rich as I am," said Luke. "I only get fourteen dollars a week. That's less than you do."

"A dollar more or less don't amount to much," said Clapp. "I'll tell you what it is, Luke," he resumed after a pause, "I'm getting sick of Centreville."

"So am I," said Luke, "but it don't make much difference. If I had fifty dollars, I'd go off and try my luck somewhere else, but I'll have to wait till I'm gray-headed before I get as much as that."

"Can't you borrow it?"

"Who'd lend it to me?"

"I don't know. If I did, I'd go in for[4] borrowing myself. I wish there was some way of my getting to California."

"California!" repeated Luke with interest. "What would you do there?"

"I'd go to the mines."

"Do you think there's money to be made there?"

"I know there is," said Clapp, emphatically.

"How do you know it?"

"There's an old school-mate of mine—Ralph Smith—went out there two years ago. Last week he returned home—I heard it in a letter—and how much do you think he brought with him?"

"How much?"

"Eight thousand dollars!"

"Eight thousand dollars! He didn't make it all at the mines, did he?"

"Yes, he did. When he went out there, he had just money enough to pay his passage. Now, after only two years, he can lay off and live like a gentleman."

"He's been lucky, and no mistake[5]."

"You bet he has. But we might be as lucky if we were only out

---

3) Just my luck! : 나는 언제나 운이 나쁘다, 또 글렀다!

4) go in for : 열중하다, 골몰하다.

5) and no mistake : 확실, 꼭. 확실히.

there."

"Ay, there's the rub[6]. A fellow can't travel for nothing."

At this point in their conversation, a well-dressed young man, evidently a stranger in the village, met them, and stopping, asked politely for a light.

This Clapp afforded him.

"You are a stranger in the village?" he said, with some curiosity.

"Yes, I was never here before. I come from New York."

"Indeed! If I lived in New York I'd stay there, and not come to such a beastly place as Centreville."

"Do you live here?" asked the stranger.

"Yes."

"I wonder you live in such a beastly place," he said, with a smile.

"You wouldn't, if you knew the reason."

"What is the reason?"

"I can't get away."

The stranger laughed.

"Cruel parents?" he asked.

"Not much[7]," said Clapp. "The plain reason is, that I haven't got money enough to get me out of town."

"It's the same with me," said Luke Harrison.

"Gentlemen, we are well met," said the stranger. "I'm hard up[8] myself."

"You don't look like it," said Luke, glancing at his rather flashy attire.

"These clothes are not paid for," said the stranger, laughing; "and what's more, I don't think they are likely to be. But, I take it, you gentlemen are better off than I in one respect. You've got situations[9]—something to do."

"Yes, but on starvation pay," said Clapp. "I'm in the office of the 'Centreville Gazette.'"

"And I'm in a shoemaker's shop. It's a beastly business for a young man of spirit," said Luke.

---

6) the rub : 장애(물), 문제점.
7) not much : 당치도 않아, 말도 안돼.
8) be hard up : 돈에 궁하다
9) situation : 일자리

"Well, I'm a gentleman at large, living on my wits[10], and pretty poor living it is sometimes," said the stranger. "As I think we'll agree together pretty well, I'm glad I've met you. We ought to know each other better. There's my card."

He drew from his pocket a highly glazed piece of pasteboard, bearing the name,

FREDERICK B. KENSINGTON.

"I haven't any cards with me," said Clapp, "but my name is John Clapp."

"And mine is Luke Harrison," said the bearer of that appellation.

"I'm proud to know you, gentlemen. If you have no objection, we'll walk on together."

To this Clapp and Luke acceded readily. Indeed, they were rather proud of being seen in company with a young man so dashing in manner, and fashionably dressed, though in a pecuniary way their new acquaintance, by his own confession, was scarcely as well off as themselves.

"Where are you staying, Mr. Kensington?" said Clapp.

"At the hotel. It's a poor place. No style."

"Of course not. I can't help wondering, Mr. Kensington, what can bring you to such a one-horse[11] place as this."

"I don't mind telling you, then. The fact is, I've got an old aunt living about two miles from here. She's alone in the world—got neither chick nor child[12]—and is worth at least ten thousand dollars. Do you see?"

"I think I do," said Clapp. "You want to come in for a share of[13] the stamps."

"Yes; I want to see if I can't get something out of the old girl," said Kensington, carelessly.

"Do you think the chance is good?"

"I don't know. I hear she's pretty tight-fisted. But I've run on here on the chance of doing something. If she will only make me her heir, and give me five hundred dollars in hand, I'll go to California, and see what'll turn up[14]."

---

10) live on one's wits : (직업 없이) 변통수로 이럭저럭 살아가다.
11) one-horse : second-rate
12) get(have) neither chick nor child : 아이가 하나도 없다.
13) come in for a ashare of : ~의 몫을 받다.
14) turn up : happen

"California!" repeated John Clapp and Luke in unison.

"Yes; were you ever there?"

"No; but we were talking of going there just as you came up," said John. "An old school-mate of mine has just returned from there with eight thousand dollars in gold."

"Lucky fellow! That's the kind of haul I'd like to make."

"Do you know how much it costs to go out there?"

"The prices are down just at present. You can go for a hundred dollars—second cabin."

"It might as well be a thousand!" said Luke. "Clapp and I can't raise a hundred dollars apiece to save our lives."

"I'll tell you what," said Kensington. "You two fellows are just the company I'd like. If I can raise five hundred dollars out of the old girl, I'll take you along with me, and you can pay me after you get out there."

John Clapp and Luke Harrison were astounded at this liberal offer from a perfect stranger, but they had no motives of delicacy about accepting it. They grasped the hand of their new friend, and assured him that nothing would suit them so well.

"All right!" said Kensington. "Then it's agreed. Now, boys, suppose we go round to the tavern, and ratify our compact by a drink."

"I say amen to that[15)]," answered Clapp, "but I insist on standing treat[16)]."

"Just as you say," said Kensington. "Come along."

It was late when the three parted company. Luke and John Clapp were delighted with their new friend, and, as they staggered home with uncertain steps, they indulged in[17)] bright visions of future prosperity.

---

15) say amen to~ : ~에 동의하다.
16) stand treat : 한턱내다.
17) indulge in : 탐닉하다, ~에 빠지다.

CHAPTER XVII.

AUNT DEBORAH.

Miss Deborah Kensington sat in an old-fashioned rocking-chair covered with a cheap print[1], industriously engaged in footing[2] a stocking. She was a maiden lady of about sixty, with a thin face, thick[3] seamed with wrinkles, a prominent nose, bridged by spectacles, sharp gray eyes, and thin lips. She was a shrewd New England woman, who knew very well how to take care of and increase the property which she had inherited. Her nephew had been correctly informed as to her being close-fisted. All her establishment[4] was carried on with due regard to economy, and though her income in the eyes of a city man would be counted small, she saved half of it every year, thus increasing her accumulations.

As she sat placidly knitting, an interruption came in the shape of a knock at the front door.

"I'll go myself," she said, rising, and laying down the stocking. "Hannah's out in the back room, and won't hear. I hope it aint Mrs. Smith, come to borrow some butter. She aint returned that last half-pound she borrowed. She seems to think her neighbors have got to support her."

These thoughts were in her mind as she opened the door. But no Mrs. Smith presented her figure to the old lady's gaze. She saw instead, with considerable surprise, a stylish young man with a book under his arm. She jumped to the conclusion that he was a book-pedler, having been annoyed by several persistent specimens of that class of travelling merchants.

"If you've got books to sell," she said, opening the attack, "you may as well go away. I aint got no money to throw away."

Mr. Ferdinand B. Kensington—for he was the young man in question—

---

1) print : 날염포, 사라사.
2) foot : 발 부분을 붙이다.
3) thick : 짙게
4) establishment : household, 가정, 세대.

laughed heartily, while the old lady stared at him half amazed, half angry.

"I don't see what there is to laugh at," said she, offended.

"I was laughing at the idea of my being taken for a book-pedler."

"Well, aint you one?" she retorted. "If you aint, what be you?"

"Aunt Deborah, don't you know me?" asked the young man, familiarly.

"Who are you that calls me aunt?" demanded the old lady, puzzled.

"I'm your brother Henry's son. My name is Ferdinand."

"You don't say so!"[5] ejaculated the old lady. "Why, I'd never 'ave thought it. I aint seen you since you was a little boy."

"This don't look as if I was a little boy, aunt," said the young man, touching his luxuriant whiskers.

"How time passes, I do declare![6]" said Deborah. "Well, come in, and we'll talk over old times. Where did you come from?"

"From the city of New York. That's where I've been living for some time."

"You don't say! Well, what brings you this way?"

"To see you, Aunt Deborah. It's so long since I've seen you that I thought I'd like to come."

"I'm glad to see you, Ferdinand," said the old lady, flattered by such a degree of dutiful attention from a fine-looking young man. "So your poor father's dead?"

"Yes, aunt, he's been dead three years."

"I suppose he didn't leave much. He wasn't very forehanded.[7]"

"No, aunt; he left next to nothing."

"Well, it didn't matter much, seein' as you was the only child, and big enough to take care of yourself."

"Still, aunt, it would have been comfortable if he had left me a few thousand dollars."

"Aint you doin' well? You look as if you was," said Deborah, surveying critically[8] her nephew's good clothes.

"Well, I've been earning a fair salary, but it's very expensive living

---

5) you don't say(so)! : 설마, 그럴 리가 없다.
6) I (do) declare! : (문장 끝에서) ~이고 말고, 정말 ~이다.
7) forehanded : well-to-do, 장래에 대비한
8) critically : 정밀하게

in a great city like New York."

"Humph[9]! that's accordin' as you manage. If you live snug, you can get along there cheap as well as anywhere, I reckon. What was you doin'?"

"I was a salesman for A. T. Stewart, our leading dry-goods merchant."
"What pay did you get?"

"A thousand dollars a year."

"Why, that's a fine salary. You'd ought to save up a good deal."

"You don't realize how much it costs to live in New York, aunt. Of course, if I lived here, I could live on half the sum, but I have to pay high prices for everything in New York."

"You don't need to spend such a sight[10] on dress," said Deborah, disapprovingly.

"I beg your pardon, Aunt Deborah; that's where you are mistaken. The store-keepers in New York expect you to dress tip-top[11] and look genteel, so as to do credit to them. If it hadn't been for that, I shouldn't have spent half so much for dress. Then, board's very expensive."

"You can get boarded here for two dollars and a half a week," said Aunt Deborah.

"Two dollars and a half! Why, I never paid less than eight dollars a week in the city, and you can only get poor board for that."

"The boarding-houses must make a great deal of money," said Deborah. "If I was younger, I'd maybe go to New York, and keep one myself."

"You're rich, aunt. You don't need to do that."

"Who told you I was rich?" said the old lady, quickly.

"Why, you've only got yourself to take care of, and you own this farm, don't you?"

"Yes, but farmin' don't pay much."

"I always heard you were pretty comfortable."

"So I am," said the old lady, "and maybe I save something; but my income aint as great as yours."

"You have only yourself to look after, and it is cheap living in

---

9) humph! : (불신, 불안, 경멸의 표시) 흥!
10) a sight : 거액
11) tip-top : perfectly

Centreville."

"I don't fling money away. I don't spend quarter as much as you on dress."

Looking at the old lady's faded bombazine dress, Ferdinand was very ready to believe this.

"You don't have to dress here, I suppose," he answered. "But, aunt, we won't talk about money matters just yet. It was funny you took me for a book-pedler."

"It was that book you had, that made me think so."

"It's a book I brought as a present to you, Aunt Deborah."

"You don't say!" said the old lady, gratified. "What is it? Let me look at it."

"It's a copy of 'Pilgrim's Progress[12),' illustrated. I knew you wouldn't like the trashy[13) books they write nowadays, so I brought you this."

"Really, Ferdinand, you're very considerate," said Aunt Deborah, turning over the leaves with manifest pleasure. "It's a good book, and I shall be glad to have it. Where are you stoppin'?"

"At the hotel in the village."

"You must come and stay here. You can get 'em to send round your things any time."

"Thank you, aunt, I shall be delighted to do so. It seems so pleasant to see you again after so many years. You don't look any older than when I saw you last."

Miss Deborah knew very well that she did look older, but still she was pleased by the compliment. Is there any one who does not like to receive the same assurance?

"I'm afraid your eyes aint very sharp, Ferdinand," she said. "I feel I'm gettin' old. Why, I'm sixty-one, come October."

"Are you? I shouldn't call you over fifty, from your looks, aunt. Really I shouldn't."

"I'm afraid you tell fibs[14) sometimes," said Aunt Deborah, but she

---

12) Pilgrim's Progress : 영국의 John Bunyan이 1684년에 쓴 종교적 우화소설. 『천로역정』으로 번역되었다.

13) trashy : rubbishy, 시시한

14) fibs : 악의 없는 거짓말

said it very graciously, and surveyed her nephew very kindly. "Heigh ho![15] it's a good while since your poor father and I were children together, and went to the school-house on the hill. Now he's gone, and I'm left alone."

"Not alone, aunt. If he is dead, you have got a nephew."

"Well, Ferdinand, I'm glad to see you, and I shall be glad to have you pay me a good long visit. But how can you be away from your place so long? Did Mr. Stewart give you a vacation?"

"No, aunt; I left him."

"For good?"

"Yes."

"Left a place where you was gettin' a thousand dollars a year!" said the old lady in accents of strong disapproval.

"Yes, aunt."

"Then I think you was very foolish," said Deborah with emphasis.

"Perhaps you won't, when you know why I left it."

"Why did you?"

"Because I could do better."

"Better than a thousand dollars a year!" said Deborah with surprise.

"Yes, I am offered two thousand dollars in San Francisco."

"You don't say!" ejaculated Deborah, letting her stocking drop in sheer amazement.

"Yes, I do. It's a positive fact."

"You must be a smart clerk!"

"Well, it isn't for me to say," said Ferdinand, laughing.

"When be you goin' out?"

"In a week, but I thought I must come and bid you good-by first."

"I'm real glad to see you, Ferdinand," said Aunt Deborah, the more warmly because she considered him so prosperous that she would have no call to help him. But here she was destined to find herself mistaken.

---

15) Heigh ho! : 힘내!

CHAPTER XVIII.

AUNT AND NEPHEW.

"I don't think I can come here till to-morrow, Aunt Deborah," said Ferdinand, a little later. "I'll stay at the hotel to-night, and come round with my baggage in the morning."

"Very well, nephew, but now you're here, you must stay to tea."

"Thank you, aunt, I will."

"I little thought this mornin', I should have Henry's son to tea," said Aunt Deborah, half to herself. "You don't look any like him, Ferdinand."

"No, I don't think I do."

"It's curious too, for you was his very picter[1] when you was a boy."

"I've changed a good deal since then, Aunt Deborah," said her nephew, a little uneasily.

"So you have, to be sure. Now there's your hair used to be almost black, now it's brown. Really I can't account for it," and Aunt Deborah surveyed the young man over her spectacles.

"You've got a good memory, aunt," said Ferdinand with a forced laugh.

"Now ef your hair had grown darker, I shouldn't have wondered," pursued Aunt Deborah; "but it aint often black turns to brown."

"That's so, aunt, but I can explain it," said Ferdinand, after a slight pause.

"How was it?"

"You know the French barbers can change your hair to any shade[2] you want."

"Can they?"

"Yes, to be sure. Now—don't laugh at me, aunt—a young lady I used to like didn't fancy dark hair, so I went to a French barber, and he changed the color for me in three months."

"You don't say!"

"Fact, aunt; but he made me pay him well too."

---

1) picter : picture, counterpart, 꼭 닮은 사람.

2) shade : (검은 빛깔을 섞어서 생기는) 명암의 정도, 농담의 색조

"How much did you give him?"

"Fifty dollars, aunt."

"That's what I call wasteful," said Aunt Deborah, disapprovingly. "Couldn't you be satisfied with the nat'ral color of your hair? To my mind black's handsomer than brown."

"You're right, aunt. I wouldn't have done it if it hadn't been for Miss Percival."

"Are you engaged to her?"

"No, Aunt Deborah. The fact was, I found she wasn't domestic, and didn't know anything about keeping house, but only cared for dress, so I drew off,[3] and she's married to somebody else now."

"I'm glad to hear it," said Deborah, emphatically. "The jade![4] She wouldn't have been a proper wife for you. You want some good girl that's willin' to go into the kitchen, and look after things, and not carry all she's worth on her back."

"I agree with you, aunt," said Ferdinand, who thought it politic, in view of the request he meant to make by and by, to agree with his aunt in her views of what a wife should be.

Aunt Deborah began to regard her nephew as quite a sensible young man, and to look upon him with complacency.

"I wish, Ferdinand," she said, "you liked farmin'."

"Why, aunt?"

"You could stay here, and manage my farm for me."

"Heaven forbid![5]" thought the young man with a shudder. "I should be bored to death. Does the old lady think I would put on a frock and overalls, and go out and plough, or hoe potatoes?"

"It's a good, healthy business," pursued Aunt Deborah, unconscious of the thoughts which were passing through her nephew's mind, "and you wouldn't have to spend much for dress. Then I'm gittin' old, and though I don't want to make no promises, I'd very likely will[6] it to you, ef I was satisfied with the way you managed."

"You're very kind, aunt," said Ferdinand, "but I'm afraid I wasn't

---

3) draw off : 손을 떼다.
4) the jade : 닳고 닳은 (굴러먹은) 여자.
5) Heaven forbid! : 당치도 않다.
6) will : 유산으로 물려주다.

cut out for[7] farming. You know I never lived in the country."

"Why, yes, you did," said the old lady. "You was born in the country, and lived there till you was ten years old."

"To be sure," said Ferdinand, hastily, "but I was too young then to take notice of farming. What does a boy of ten know of such things?"

"To be sure. You're right there."

"The fact is, Aunt Deborah, some men are born to be farmers, and some are born to be traders. Now, I've got a talent for trading. That's the reason I've got such a good offer from San Francisco."

"How did you get it? Did you know the man?"

"He used to be in business in New York. He was the first man I worked for, and he knew what I was. San Francisco is full of money, and traders make more than they do here. That's the reason he can afford to offer me so large a salary."

"When did he send for you?"

"I got the letter last week."

"Have you got it with you?"

"No, aunt; I may have it at the hotel," said the young man, hesitating, "but I am not certain."

"Well, it's a good offer. There isn't nobody in Centreville gets so large a salary."

"No, I suppose not. They don't need it, as it is cheap living here."

"I hope when you get out there, Ferdinand, you'll save up money. You'd ought to save two-thirds of your pay."

"I will try to, aunt."

"You'll be wantin' to get married bimeby[8], and then it'll be convenient to have some money to begin with."

"To be sure, aunt. I see you know how to manage."

"I was always considered a good manager," said Deborah, complacently. "Ef your poor father had had *my* faculty[9], he wouldn't have died as poor as he did, I can tell you."

"What a conceited old woman she is, with her faculty!" thought Ferdinand, but what he said was quite different.

---

7) be cut out for : 천성이 ~에 맞다.
8) bimeby : by and by, soon
9) faculty : 재능, 재간

"I wish he had had, aunt. It would have been better for me."

"Well, you ought to get along, with your prospects."

"Little the old woman knows what my real prospects are!" thought the young man.

"Of course I ought," he said.

"Excuse me a few minutes, nephew," said Aunt Deborah, gathering up her knitting and rising from her chair. "I must go out and see about tea. Maybe you'd like to read that nice book you brought."

"No, I thank you, aunt. I think I'll take a little walk round your place, if you'll allow me."

"Sartin, Ferdinand. Only come back in half an hour; tea'll be ready then."

"Yea, aunt, I'll remember."

So while Deborah was in the kitchen, Ferdinand took a walk in the fields, laughing to himself from time to time, as if something amused him.

He returned in due time, and sat down to supper Aunt Deborah had provided her best, and, though the dishes were plain, they were quite palatable.[10)]

When supper was over, the young man said,—

"Now, aunt, I think I will be getting back to the hotel."

"You'll come over in the morning, Ferdinand, and fetch your trunk?"

"Yes, aunt. Good-night."

"Good-night."

"Well," thought the young man, as he tramped back to the hotel, I've opened the campaign, and made, I believe, a favorable impression. But what a pack of lies I have had to tell, to be sure! The old lady came near catching me once or twice, particularly about the color of my hair. It was a lucky thought, that about the French barber. It deceived the poor old soul. I don't think she could ever have been very handsome. If she was she must have changed fearfully."

In the evening, John Clapp and Luke Harrison came round to the hotel to see him.

"Have you been to see your aunt?" asked Clapp.

---

10) palatable : tasty, savory

"Yes, I took tea there."

"Have a good time?"

"Oh, I played the dutiful nephew to perfection[11]. The old lady thinks a sight of me."

"How did you do it?"

"I agreed with all she said, told her how young she looked, and humbugged her generally."

Clapp laughed.

"The best part of the joke is—will you promise to keep dark[12]?"

"Of course."

"Don't breathe[13] it to a living soul, you two fellows. *She isn't my aunt of all*!"

"Isn't your aunt?"

"No, her true nephew is in New York—I know him.—but I know enough of family matters to gull[14] the old lady, and, I hope, raise a few hundred dollars out of her."

This was a joke which Luke and Clapp could appreciate, and they laughed heartily at the deception which was being practised on simple Aunt Deborah, particularly when Ferdinand explained how he got over the difficulty of having different colored hair from the real owner of the name he assumed.

"We must have a drink on that," said Luke. "Walk up[15], gentlemen."

"I'm agreeable," said Ferdinand.

"And I," said Clapp. "Never refuse a good offer, say I."

Poor Aunt Deborah! She little dreamed that she was the dupe of a designing adventurer who bore no relationship to her.

---

11) to perfection : completely, 더할 나위 없이.

12) keep dark : 비밀에 붙여두다.

13) breathe : whisper , 말해 주다.

14) gull : humbag, cheat

15) walk up : 어서 오십시오.

CHAPTER XIX.

THE ROMANCE OF A RING.

Ferdinand B. Kensington, as he called himself, removed the next morning to the house of Aunt Deborah. The latter received him very cordially, partly because it was a pleasant relief to her solitude to have a lively and active young man in the house, partly because she was not forced to look upon him as a poor relation in need of pecuniary assistance. She even felt considerable respect for the prospective recipient of an income of two thousand dollars, which in her eyes was a magnificent salary.

Ferdinand, on his part, spared no pains to make himself agreeable to the old lady, whom he had a mercenary object in pleasing. Finding that she was curious to hear about the great city, which to her was as unknown as London or Paris, he gratified her by long accounts, chiefly of as imaginative character, to which she listened greedily. These included some personal adventures, in all of which he figured[1)] very creditably.

Here is a specimen:

"By the way, Aunt Deborah," he said, casually, "have you noticed this ring on my middle finger?"

"No, I didn't notice it before, Ferdinand. It's very handsome."

"I should think it ought to be, Aunt Deborah," said the young man.

"Why?"

"It cost enough to be handsome."

"How much did it cost?" asked the old lady, not without curiosity.

"Guess."

"I aint no judge of such things; I've only got this plain gold ring. Yours has got some sort of a stone in it."

"That stone is a diamond, Aunt Deborah!"

"You don't say so! Let me look at it. It aint got no color. Looks like glass."

"It's very expensive, though. How much do you think it cost?"

---

1) figure : 통하다, 나타나다.

"Well, maybe five dollars."

"Five dollars!" ejaculated the young man. "Why, what can you be thinking of, Aunt Deborah?"

"I shouldn't have guessed so much," said the old lady, misunderstanding him, "only you said it was expensive."

"So it is. Five dollars would be nothing at all."

"You don't say it cost more?"

"A great deal more."

"Did it cost ten dollars?"

"More."

"Fifteen?"

"I see, aunt, you have no idea of the cost of diamond rings! You may believe me or not, but that ring cost six hundred and fifty dollars."

"What!" almost screamed Aunt Deborah, letting fall her knitting in her surprise.

"It's true."

"Six hundred and fifty dollars for a little piece of gold and glass!" ejaculated the old lady.

"Diamond, aunt, not glass."

"Well, it don't look a bit better'n glass, and I do say," proceeded Deborah, with energy, "that it's a sin and a shame to pay so much money for a ring. Why, it was more than half your year's salary, Ferdinand."

"I agree with you, aunt; it would have been very foolish and wrong for a young man on a small salary like mine to buy so expensive a ring as this. I hope, Aunt Deborah, I have inherited too much of your good sense to do that."

"Then where did you get it?" asked the old lady, moderating her tone.

"It was given to me."

"Given to you! Who would give you such a costly present?"

"A rich man whose life I once saved, Aunt Deborah."

"You don't say so, Ferdinand!" said Aunt Deborah, interested. "Tell me all about it."

"So I will, aunt, though I don't often speak of it," said Ferdinand, modestly. "It seems like boasting, you know, and I never like to do that. But this is the way it happened.

"Now for a good tough lie!" said Ferdinand to himself, as the old lady suspended her work, and bent forward with eager attention.

"You know, of course, that New York and Brooklyn are on opposite sides of the river, and that people have to go across in ferry-boats."

"Yes, I've heard that, Ferdinand."

"I'm glad of that, because now you'll know that my story is correct. Well, one summer I boarded over in Brooklyn—on the Heights—and used to cross the ferry morning and night. It was the Wall street ferry, and a great many bankers and rich merchants used to cross daily also. One of these was a Mr. Clayton, a wholesale dry-goods merchant, immensely rich, whom I knew by sight, though I had never spoken to him. It was one Thursday morning—I remember even the day of the week—when the boat was unusually full. Mr. Clayton was leaning against the side-railing talking to a friend, when all at once[2] the railing gave way[3], and he fell backward into the water, which immediately swallowed him up."

"Merciful man![4]" ejaculated Aunt Deborah, intensely interested. "Go on, Ferdinand."

"Of course there was a scene of confusion and excitement," continued Ferdinand, dramatically. 'Man overboard![5] Who will save him?' said more than one. 'I will,' I exclaimed, and in an instant I had sprang over the railing into the boiling current."

"Weren't you frightened to death?" asked the old lady. "Could you swim?"

"Of course I could. More than once I have swum all the way from New York to Brooklyn. I caught Mr. Clayton by the collar, as he was sinking for the third time, and shouted to a boatman near by to come to my help. Well, there isn't much more to tell. We were taken on board the boat, and rowed to shore. Mr. Clayton recovered his senses so far as to realize that I had saved his life.

"'What is your name, young man?' he asked, grasping my hand.

"'Ferdinand B. Kensington,' I answered modestly.

"'You have saved my life,' he said warmly.

---

2) all at once : suddenly
3) give way : 무너지다, 부서지다
4) merciful man! : 저런!
5) Man overboard! : 사람이 빠졌어!

"'I am very glad of it,' said I.

"'You have shown wonderful bravery."

"'Oh no,' I answered. 'I know how to swim, and I wasn't going to see you drown before my eyes.'

"'I shall never cease to be grateful to you.'

"'Oh, don't think of it,' said I.

"'But I must think of it,' he answered. 'But for you I should now be a senseless corpse lying in the bottom of the river,' and he shuddered.

"'Mr. Clayton,' said I, 'let me advise you to get home as soon as possible, or you will catch your death of cold.'

"'So will you,' he said. 'You must come with me.'

"He insisted, so I went, and was handsomely treated, you may depend. Mr. Clayton gave me a new suit of clothes, and the next morning he took me to Tiffany's—that's the best jeweller in New York—and bought me this diamond ring. He first offered me money, but I felt delicate about taking money for such a service, and told him so. So he bought me this ring."

"Well, I declare!" ejaculated Aunt Deborah.

"That was an adventure. But it seems to me, Ferdinand, I would have taken the money."

"As to that, aunt, I can sell this ring, if ever I get hard up, but I hope I sha'n't be obliged to."

"You certainly behaved very well, Ferdinand. Do you ever see Mr. Clayton now?"

"Sometimes, but I don't seek his society[6)], for fear he would think I wanted to get something more out of him."

"How much money do you think he'd have given you?" asked Aunt Deborah, who was of a practical nature.

"A thousand dollars, perhaps more."

"Seems to me I would have taken it."

"If I had, people would have said that's why I jumped into the water, whereas I wasn't thinking anything about getting a reward. So now, aunt, you won't think it very strange that I wear such an expensive ring."

"Of course it makes a difference, as you didn't buy it yourself. I

---

6) society : 교제, 함께 있기

don't see how folks can be such fools as to throw away hundreds of dollars for such a trifle."

"Well, aunt, everybody isn't as sensible and practical as you. Now I agree with you; I think it's very foolish. Still I'm glad I've got the ring, because I can turn it into money when I need to. Only, you see, I don't like to part with a gift, although I don't think Mr. Clayton would blame me."

"Of course he wouldn't, Ferdinand. But I don't see why you should need money when you're goin' to get such a handsome salary in San Francisco."

"To be sure, aunt, but there's something else. However, I won't speak of it to-day. To-morrow I may want to ask your advice on a matter of business."

"I'll advise you the best I can, Ferdinand," said the flattered spinster.

"You see, aunt, you're so clear-headed, I shall place great dependence on your advice. But I think I'll take a little walk now, just to stretch my limbs."

"I've made good progress," said the young man to himself, as he lounged over the farm. "The old lady swallows[7] it all. To-morrow must come my grand stroke[8]. I thought I wouldn't propose it to-day, for fear she'd suspect the ring story."

---

7) swallow : (의심 없이) ~을 받아들이다.

8) stroke : 우연한 행운

CHAPTER XX.

A BUSINESS TRANSACTION.

Ferdinand found life at the farm-house rather slow, nor did he particularly enjoy the society of the spinster whom he called aunt. But he was playing for a valuable stake, and meant to play out[1] his game.

"Strike while the iron is hot!" said he to himself; "That's a good rule; but how shall I know when it is hot? However, I must risk something, and take my chances[2] with the old lady."

Aunt Deborah herself hastened his action. Her curiosity had been aroused by Ferdinand's intimation that he wished her advice on a matter of business, and the next morning, after breakfast, she said, "Ferdinand, what was that you wanted to consult me about? You may as well tell me now as any time."

"Here goes, then![3]" thought the young man.

"I'll tell you, aunt. You know I am offered a large salary in San Francisco?"

"Yes, you told me so."

"And, as you said the other day, I can lay up half my salary, and in time become a rich man."

"To be sure you can."

"But there is one difficulty in the way."

"What is that?"

"I must go out there."

"Of course you must," said the old lady, who did not yet see the point.

"And unfortunately it costs considerable money."

"Haven't you got enough money to pay your fare out there?"

"No, aunt; it is very expensive living in New York, and I was unable to save anything from my salary."

"How much does it cost to go out there?"

---

1) play out : finish, 마지막 수단까지 다 쓰다.
2) take one's chance : 흥하건 망하건 해보다.
3) Here goes, then! : 자, 그러면, 간다!

"About two hundred and fifty dollars."

"That's a good deal of money."

"So it is; but it will be a great deal better to pay it than to lose so good a place."

"I hope," said the old lady, sharply, "you don't expect me to pay your expenses out there."

"My dear aunt," said Ferdinand, hastily, "how can you suspect such a thing?"

"Then what do you propose to do?" asked the spinster, somewhat relieved.

"I wanted to ask your advice."

"Sell your ring. It's worth over six hundred dollars."

"Very true; but I should hardly like to part with it. I'll tell you what I have thought of. It cost six hundred and fifty dollars. I will give it as security[4] to any one who will lend me five hundred dollars, with permission to sell it if I fail to pay up the note in six months. By the way, aunt, why can't you accommodate me in this matter? You will lose nothing, and I will pay handsome interest."

"How do you know I have the money?"

"I don't know; but I think you must have. But, although I am your nephew, I wouldn't think of asking you to lend me money without security. Business is business, so I say."

"Very true, Ferdinand."

"I ask nothing on the score of[5] relationship, but I will make a business proposal."

"I don't believe the ring would fetch over six hundred dollars."

"It would bring just about that. The other fifty dollars represent the profit. Now, aunt, I'll make you a regular business proposal. If you'll lend me five hundred dollars, I'll give you my note for five hundred and fifty, bearing interest at six per cent., payable in six months, or, to make all sure, say in a year. I place the ring in your hands, with leave to sell it at the end of that time if I fail to carry out my agreement. But I sha'n't if I keep my health."

---

4) security : 담보물, 저당물

5) on the score of :~ 을 이유로.

The old lady was attracted by the idea of making a bonus of fifty dollars, but she was cautious, and averse to parting with her money.

"I don't know what to say, Ferdinand," she replied. "Five hundred dollars is a good deal of money."

"So it is, aunt. Well, I don't know but I can offer you a little better terms. Give me four hundred and seventy-five, and I'll give you a note for five hundred and fifty. You can't make as much interest anywhere else."

"I'd like to accommodate you," said the old lady, hesitating, for, like most avaricious persons, she was captivated by the prospect of making extra-legal interest.

"I know you would. Aunt Deborah, but I don't want to ask the money as a favor. It is a strictly business transaction."

"I am afraid I couldn't spare more than four hundred and fifty."

"Very well, I won't dispute about the extra twenty-five dollars. Considering how much income I'm going to get, it isn't of any great importance."

"And you'll give me a note for five hundred and fifty?"

"Yes, certainly."

"I don't know as I ought to take so much interest."

"It's worth that to me, for though, of course, I could raise it by selling the ring, I don't like to do that."

"Well, I don't know but I'll do it. I'll get some ink, and you can write me the due bill[6]."

"Why, Aunt Deborah, you haven't got the money here, have you?"

"Yes, I've got it in the house. A man paid up a mortgage last week, and I haven't yet invested the money. I meant to put it in the savings bank."

"You wouldn't get but six per cent there. Now the bonus I offer you will be equal to about twenty per cent."

"And you really feel able to pay so much?"

"Yes, aunt; as I told you, it will be worth more than that to me."

"Well, Ferdinand, we'll settle the matter now. I'll go and get the money, and you shall give me the note and the ring."

---

6) due bill : 차용증서

"Triumph!" said the young man to himself, when the old lady had left the room. "You're badly sold[7], Aunt Deborah, but it's a good job for me. I didn't think I would have so little trouble."

Within fifteen minutes the money was handed over, and Aunt Deborah took charge of the note and the valuable diamond ring.

"Be careful of the ring, Aunt Deborah," said Ferdinand. "Remember, I expect to redeem it again."

"I'll take good care of it, nephew, never fear!"

"If it were a little smaller, you could wear it, yourself."

"How would Deborah Kensington look with a diamond ring? The neighbors would think I was crazy. No: I'll keep it in a safe place, but I won't wear it."

"Now, Aunt Deborah, I must speak about other arrangements. Don't you think it would be well to start for San Francisco as soon as possible? You know I enter upon my duties as soon as I get there."

"Yes, Ferdinand, I think you ought to."

"I wish I could spare the time to spend a week with you, aunt; but business is business, and my motto is, business before pleasure."

"And very proper, too, Ferdinand," said the old lady, approvingly.

"So I think I had better leave Centreville tomorrow."

"May be you had. You must write and let me know when you get there, and how you like your place."

"So I will, and I shall be glad to know that you take an interest in me. Now, aunt, as I have some errands to do, I will walk to the village and come back about the middle of the afternoon."

"Won't you be back to dinner?"

"No, I think not, aunt."

"Very well, Ferdinand. Come as soon as you can."

Half an hour later, Ferdinand entered the office of the "Centreville Gazette."

"How do you do, Mr. Kensington?" said Clapp, eagerly. "Anything new?"

"I should like to speak with you a moment in private[8], Mr. Clapp."

---

7) be badly sold : 배신당하다.
8) in private : secretly, 살짝, 은밀히.

"All right!"

Clapp put on his coat, and went outside, shutting the door behind him.

"Well," said Ferdinand, "I've succeeded."

"Have you got the money?"

"Yes, but not quite as much as I anticipated."

"Can't you carry out your plan?" asked Clapp, soberly, fearing he was to be left out in the cold[9].

"I've formed a new one. Instead of going to California, which is very expensive, we'll go out West, say to St. Louis, and try our fortune there. What do you say?[10]"

"I'm agreed. Can Luke go too?"

"Yes. I'll take you both out there, and lend you fifty dollars each besides, and you shall pay me back as soon as you are able. Will you let your friend know?"

"Yes, I'll undertake that; but when do you propose to start?"

"To-morrow morning."

"Whew! That's short notice."

"I want to get away as soon as possible, for fear the old lady should change her mind, and want her money back."

"That's where you're right."

"Of course you must give up your situation at once, as there is short time to get ready."F

"No trouble about that," said Clapp. "I've hated the business for a long time, and shall be only too glad to leave. It's the same with Luke. He won't shed many tears at leaving Centreville."

"Well, we'll all meet this evening at the hotel. I depend upon your both being ready to start in the morning."

"All right, I'll let Luke know."

It may be thought singular that Ferdinand should have made so liberal[11] an offer to two comparative strangers; but, to do the young man justice, though he had plenty of faults, he was disposed to be generous when he had money, though he was not particular how he obtained it. Clapp

---

9) out in the cold : 따돌림 당한, 무시당해

10) What do you say? : 어떨까?

11) liberal : generous, 후한, 아끼지 않는

and Luke Harrison he recognized as congenial spirits[12], and he was willing to sacrifice something to obtain their companionship. How long his fancy was likely to last was perhaps doubtful; but for the present he was eager to associate them with his own plans.

12) congenial spirits : 성미가 맞는 사람, 인물.

CHAPTER XXI.

HARRY IS PROMOTED.

Clapp re-entered the printing office highly elated.

"Mr. Anderson," said he to the editor, "I am going to leave you."

Ferguson and Harry Walton looked up in surprise, and Mr. Anderson asked,—

"Have you got another place?"

"No; I am going West."

"Indeed! How long have you had that in view?[1)]"

"Not long. I am going with Mr. Kensington."

"The one who just called on you?"

"Yes."

"How soon do you want to leave?"

"Now."

"That is rather short notice."

"I know it, but I leave town to-morrow morning."

"Well, I wish you success. Here is the money I owe you."

"Sha'n't we see you again, Clapp?" asked Ferguson.

"Yes; I'll just look in and say good-by. Now I must go home and get ready."

"Well, Ferguson," said Mr. Andersen, after Clapp's departure, "that is rather sudden."

"So I think."

"How can we get along with only two hands?[2)]"

"Very well, sir. I'm willing to work a little longer, and Harry here is a pretty quick compositor now. The fact is, there isn't enough work for three."

"Then you think I needn't hire another journeyman?"

"No."

"If you both work harder I must increase your wages, and then I shall save money."

---

1) have~ in view : ~을 고려하다.

2) hand : 일손, laborer

"I sha'n't object to that," said Ferguson, smiling.

"Nor I," said Harry.

"I was intending at any rate to raise Harry's wages, as I find he does nearly as much as a journeyman. Hereafter I will give you five dollars a week besides your board."

"Oh, thank you, sir!" said Harry, overjoyed at his good fortune.

"As for you, Ferguson, if you will give me an hour more daily, I will add three dollars a week to your pay."

"Thank you, sir. I think I can afford now to give Mrs. Ferguson the new bonnet she was asking for this morning."

"I don't want to overwork you two, but if that arrangement proves satisfactory, we will continue it."

"I suppose you will be buying your wife a new bonnet too; eh, Harry?" said Ferguson.

"I may buy myself a new hat. Luke Harrison turned up his nose at my old one the other day."

"What will Luke do without Clapp? They were always together."

"Perhaps he is going too."

"I don't know where he will raise the money, nor Clapp either, for that matter."

"Perhaps their new friend furnishes the money."

"If he does, he is indeed a friend."

"Well, it has turned out to our advantage, at any rate, Harry. Suppose you celebrate it by coming round and taking supper with me?"

"With the greatest pleasure[3]."

Harry was indeed made happy by his promotion. Having been employed for some months on board-wages, he had been compelled to trench upon[4] the small stock of money which he had saved up when in the employ of Prof. Henderson, and he had been unable to send any money to his father, whose circumstances were straitened, and who found it very hard to make both ends meet. That evening he wrote a letter to his father, in which he inclosed ten dollars remaining to him from his fund of savings, at the same time informing him of his

---

3) with the greatest pleasure : 좋고말고요.
4) trench upon : 침해하다.

promotion. A few days later, he received the following reply:—

"MY DEAR SON:

"Your letter has given me great satisfaction, for I conclude from your promotion that you have done your duty faithfully, and won the approbation[5] of your employer. The wages you now earn will amply pay your expenses, while you may reasonably hope that they will be still further increased, as you become more skilful and experienced. I am glad to hear that you are using your leisure hours to such good purpose, and are trying daily to improve your education. In this way you may hope in time to qualify yourself for the position of an editor, which is an honorable and influential profession, to which I should be proud to have you belong.

"The money which you so considerately inclose comes at the right time. Your brother needs some new clothes, and this will enable me to provide them. We all send love, and hope to hear from you often.

"Your affectionate father,

"HIRAM WALTON."

Harry's promotion took place just before the beginning of September. During the next week the fall term of the Prescott Academy commenced, and the village streets again became lively with returning students. Harry was busy at the case, when Oscar Vincent entered the printing office, and greeted him warmly.

"How are you, Oscar?" said Harry, his face lighting up with pleasure. "I am glad to see you back. I would shake hands, but I am afraid you wouldn't like it," and Harry displayed his hands soiled with printer's ink.

"Well, we'll shake hands in spirit, then, Harry. How have you passed the time?"

"I have been very busy, Oscar."

"And I have been very lazy. I have scarcely opened a book, that is, a study-book, during the vacation. How much have you done in French?"

"I have nearly finished Telemachus."

5) win the approbation : 인정받다, 칭찬받다.

"You have! Then you have done splendidly. By the way, Harry, I received the paper you sent, containing your essay. It does you credit[6], my boy."

Mr. Anderson, who was sitting at his desk, caught the last words. "What is that, Harry?" he asked. "Have you been writing for the papers?"

Harry blushed.

"Yes, sir," he replied. "I have written two or three articles for the 'Boston Weekly Standard.'"

"Indeed! I should like to see them."

"You republished one of them in the 'Gazette,' Mr. Anderson," said Ferguson.

"What do you refer to?"

"Don't you remember an article on 'Ambition,' which you inserted some weeks ago?"

"Yes, it was a good article. Did you write it, Walton?"

"Yes, air."

"Why didn't you tell me of it?"

"He was too bashful," said Ferguson.

"I am glad to know that you can write," said the editor. "I shall call upon you for[7] assistance, in getting up paragraphs occasionally."

"I shall be very glad to do what I can," said Harry, gratified.

"Harry is learning to be an editor," said Ferguson.

"I will give him a chance for practice, then," and Mr. Anderson returned to his exchanges.

"By the way, Oscar," said Harry, "I am not a printer's devil any longer. I am promoted to be a journeyman."

"I congratulate you, Harry, but what will Fitz do now? He used to take so much pleasure in speaking of you as a printer's devil."

"I am sorry to deprive him of that pleasure. Did you see much of him in vacation, Oscar?"

"I used to meet him almost every day walking down Washington Street, swinging a light cane, and wearing a stunning necktie, as usual."

"Is he coming back this term?"

---

6) do one credit : ~에게 명예가 되다.

7) call upon~ for : ~에게 ~을 부탁하다; request

"Yes, he came on the same train with me. Hasn't he called to pay his respects to you?[8]"

"No," answered Harry, with a smile. "He hasn't done me that honor. He probably expects me to make the first call."

"Well, Harry, I suppose you will be on hand[9] next week, when the Clionian holds its first meeting?"

"Yes, I will be there."

"And don't forget to call at my room before that time. I want to examine you in French, and see how much progress you have made."

"Thank you, Oscar."

"Now I must be going. I have got a tough Greek lesson to prepare for to-morrow. I suppose it will take me twice as long as usual. It is always hard to get to work again after a long vacation. So good-morning, and don't forget to call at my room soon—say to-morrow evening."

"I will come."

"What a gentlemanly fellow your friend is!" said Ferguson.

"What is his name, Harry?" asked Mr. Anderson.

"Oscar Vincent. His father is an editor in Boston."

"What! the son of John Vincent?" said Mr. Anderson, surprised.

"Yes, sir; do you know his father?"

"Only by reputation. He is a man of great ability."

"Oscar is a smart fellow, too, but not a hard student."

"I shall be glad to have you bring him round to the house some evening, Harry. I shall be glad to become better acquainted with him."

"Thank you, sir. I will give him the invitation."

It is very possible that Harry rose in the estimation of his employer, from his intimacy with the son of a man who stood so high in his own profession. At all events[10], Harry found himself from this time treated with greater respect and consideration than before, and Mr. Anderson often called upon him to write paragraphs upon local matters, so that his position might be regarded except as to pay, as that of an assistant editor.

---

8) pay one's respects to~ : ~을 방문하다.
9) be on hand : 출석하여, 눈앞에
10) at all events : 여하튼, 좌우간.

CHAPTER XXII.

MISS DEBORAH's EYES ARE OPENED.

Aunt Deborah felt that she had done a good stroke of business. She had lent Ferdinand four hundred and fifty dollars, and received in return a note for five hundred and fifty, secured by a diamond ring worth even more. She plumed herself on[1] her shrewdness, though at times she felt a little twinge at the idea of the exorbitant interest which she had exacted from so near a relative.

"But he said the money was worth that to him," she said to herself in extenuation, "and he's goin' to get two thousand dollars a year. I didn't want to lend the money, I'd rather have had it in the savings bank, but I did it to obleege[2] him."

By such casuistry Aunt Deborah quieted her conscience, and carefully put the ring away among her bonds and mortgages.

"Who'd think a little ring like that should be worth so much?" she said to herself. "It's clear waste of money. But then Ferdinand didn't buy it. It was given to him, and a very foolish gift it was too. Really, it makes me nervous to have it to take care of. It's so little it might get lost easy."

Aunt Deborah plumed herself upon her shrewdness. It was not easy to get the advantage of[3] her in a bargain, and yet she had accepted the ring as security for a considerable loan without once questioning its genuineness. She relied implicitly upon her nephew's assurance of its genuineness, just as she had relied upon his assertion of relationship. But the time was soon coming when she was to be undeceived.

One day, a neighbor stopped his horse in front of her house, and jumping out of his wagon, walked up to the door and knocked.

"Good-morning, Mr. Simpson," said the old lady, answering the knock herself; "won't you come in?"

"Thank you, Miss Deborah, I can't stop this morning. I was at the

---

1) plume oneself on~ : ~을 뽐내다, 자랑하다.
2) oblige : 은혜를 베풀다.
3) get the advantage of : 유리한 입장에 서다.

post-office just now, when I saw there was a letter for you, and thought I'd bring it along."

"A letter for me!" said Aunt Deborah in some surprise, for her correspondence was very limited. "Who's it from?"

"It is post-marked New York," said Mr. Simpson.

"I don't know no one in New York," said the old lady, fumbling in her pockets for her spectacles.

"Maybe it's one of your old beaux[4]," said Mr. Simpson, humorously, a joke which brought a grim smile to the face of the old spinster. "But I must be goin'. If it's an offer of marriage, don't forget to invite me to the wedding."

Aunt Deborah went into the house, and seating herself in her accustomed place, carefully opened the letter. She turned over the page, and glanced at the signature. To her astonishment it was signed,

"Your affectionate nephew,

"FERDINAND B. KENSINGTON."

"Ferdinand!" she exclaimed in surprise. "Why, I thought he was in Californy by this time. How could he write from New York? I s'pose he'll explain. I hope he didn't lose the money I lent him."

The first sentence in the letter was destined to surprise Miss Deborah yet more.

"Dear aunt," it commenced, "it is so many years since we have met, that I am afraid you have forgotten me."

"So many years!" repeated Miss Deborah in bewilderment. "What on earth can Ferdinand mean? Why, it's only five weeks yesterday since he was here. He must be crazy."

She resumed reading.

"I have often had it in mind to make you a little visit, but I have been so engrossed by business that I have been unable to get away. I am a salesman for A. T. Stewart, whom you must have heard of, as he is the largest retail dealer in the city. I have been three years in his employ, and have been promoted by degrees, till I now receive quite a good salary, until—and that is the news I have to write you—I have felt justifed in getting married. My wedding is fixed for next week,

---

4) beaux : beau의 복수형, 애인.

Thursday. I should be very glad if you could attend, though I suppose you would consider it a long journey. But at any rate I can assure you that I should be delighted to see you present on the occasion, and so would Maria. If you can't come, write to me, at any rate, in memory of old times. It is just possible that during our bridal tour—we are to go to the White Mountains for a week—we shall call on you. Let me know if it will be convenient for you to receive us for a day.

"Your affectionate nephew,

"FERDINAND B. KENSINGTON."

Miss Deborah read this letter like one dazed. She had to read it a second time before she could comprehend its purport.

"Ferdinand going to be married! He never said a word about it when he was here. And he don't say a word about Californy. Then again he says he hasn't seen me for years. Merciful man! I see it now—the other fellow was an impostor!" exclaimed Miss Deborah, jumping to her feet in excitement. "What did he want to deceive an old woman for?"

It flashed upon her at once. He came after money, and he had succeeded only too well. He had carried away four hundred and fifty dollars with him. True, he had left a note, and security. But another terrible suspicion had entered the old lady's mind; the ring might not be genuine.

"I must know at once," exclaimed the disturbed spinster. "I'll go over to Brandon, to the jeweller's, and inquire. If it's paste,[5] then, Deborah Kensington, you're the biggest fool in Centreville."

Miss Deborah summoned Abner, her farm servant from the field, and ordered him instantly to harness the horse, as she wanted to go to Brandon.

"Do you want me to go with you?" asked Abner.

"To be sure, I can't drive so fur, and take care of the horse."

"It'll interrupt the work," objected Abner.

"Never mind about the work," said Deborah, impatiently. "I must go right off. It's on very important business."

"Wouldn't it be best to go after dinner?"

"No, we'll get some dinner over there, at the tavern."

5) paste : 모조 보석

"What's got into the old woman?" thought Abner. "It isn't like her to spend money at a tavern for dinner, when she might as well dine at home. Interruptin' the work, too! However, it's her business!"

Deborah was ready and waiting when the horse drove up the door. She got in, and they set out. Abner tried to open a conversation, but he found Miss Deborah strangely unsocial. She appeared to take no interest in the details of farm work of which he spoke.

"Something's on her mind, I guess," thought Abner; and, as we know, he was right.

In her hand Deborah clutched the ring, of whose genuineness she had come to entertain[6] such painful doubts. It might be genuine, she tried to hope, even if it came from an impostor; but her hope was small. She felt a presentiment that it would prove as false as the man from whom she received it. As for the story of the manner in which he became possessed of it, doubtless that was as false as the rest.

"How blind I was!" groaned Deborah in secret. "I saw he didn't look like the family. What a goose[7] I was to believe that story about his changin' the color of his hair! I was an old fool, and that's all about it."

"Drive to the jeweller's," said Miss Deborah, when they reached Brandon.

In some surprise, Abner complied.

Deborah got out of the wagon hastily and entered the store.

"What can I do for you, Miss Kensington?" asked the jeweller, who recognized the old lady.

"I want to show you a ring," said Aunt Deborah, abruptly. "Tell me what it's worth."

She produced the ring which the false Ferdinand had intrusted to her.

The jeweller scanned it closely.

"It's a good imitation of a diamond ring," he said.

"Imitation!" gasped Deborah.

"Yes; you didn't think it was genuine?"

"What's it worth?"

---

6) entertain : 생각하다, 품다.

7) goose : (바보 같은) 여자, 숙맥

"The value of the gold. That appears to be genuine. It may be worth three dollars."

"Three dollars!" ejaculated Deborah. "He told me it cost six hundred and fifty."

"Whoever told you that was trying to deceive you."

"You're sure about its being imitation, are you?"

"There can be no doubt about it."

"That's what I thought," muttered the old lady, her face pale and rigid. "Is there anything to pay?"[8)]

"Oh, no; I am glad to be of service to you."

"Good-afternoon, then," said Deborah, abruptly, and she left the store.

"Drive home, Abner, as quick as you can," she said.

"I haven't had any dinner," Abner remarked, "You said you'd get some at the tavern."

"Did I? Well, drive over there. I'm not hungry myself, but I'll pay for some dinner for you."

Poor Aunt Deborah! it was not the loss alone that troubled her, though she was fond of money; but it was humiliating to think that she had fallen such an easy prey to[9)] a designing adventurer.[10)] In her present bitter mood, she would gladly have ridden fifty miles to see the false Ferdinand hanged.

---

8) Is there anything to pay? : (검사) 비용이 있나요?
9) fall prey to~ :~ 의 먹이가 되다.
10) designing adventurer : 교활한 모사꾼.

CHAPTER XXIII.

THE PLOT AGAINST FLETCHER.

The intimacy between Harry and Oscar Vincent continued, and, as during the former term, the latter volunteered to continue giving French lessons to our hero. These were now partly of a conversational character, and, as Harry was thoroughly in earnest, it was not long before he was able to speak quite creditably.

About the first of November, Fitzgerald Fletcher left the Prescott Academy, and returned to his home in Boston. It was not because he had finished his education, but because he felt that he was not appreciated by his fellow-students. He had been ambitious to be elected to an official position in the Clionian Society, but his aspirations were not gratified. He might have accepted this disappointment, and borne it as well as he could, had it not been aggravated by the elevation of Harry Walton to the presidency. To be only a common member, while a boy so far his social inferior was President, was more than Fitzgerald could stand. He was so incensed that upon the announcement of the vote he immediately rose to a point of order.[1)]

"Mr. President," he said warmly, "I must protest against this election. Walton is not a member of the Prescott Academy, and it is unconstitutional to elect him President."

"Will the gentleman point out the constitutional clause which has been violated by Walton's election?" said Oscar Vincent.

"Mr. President," said Fletcher, "this Society was founded by students of the Prescott Academy; and the offices should be confined to the members of the school."

Harry Walton rose and said: "Mr. President, my election has been a great surprise to myself. I had no idea that any one had thought of me for the position. I feel highly complimented by your kindness, and deeply grateful for it; but there is something in what Mr. Fletcher says. You have kindly allowed me to share in the benefits of the Society, and that satisfies me. I think it will be well for you to make another

---

1) rise to a point of order : 일어나서 의사·발언의 위법성을 항의하다.

choice as President."

"I will put it to vote," said the presiding officer. "Those who are ready to accept Mr. Walton's resignation will signify it in the usual way."

Fletcher raised his hand, but he was alone.

"Those who are opposed," said the President.

Every other hand except Harry's was now raised.

"Mr. Walton, your resignation is not accepted," said the presiding officer. "I call upon you to assume the duties of your new position."

Harry rose, and, modestly advanced to the chair. "I have already thanked you, gentlemen," he said, "for the honor you have conferred upon me in selecting me as your presiding officer. I have only to add that I will discharge its duties[2] to the best of my ability."

All applauded except Fletcher. He sat with an unpleasant scowl upon his face, and waited for the result of the balloting for Vice-President and Secretary. Had he been elected to either position, the Clionian would probably have retained his illustrious name upon its roll. But as these honors were conferred upon other members, he formed the heroic resolution no longer to remain a member.

"Mr. President," he said, when the last vote was announced, "I desire to terminate my connection with this Society."

"I hope Mr. Fletcher will reconsider his determination," said Harry from the chair.

"I would like to inquire the gentleman's reasons," said Tom Carver.

"I don't like the way in which the Society is managed," said Fletcher. "I predict that it will soon disband."

"I don't see any signs of it," said Oscar. "If the gentleman is really sincere, he should not desert the Clionian in the hour of danger."

"I insist upon my resignation," said Fletcher.

"I move[3] that it be accepted," said Tom Carver.

"Second[4] the motion," said the boy who sat next him.

The resignation was unanimously accepted. Fletcher ought to have felt gratified at the prompt granting of his request, but he was not. He had intended to strike dismay into the Society by his proposal to withdraw,

---

2) discharge duty : 임무를 수행하다, 이행하다.
3) move : 동의하다.
4) second : 재청하다.

but there was no consternation visible. Apparently they were willing to let him go.

He rose from his seat mortified and wrathful.

"Gentlemen," he said, "you have complied with my request, and I am deeply grateful. I no longer consider it an honor to belong to the Clionian. I trust your new President may succeed as well in his new office as he has in the capacity of a printer's devil."

Fletcher was unable to proceed, being interrupted by a storm of hisses, in the midst of which he hurriedly made his exit.

"He wanted to be President himself—that's what's the matter," said Tom Carver in a whisper to his neighbor. "But he couldn't blame us for not wanting to have him."

Other members of the Society came to the same conclusion, and it was generally said that Fletcher had done himself no good by his undignified resentment. His parting taunt levelled at[5] Harry was regarded as mean and ungenerous, and only strengthened the sentiment in favor of our hero who bore his honors modestly. In fact Tom Carver, who was fond of fun, conceived[6] a project for mortifying Fletcher, and readily obtained the co-operation of his classmates.

It must be premised that Fitz was vain of his reading and declamation. He had a secret suspicion that, if he should choose to devote his talents to the stage, he would make a second Booth. This self-conceit of his made it the more easy to play off the following joke upon him.

A fortnight later, the young ladies of the village proposed to hold a Fair to raise funds for some public object. At the head of the committee of arrangements was a sister of the doctor's wife, named Pauline Clinton. This will explain the following letter which, Fletcher received the succeeding day:—

"FITZGERALD FLETCHER, ESQ.—Dear Sir: Understanding that you are a superior reader, we should be glad of your assistance in lending *eclat*[7] to the Fair which we propose to hold on the evening of the 29th. Will you be kind enough to occupy twenty minutes by reading such

5) level at : ~를 겨냥하다.

6) conceive : devise

7) ´e clat : 영광

selections as in your opinion will be of popular interest? It is desirable that you should let me know as soon as possible what pieces you have selected, that they may be printed on the programme.

"Yours respectfully,

"PAULINE CLINTON,

"(for the Committee)."

This note reached Fletcher at a time when he was still smarting[8] from his disappointment in obtaining promotion from the Clionian Society. He read it with a flushed and triumphant face. He never thought of questioning its genuineness. Was it not true that he was a superior reader? What more natural than that he should be invited to give *eclat* to the Fair by the exercise of his talents! He felt it to be a deserved compliment. It was a greater honor to be solicited to[9] give a public reading than to be elected President of the Clionian Society.

"They won't laugh at me now," thought Fletcher.

He immediately started for Oscar's room to make known his new honors.

"How are you, Fitz?" said Oscar, who was in the secret, and guessed the errand on which he came.

"Very well, thank you, Oscar," answered Fletcher, in a stately manner.

"Anything new with you?" asked Oscar, carelessly.

"Not much," said Fletcher. "There's a note I just received."

"Whew!" exclaimed Oscar, in affected astonishment. "Are you going to accept?"

"I suppose I ought to oblige them," said Fletcher. "It won't be much trouble to me, you know."

"To be sure; it's in a good cause.[10] But how did they hear of your reading?"

"Oh, there are no secrets in a small village like this," said Fletcher.

"It's certainly a great compliment. Has anybody else been invited to read?"

"I think not," said Fletcher, proudly. "They rely upon me."

---

8) be smarting : 상심하다.

9) be solicited to~ : ~할 것을 요청받다.

10) cause : 명분

"Couldn't you get a chance for me? It would be quite an honor, and I should like it for the sake of the family."

"I shouldn't feel at liberty to[11] interfere with their arrangements," said Fletcher, who didn't wish to share the glory with any one. "Besides, you don't read well enough."

"Well, I suppose I must give it up," said Oscar, in a tone of resignation. "By the way, what have you decided to read?"

"I haven't quite made up my mind," said Fletcher, in a tone of importance.[12] "I have only just received the invitation, you know."

"Haven't you answered it yet?"

"No; but I shall as soon as I go home. Good-night, Oscar."

"Good-night, Fitz."

"How mad Fitz will be when he finds he has been sold![13]" said Oscar to himself. "But he deserves it for treating Harry so meanly."

---

11) at liberty to~ : 마음대로 ~해도 되는

12) importance : (경멸적) 거드름, 거만한 태도.

13) be sold : (감쪽같이) 속다.

CHAPTER XXIV.

READING UNDER DIFFICULTIES.

On reaching home, Fletcher looked over his "Speaker," and selected three poems which he thought he could read with best effect. The selection made, he sat down to his desk, and wrote a reply to the invitation, as follows: —

"MISS PAULINE CLINTON: I hasten to acknowledge your polite invitation to occupy twenty minutes in reading choice[1)] selections at your approaching Fair. I have paid much attention to reading, and hope to be able to give pleasure to the large numbers who will doubtless honor the occasion with their presence. I have selected three poems, —Poe's[2)] Raven, the Battle of Ivry, by Macaulay[3)], and Marco Bozarris, by Halleck[4)]. I shall be much pleased if my humble efforts add *eclat* to the occasion.

"Yours, very respectfully,

"FITZGERALD FLETCHER."

"There[5)]," said Fletcher, reading his letter through with satisfaction. "I think that will do. It is high-toned and dignified, and shows that I am highly cultured and refined. I will copy it off, and mail it."

Fletcher saw his letter deposited in the post-office, and returned to his room.

"I ought to practise reading these poems, so as to do it up handsomely," he said. "I suppose I shall get a good notice in the 'Gazette.' If I do, I will buy a dozen papers, and send to my friends. They will see that I am a person of consequence in Centreville, even if I didn't get elected to any office in the high and mighty Clionian Society."

I am sorry that I cannot reproduce the withering sarcasm which Fletcher put into his tone in the last sentence.

---

1) choice : 우수한, 정선된, 고급의
2) Poe : Edgar Allan Poe(1809~49), 미국의 시인.
3) Macaulay : Thomas B. Macaulay(1800~59), 영국의 문필가
4) Halleck : Fitz-Greene Halleck(1790~1867), 미국의 문필가.
5) There : (안도·위로) 그것 봐.

When Demosthenes[6] was practising oratory, he sought the sea-shore; but Fitzgerald repaired instead to a piece of woods about half a mile distant. It was rather an unfortunate selection, as will appear.

It so happened that Tom Carver and Hiram Huntley were strolling about the woods, when they espied Fletcher approaching with an open book in his hand.

"Hiram," said Tom, "there's fun coming. There's Fitz Fletcher with his 'Speaker' in his hand. He's going to practise reading in the woods. Let us hide, and hear the fun."

"I'm in for it," said Hiram, "but where will be the best place to hide?"

"Here in this hollow tree. He'll be very apt to halt here."

"All right! Go ahead, I'll follow."

They quickly concealed themselves in the tree, unobserved by Fletcher, whose eyes were on his book.

About ten feet from the tree he paused.

"I guess this'll be a good place," he said aloud. "There's no one to disturb me here. Now, which shall I begin with? I think I'll try The Raven. But first it may be well to practise an appropriate little speech. Something like this:"—

Fletcher made a low bow to the assembled trees, cleared his throat, and commenced,—

"Ladies and Gentlemen: It gives me great pleasure to appear before you this evening, in compliance with[7] the request of the committee, who have thought that my humble efforts would give *eclat* to the fair. I am not a professional reader, but I have ever found pleasure in reciting the noble productions of our best authors, and I hope to give you pleasure."

"That'll do[8], I think," said Fletcher, complacently. "Now I'll try The Raven."

In a deep, sepulchral tone, Fletcher read the first verse, which is quoted below:—

"Once upon a midnight dreary, while I pondered weak and weary,

---

6) Demosthenes : 데모스테네스(384?~ 322. B.C.), 고대 아테네의 정치가, 웅변가.
7) in compliance with~ : ~에 따라, 응하여.
8) that'll do : 그만하면 됐다.

Over many a quaint and curious volume of forgotten lore,
While I nodded, nearly napping, suddenly there came a tapping,
As of some one gently rapping, rapping at my chamber door.
"Tis some visitor,' I muttered, 'tapping at my chamber door—
Only this and nothing more.'"

Was it fancy, or did Fletcher really hear a slow, measured tapping near him—upon one of the trees, as it seemed? He started, and looked nervously; but the noise stopped, and he decided that he had been deceived, since no one was visible.

The boys within the tree made no other demonstration till Fletcher had read the following verse:—

"Back into the chamber turning, all my soul within me burning,
Soon again I heard a tapping, something louder than before.
'Surely,' said I, 'surely that is something at my window lattice;
Let me see then what thereat is, and this mystery explore—
Let my heart be still a moment, and this mystery explore;
'Tis the wind, and nothing more.'"

Here an indescribable, unearthly noise was heard from the interior of the tree, like the wailing of some discontented ghost.

"Good heavens![9] what's that?" ejaculated Fletcher, turning pale, and looking nervously around him.

It was growing late, and the branches above him, partially stripped of their leaves, rustled in the wind. Fletcher was somewhat nervous, and the weird character of the poem probably increased this feeling, and made him very uncomfortable. He summoned u[10]p courage enough, however, to go on, though his voice shook a little. He was permitted to go on without interruption to the end. Those who are familiar with the poem, know that it becomes more and more wild and weird as it draws to the conclusion. This, with his gloomy surroundings, had its effect upon the mind of Fletcher. Scarcely had he uttered the last words,

---

9) Good heavens! : (놀람, 동정) 어머나! 저런!
10) summon up : ~을 불러일으키다.

when a burst of wild and sepulchral laughter was heard within a few feet of him. A cry of fear proceeded from Fletcher, and, clutching his book, he ran at wild speed from the enchanted spot, not daring to look behind him. Indeed, he never stopped running till he passed out of the shadow of the woods, and was well on his way homeward.

Tom Carver and Hiram crept out from their place of concealment. They threw themselves on the ground, and roared with laughter.

"I never had such fun in my life," said Tom.

"Nor I."

"I wonder what Fitz thought."

"That the wood was enchanted, probably; he left in a hurry."

"Yes; he stood not on the order of his going, but went at once."

"I wish I could have seen him. We must have made a fearful noise."

"I was almost frightened myself. He must be almost home by this time."

"When do you think he'll find out about the trick?"

"About the invitation? Not till he gets a letter from Miss Clinton, telling him it is all a mistake. He will be terribly mortified."

Meanwhile Fletcher reached home, tired and out of breath. His temporary fear was over, but he was quite at sea[11] as to the cause of the noises he had heard. He could not suspect any of his school-fellows, for no one was visible, nor had he any idea that any were in the wood at the time.

"I wonder if it was an animal," he reflected. "It was a fearful noise. I must find some other place to practise reading in. I wouldn't go to that wood again for fifty dollars[12]."

But Fletcher's readings were not destined to be long continued. When he got home from school the next day, he found the following note, which had been left for him during the forenoon:—

"MR. FITZGERALD FLETCHER,—Dear Sir: I beg to thank you for your kind proposal to read at our Fair; but I think there must be some mistake in the matter, as we have never contemplated having any

11) be at sea : 어쩔 줄 모르는
12) for fifty dollars : 아무리 많은 돈을 준다 해도.

readings, nor have I written to you on the subject, as you intimate. I fear that we shall not have time to spare for such a feature[13], though, under other circumstances, it might be attractive. In behalf of the committee, I beg to tender thanks for your kind proposal.

"Yours respectfully,

"PAULINE CLINTON."

Fletcher read this letter with feelings which can better be imagined than described. He had already written home in the most boastful manner about the invitation he had received, and he knew that before he could contradict it, it would have been generally reported by his gratified parents to his city friends. And now he would be compelled to explain that he had been duped, besides enduring the jeers of those who had planned the trick.

This was more than he could endure. He formed a sudden resolution. He would feign illness, and go home the next day. He could let it be inferred that it was sickness alone which had compelled him to give up the idea of appearing as a public reader.

Fitz immediately acted upon his decision, and the next day found him on the way to Boston. He never returned to the Prescott Academy as a student.

---

13) a feature : 볼거리

CHAPTER XXV.

AN INVITATION TO BOSTON.

Harry was doubly glad that he was now in receipt of[1] a moderate salary. He welcomed it as an evidence that he was rising in the estimation of his employer, which was of itself satisfactory, and also because in his circumstances the money was likely to be useful.

"Five dollars a week!" said Harry to himself. "Half of that ought to be enough to pay for my clothes and miscellaneous expenses, and the rest I will give to father. It will help him take care of the rest of the family."

Our hero at once made this proposal by letter. This is a paragraph from his father's letter in reply:—

"I am glad, my dear son, to find you so considerate and dutiful, as your offer indicates. I have indeed had a hard time in supporting my family, and have not always been able to give them the comforts I desired. Perhaps it is my own fault in part. I am afraid I have not the faculty of getting along and making money that many others have. But I have had an unexpected stroke of good fortune. Last evening a letter reached your mother, stating that her cousin Nancy had recently died at St. Albans, Vermont, and that, in accordance with her will, your mother is to receive a legacy of four thousand dollars. With your mother's consent, one-fourth of this is to be devoted to the purchase of the ten acres adjoining my little farm, and the balance[2] will be so invested as to yield us an annual income of one hundred and eighty dollars. Many would think this a small addition to an income, but it will enable us to live much more comfortably. You remember the ten-acre lot to the east of us, belonging to the heirs of Reuben Todd. It is excellent land, well adapted for cultivation, and will fully double the value of my farm.

"You see, therefore, my dear son, that a new era of prosperity has opened for us. I am now relieved from the care and anxiety which for years have oppressed me, and feel sure of a comfortable support. Instead

---

1) be in receipt of : receive
2) the balance : 나머지, 잔여분.

of accepting the half of your salary, I desire you, if possible, to save it, depositing in some reliable savings institution. If you do this every year till you are twenty-one, you will have a little capital to start you in business, and will be able to lead a more prosperous career than your father. Knowing you as well as I do, I do not feel it necessary to caution you against unnecessary expenditures. I will only remind you that extravagance is comparative, and that what would be only reasonable expenditure for one richer than yourself would be imprudent in you."

Harry read this letter with great joy. He was warmly attached to the little home circle, and the thought that they were comparatively provided for gave him fresh courage. He decided to adopt his father's suggestion, and the very next week deposited three dollars in the savings bank.

"That is to begin an account," he thought. "If I can only keep that up, I shall feel quite rich at the end of a year."

Several weeks rolled by, and Thanksgiving approached.

Harry was toiling at his case one day, when Oscar Vincent entered the office.

"Hard at work, I see, Harry," he said.

"Yes," said Harry; "I can't afford to be idle."

"I want you to be idle for three days," said Oscar.

Harry looked up in surprise.

"How is that?" he asked.

"You know we have a vacation from Wednesday to Monday at the Academy."

"Over Thanksgiving?"

"Yes."

"Well, I am going home to spend that time, and I want you to go with me."

"What, to Boston?" asked Harry, startled, for to him, inexperienced as he was, that seemed a very long journey.

"Yes. Father and mother gave me permission to invite you. Shall I show you the letter?"

"I'll take it for granted, Oscar, but I am afraid I can't go."

"Nonsense![3] What's to prevent?"

---

3) Nonsense! : 바보 같은! 시시한!

"In the first place, Mr. Anderson can't spare me."

"Ask him."

"What's that?" asked the editor, hearing his name mentioned.

"I have invited Harry to spend the Thanksgiving vacation with me in Boston, and he is afraid you can't spare him?"

"Does your father sanction your invitation?"

"Yes, he wrote me this morning—that is, I got the letter this morning—telling me to ask Harry to come."

Now the country editor had a great respect for the city editor, who was indeed known by reputation throughout New England as a man of influence and ability, and he felt disposed to accede to any request of his.

So he said pleasantly, "Of course, Harry, we shall miss you, but if Mr. Ferguson is disposed to[4)] do a little additional work, we will get along till Monday. What do you say, Mr. Ferguson?"

"I shall be very glad to oblige Harry," said the older workman, "and I hope he will have a good time."

"That settles the question, Harry," said Oscar, joyfully. "So all you've got to do is to pack up and be ready to start to-morrow morning. It's Tuesday, you know, already."

Harry hesitated, and Oscar observed it.

"Well, what's the matter now?" he said; "out with it."[5)]

"I'll tell you, Oscar," said Harry, coloring a little. "Your father is a rich man, and lives handsomely. I haven't any clothes good enough to wear on a visit to your house."

"Oh, hang your clothes!" said Oscar, impetuously. "It isn't your clothes we invite. It's yourself."

"Still, Oscar—"

"Come,[6)] I see you think I am like Fitz Fletcher, after all. Say you think me a snob, and done with it."

"But I don't," said Harry, smiling.

"Then don't make any more ridiculous objections. Don't you think they are ridiculous, Mr. Ferguson?"

---

4) be disposed to : ~의 경향이 있는.
5) Out with it : bring out, utter.
6) come, : 이봐, 자.

"They wouldn't be in some places," said Ferguson, "but here I think they are out of place. I feel sure you are right, and that you value Harry more than the clothes he wears."

"Well, Harry, do you surrender at discretion?"[7] said Oscar. "You see Ferguson is on my side."

"I suppose I shall have to," said Harry, "as long as you are not ashamed of me."

"None of that, Harry."

"I'll go."

"The first sensible words you've spoken this morning."

"I want to tell you how much I appreciate your kindness, Oscar," said Harry, earnestly.

"Why shouldn't I be kind to my friend?"

"Even if he was once a printer's devil."

"Very true. It is a great objection, but still I will overlook it. By the way, there is one inducement I didn't mention."

"What is that?"

"We may very likely see Fitz in the city. He is studying at home now, I hear. Who knows but he may get up a great party[8] in your honor?"

"Do you think it likely?" asked Harry, smiling.

"It might not happen to occur to him, I admit. Still, if we made him a ceremonious call—"

"I am afraid he might send word that he was not at home."

"That would be a loss to him, no doubt. However, we will leave time to settle that question. Be sure to be on hand[9] in time for the morning train."

"All right, Oscar."

Harry had all the love of new scenes natural to a boy of sixteen. He had heard so much of Boston that he felt a strong curiosity to see it. Besides, was not that the city where the "Weekly Standard" was printed, the paper in which he had already appeared as an author? In connection with this, I must here divulge a secret of Harry's. He was ambi-

---

7) at discretion : 무조건.
8) get up a party : 파티를 열다.
9) be on hand : 출석하여.

tious not only to contribute to the literary papers, but to be paid for his contributions. He judged that essays were not very marketable, and he had therefore in his leisure moments written a humorous sketch, entitled "The Tin Pedler's Daughter." I shall not give any idea of the plot here; I will only say that it was really humorous, and did not betray[10] as much of the novice as might have been expected. Harry had copied it out in his best hand, and resolved to carry it to Boston, and offer it in person to the editor of the "Standard" with an effort, if accepted, to obtain compensation for it.

10) betray : ~을 무심코 드러내다.

CHAPTER XXVI.

THE VINCENTS AT HOME.

When Harry rather bashfully imparted to Oscar his plans respecting[1] the manuscript, the latter entered enthusiastically into them, and at once requested the privilege of reading the story. Harry awaited his judgment with some anxiety.

"Why, Harry, this is capital," said Oscar, looking up from the perusal.

"Do you really think so, Oscar?"

"If I didn't think so, I wouldn't say so."

"I thought you might say so out of friendship."

"I don't say it is the best I ever read, mind you,[2] but I have read a good many that are worse. I think you managed the *denouement* (you're a French scholar, so I'll venture on the word) admirably."

"I only hope the editor of the 'Standard' will think so."

"If he doesn't, there are other papers in Boston; the 'Argus' for instance."

"I'll try the 'Standard' first, because I have already written for it."

"All right. Don't you want me to go to the office with you?"

"I wish you would. I shall be bashful."

"I am not troubled that way. Besides, my father's name is well known, and I'll take care to mention it. Sometimes influence goes farther than merit, you know."

"I should like to increase my income by writing for the city papers. Even if I only made fifty dollars a year, it would all be clear[3] gain."

Harry's desire was natural. He had no idea how many shared it. Every editor of a successful weekly could give information on this subject. Certainly there is no dearth of aspiring young writers—Scotts and Shakspeares in embryo[4]—in our country, and if all that were written for publication succeeded in getting into print, the world would scarcely

---

1) respecting : ~에 관하여.
2) mind you : 잘 들어둬 (다짐을 할 때).
3) clear : net, 순익의.
4) in embryo : 초기 상태의.

contain the books and papers which would pour in uncounted thousands from the groaning press.

When the two boys arrived in Boston they took a carriage to Oscar's house. It was situated on Beacon Street, not far from the Common,—a handsome brick house with a swell front, such as they used to build in Boston. No one of the family was in, and Oscar and Harry went up at once to the room of the former, which they were to share together. It was luxuriously furnished, so Harry thought, but then our hero had been always accustomed to the plainness of a country home.

"Now, old fellow, make yourself at home," said Oscar. "You can get yourself up[5] for dinner. There's water and towels, and a brush."

"I don't expect to look very magnificent," said Harry. "You must tell your mother I am from the country."

"I would make you an offer if I dared," said Oscar.

"I am always open to a good offer."

"It's this: I'm one size larger than you, and my last year's suits are in that wardrobe. If any will fit you, they are yours."

"Thank you, Oscar," said Harry; "I'll accept your offer to-morrow."

"Why not to-day?"

"You may not understand me, but when I first appear before your family, I don't want to wear false colors."[6]

"I understand," said Oscar, with instinctive delicacy.

An hour later, the bell rang for dinner.

Harry went down, and was introduced to his friend's mother and sister. The former was a true lady, refined and kindly, and her smile made our hero feel quite at home.

"I am glad to meet you, Mr. Walton," she said. "Oscar has spoken of you frequently."

With Oscar's sister Maud—a beautiful girl two years younger than himself—Harry felt a little more bashful; but the young lady soon entered into an animated conversation with him.

"Do you often come to Boston, Mr. Walton?" she asked.

"This is my first visit," said Harry.

---

5) get oneself up : (옷차림을) 단정히 하다.
6) colors: 외관, 겉치레.

"Then I dare say Oscar will play all sorts of tricks upon you. We had a cousin visit us from the country, and the poor fellow had a hard time."

"Yes," said Oscar, laughing, "I used to leave him at a street corner, and dodge into a doorway. It was amusing to see his perplexity when he looked about, and couldn't find me."

"Shall you try that on me?" asked Harry.

"Very likely."

"Then I'll be prepared."

"You might tie him with a rope, Mr. Walton," said Maud, "and keep firm hold."

"I will, if Oscar consents."

"I will see about[7] it. But here is my father. Father, this is my friend, Harry Walton."

"I am glad to see you, Mr. Walton," said Mr. Vincent. "Then you belong to my profession?"

"I hope to, some time, sir; but I am only a printer as yet."

"You are yet to rise from the ranks. I know all about that. I was once a compositor."

Harry looked at the editor with great respect. He was stout, squarely built, with a massive head and a thoughtful expression. His appearance was up to[8] Harry's anticipations. He felt that he would be prouder to be Mr. Vincent than any man in Boston, He could hardly believe that this man, who controlled so influential an organ,[9] and was so honored in the community, was once a printer boy like himself.

"What paper are you connected with?" asked Mr. Vincent.

"The 'Centreville Gazette.'"

"I have seen it. It is quite a respectable paper."

"But how different," thought Harry, "from a great city daily!"

"Let us go out to dinner," said Mr. Vincent, consulting his watch. "I have an engagement immediately afterward."

At table Harry sat between Maud and Oscar. If at first he felt a little bashful, the feeling soon wore away. The dinner hour passed very

---

7) see about~ : (결정하기 전에) 잘 생각하다.
8) be up to~ : ~에 필적하여, 나란히.
9) organ : 기관지.

pleasantly. Mr. Vincent chatted very agreeably about men and things. There is no one better qualified to shine in this kind of conversation than the editor of a city daily, who is compelled to be exceptionally well informed. Harry listened with such interest that he almost forgot to eat, till Oscar charged him with want of appetite.

"I must leave in haste," said Mr. Vincent, when dinner was over. "Oscar, I take it for granted that you will take care of your friend."

"Certainly, father. I shall look upon myself as his guardian, adviser and friend."

"You are not very well fitted to be a mentor, Oscar," said Maud.

"Why not, young lady?"

"You need a guardian yourself. You are young and frivolous."

"And you, I suppose, are old and judicious."

"Thank you. I will own to the last, and the first will come in time."

"Isn't it singular, Harry, that my sister should have so much conceit, whereas I am remarkably modest?"

"I never discovered it, Oscar," said Harry, smiling.

"That is right, Mr. Walton," said Maud. "I see you are on my side. Look after my brother, Mr. Walton. He needs an experienced friend."

"I am afraid I don't answer[10] the description, Miss Maud."

"I don't doubt you will prove competent. I wish you a pleasant walk."

"My sister's a jolly girl, don't you think so?" asked Oscar, as Maud left the room.

"That isn't exactly what I should say of her, but I can describe her as even more attractive than her brother."

"You couldn't pay her a higher compliment. But come; we'll take a walk on the Common."

They were soon on the Common, dear to every Bostonian, and sauntered along the walks, under the pleasant shade of the stately elms.

"Look there," said Oscar, suddenly; "isn't that Fitz Fletcher?"

"Yes," said Harry, "but he doesn't see us."

"We'll join him. How are you, Fitz?"

"Glad to see you, Oscar," said Fletcher, extending a gloved band, while in the other he tossed a light cane. "When did you arrive?"

---

10) answer : correspond to, ~에 합치하다.

"Only this morning; but you don't see Harry Walton."

Fletcher arched his brows in surprise, and said coldly, "Indeed, I was not aware Mr. Walton was in the city."

"He is visiting me," said Oscar.

Fletcher looked surprised. He knew the Vincents stood high socially, and it seemed extraordinary that they should receive a printer's devil as a guest.

"Have you given up the printing business?" he asked superciliously.[11)]

"No; I only have a little vacation from it."

"Ah, indeed! It's a very dirty business. I would as soon be a chimney-sweep."

"Each to his taste, Fitz," said Oscar. "If you have a taste for chimneys, I hope your father won't interfere."

"I haven't a taste for such a low business," said Fletcher, haughtily. "I should like it as well as being a printer's devil though."

"Would you? At any rate, if you take it up, you'll be sure to be well *sooted*."

Fletcher did not laugh at the joke. He never could see any wit in jokes directed at himself.

"How long are you going to stay at that beastly school?" he asked.

"I am not staying at any beastly school."

"I mean the Academy."

"Till I am ready for college. Where are you studying?"

"I recite to a private tutor."

"Well, we shall meet at 'Harvard' if we are lucky enough to get in."

Fletcher rather hoped Oscar would invite him to call at his house, for he liked to visit a family of high social position; but he waited in vain.

"What a fool Oscar makes of himself about that country clod-hopper!" thought the stylish young man, as he walked away. "The idea of associating with a printer's devil! I hope I know what is due to myself better."

---

11) superciliously : haughtily

Chapter XXVII.

THE OFFICE OF THE "STANDARD."

On the day after Thanksgiving, Harry brought out from his carpet-bag his manuscript story, and started with Oscar for the office of the "Weekly Standard." He bought the last copy of the paper, and thus ascertained the location of the office.

Oscar turned the last page, and ran through a sketch of about the same length as Harry's.

"Yours is fully as good as this, Harry," he said.

"The editor may not think so."

"Then he ought to."

"This story is by one of his regular contributors, Kenella Kent."

"You'll have to take a name yourself,—a *nom de plume*, I mean."

"I have written so far over the name of Franklin."

"That will do very well for essays, but is not appropriate for stories."

"Suppose you suggest a name, Oscar."

"How will 'Fitz Fletcher' do?"

"Mr. Fletcher would not permit me to take such a liberty."

"And you wouldn't want to take it."

"Not much."

"Let me see. I suppose I must task my invention, then. How will Old Nick do?"

"People would think you wrote the story."

"A fair hit. Hold on, I've got just the name. Frank Lynn."

"I thought you objected to that name."

"You don't understand me. I mean two names, not one. Frank Lynn! Don't you see?"

"Yes, it's a good plan. I'll adopt it."

"Who knows but you may make the name illustrious, Harry?"

"If I do, I'll dedicate my first boot to Oscar Vincent."

"Shake hands on that. I accept the dedication with mingled feelings of gratitude and pleasure."

"Better wait till you get it," said Harry, laughing. "Don't count your chickens before they're hatched."[1]

"The first egg is laid, and that's something. But here we are at the office."

It was a building containing a large number of offices. The names of the respective occupants were printed on slips of black tin at the entrance. From this, Harry found that the office of the "Weekly Standard" was located at No. 6.

"My heart begins to beat, Oscar," said Harry, naturally excited in anticipation of an interview with one who could open the gates of authorship to him.

"Does it?" asked Oscar. "Mine has been beating for a number of years."

"You are too matter-of-fact for me, Oscar. If it was your own story, you might feel differently."

"Shall I pass it off as my own, and make the negotiation?"

Harry was half tempted to say yes, but it occurred to him that this might prove an embarrassment in the future, and he declined the proposal.

They climbed rather a dark, and not very elegant staircase, and found themselves before No. 6.

Harry knocked, or was about to do so, when a young lady with long ringlets, and a roll of manuscript in her hand, who had followed them upstairs advanced confidently, and, opening the door, went in. The two boys followed, thinking the ceremony of knocking needless.

They found themselves in a large room, one corner of which was partitioned off for the editor's sanctum. A middle-aged man was directing papers in the larger room, while piles of papers were ranged on shelves at the sides of the apartment.

The two boys hesitated to advance, but the young lady in ringlets went on, and entered the office through the open door.

"We'll wait till she is through," said Harry.

It was easy to hear the conversation that passed between the young lady and the editor, whom they could not see.

"Good-morning, Mr. Houghton," she said.

---

1) Don't count your chicken before they're hatched. : 김칫국부터 마시지 마라.

"Good-morning. Take a seat, please," said the editor, pleasantly. "Are you one of our contributors?"

"No, sir, not yet," answered the young lady, "but I would become so."

"We are not engaging any new contributors at present, but still if you have brought anything for examination you may leave it."

"I am not wholly unknown to fame," said the young lady, with an air of consequence.[2] "You have probably heard of Prunella Prune."

"Possibly, but I don't at present recall it. We editors meet with so many names, you know. What is the character of your articles?"

"I am a poetess, sir, and I also write stories."

"Poetry is a drug in the market.[3] We have twice as much offered us as we can accept. Still we are always glad to welcome really meritorious poems."

"I trust my humble efforts will please you," said Prunella. "I have here some lines to a nightingale, which have been very much praised in our village. Shall I read them?"

"If you wish," said the editor, by no means cheerfully. Miss Prune raised her voice, and commenced:—

"O star-eyed Nightingale,
How nobly thou dost[4] sail
Through the air!
No other bird can compare
With the tuneful song
Which to thee doth belong.
I sit and hear thee sing,
While with tireless wing
Thou dost fly.
And it makes me feel so sad,
It makes me feel so bad,
I know not why,
And I heave so many sighs,
O warbler of the skies!"

---

2) consequence : self-importance, 잘난 체함.
3) a drug in the market : 남아돌아서 팔리지 않는 상품, 체화.
4) thou dost : you do

"Is there much more?" asked the editor.

"That is the first verse. There are fifteen more," said Prunella.

"Then I think I shall not have time at present to hear you read it all. You may leave it, and I will look it over at my leisure."[5)]

"If it suits you," said Prunella, "how much will it be worth?"

"I don't understand."

"How much would you be willing to pay for it?"

"Oh, we never pay for poems," said Mr. Houghton.

"Why not?" asked Miss Prune, evidently disappointed.

"Our contributors are kind enough to send them gratuitously."

"Is that fostering American talent?" demanded Prunella, indignantly.

"American poetical talent doesn't require fostering, judging from the loads of poems which are sent in to us."

"You pay for stories, I presume?"

"Yes, we pay for good, popular stories."

"I have one here," said Prunella, untying her manuscript, "which I should like to read to you."

"You may read the first paragraph, if you please. I haven't time to hear more. What is the title?"

"'The Bandit's Bride.' This is the way it opens:—

"'The night was tempestuous. Lightnings flashed in the cerulean sky, and the deep-voiced thunder rolled from one end of the firmament to the other. It was a landscape in Spain. From a rocky defile gayly pranced forth a masked cavalier, Roderigo di Lima, a famous bandit chief.

"'"Ha! ha!" he laughed in demoniac glee, "the night is well fitted to my purpose. Ere it passes, Isabella Gomez shall be mine."'"

"I think that will do," said Mr. Houghton, hastily. "I am afraid that style won't suit our readers."

"Why not?" demanded Prunella, sharply. "I can assure you, sir, that it has been praised by *excellent* judges in our village."

"It is too exciting for our readers. You had better carry it to 'The Weekly Corsair.'"[6)]

"Do they pay well for contributions?"

---

5) at one's leisure : 틈이 있을 때.

6) corsair : 해적(선)

"I really can't say. How much do you expect?"

"This story will make about five columns. I think twenty-five dollars will be about right."

"I am afraid you will be disappointed. We can't afford to pay such prices, and the 'Corsair' has a smaller circulation[7] than our paper."

"How much do you pay?"

"Two dollars a column."

"I expected more," said Prunella, "but I will write for you at that price."

"Send us something suited to our paper, and we will pay for it at that price."

"I will write you a story to-morrow. Good-morning, sir."

"Good-morning, Miss Prune."

The young lady with ringlets sailed out of the editor's room, and Oscar, nudging Harry, said, "Now it is our turn. Come along. Follow me, and don't be frightened."

---

7) circulation : 보급, 배포.

Chapter XXVIII.

ACCEPTED.

The editor of the "Standard" looked with some surprise at the two boys. As editor, he was not accustomed to receive such young visitors. He was courteous, however, and said, pleasantly:—

"What can I do for you, young gentlemen?"

"Are you the editor of the 'Standard'?" asked Harry, diffidently.

"I am. Do you wish to subscribe?"

"I have already written something for your paper," Harry continued.

"Indeed!" said the editor. "Was it poetry or prose?"

Harry felt flattered by the question. To be mistaken for a poet he felt to be very complimentary. If he had known how much trash weekly found its way to the "Standard" office, under the guise of[1] poetry, he would have felt less flattered.

"I have written some essays over the name of 'Franklin,'" he hastened to say.

"Ah, yes, I remember, and very sensible essays too. You are young to write."

"Yes, sir; I hope to improve as I grow older."

By this time Oscar felt impelled to speak for his friend. It seemed to him that Harry was too modest.

"My friend is assistant editor of a New Hampshire paper,—'The Centreville Gazette,'" he announced.

"Indeed!" said the editor, looking surprised. "He is certainly young for an editor."

"My friend is not quite right," said Harry, hastily. "I am one of the compositors on that paper."

"But you write editorial paragraphs," said Oscar.

"Yes, unimportant ones."

"And are you, too, an editor?" asked the editor of the "Standard," addressing Oscar with a smile.

"Not exactly," said Oscar; "but I am an editor's son. Perhaps you

---

1) under the guise of: ~을 가장하여.

are acquainted with my father,—John Vincent of this city."

"Are you his son?" said the editor, respectfully. "I know your father slightly. He is one of our ablest journalists."

"Thank you, sir."

"I am very glad to receive a visit from you, and should be glad to print anything from your pen."

"I am not sure about that," said Oscar, smiling. "If I have a talent for writing, it hasn't developed itself yet. But my friend here takes to[2] it as naturally as a duck takes to water."

"Have you brought me another essay, Mr. 'Franklin'?" asked the editor, turning to Harry. "I address you by your *nom de plume*, not knowing your real name."

"Permit me to introduce my friend, Harry Walton," said Oscar. "Harry, where is your story?"

"I have brought you in a story," said Harry, blushing. "It is my first attempt, and may not suit you, but I shall be glad if you will take the trouble to examine it."

"With pleasure," said the editor. "Is it long?"

"About two columns. It is of a humorous character."

The editor reached out his hand, and, taking the manuscript, unrolled it. He read the first few lines, and they seemed to strike his attention.

"If you will amuse yourselves for a few minutes, I will read it at once," he said. "I don't often do it, but I will break over my custom this time."

"Thank you, sir," said Harry.

"There are some of my exchanges," said the editor, pointing to a pile on the floor. "You may find something to interest you in some of them."

They picked up some papers, and began to read. But Harry could not help thinking of the verdict that was to be pronounced on his manuscript. Upon that a great deal hinged.[3] If he could feel that he was able to produce anything that would command[4] compensation, however small, it would make him proud and happy. He tried, as he gazed furtively

---

2) take to~ : ~에 몰두하다, ~이 습관이 되다.
3) hinge on : depend on.
4) command : deserve.

over his paper at the editor's face, to anticipate his decision, but the latter was too much accustomed to reading manuscript to show the impression made upon him.

Fifteen minutes passed, and he looked up.

"Well, Mr. Walton," he said, "your first attempt is a success."

Harry's face brightened.

"May I ask if the plot is original?"

"It is so far as I know, sir. I don't think I ever read anything like it."

"Of course there are some faults in the construction, and the dialogue might be amended here and there. But it is very creditable, and I will use it in the 'Standard' if you desire it."

"I do, sir."

"And how much are you willing to pay for it?" Oscar struck in.

The editor hesitated.

"It is not our custom to pay novices just at first," he said. "If Mr. Walton keeps on writing, he would soon command compensation."

Harry would not have dared to press the matter, but Oscar was not so diffident. Indeed, it is easier to be bold in a friend's cause than one's own.

"Don't you think it is worth being paid for, if it is worth printing?" he persisted.

"Upon that principle, we should feel obliged to pay for poetry," said the editor.

"Oh," said Oscar, "poets don't need money. They live on flowers and dew-drops."

The editor smiled.

"You think prose-writers require something more substantial?"

"Yes, sir."

"I will tell you how the matter stands,"[5] said the editor. "Mr. Walton is a beginner. He has his reputation to make. When it is made he will be worth a fair price to me, or any of my brother editors."

"I see," said Oscar; "but his story must be worth something. It will fill up two columns. If you didn't print it, you would have to pay somebody for writing these two columns."

---

5) how the matter stands : 사정이 어떤지.

"You have some reason in what you say. Still our ordinary rule is based on justice. A distinction should be made between new contributors and old favorites."

"Yes, sir. Pay the first smaller sums."

If the speaker had not been John Vincent's son, it would have been doubtful if his reasoning would have prevailed. As it was, the editor yielded.

"I may break over my rule in the case of your friend," said the editor; "but he must be satisfied with a very small sum for the present."

"Anything will satisfy me, sir," said Harry, eagerly.

"Your story will fill two columns. I commonly pay two dollars a column for such articles, if by practised writers. I will give you half that."

"Thank you, sir. I accept it," said Harry, promptly.

"In a year or so I may see my way clear to paying you more, Mr. Walton; but you must consider that I give you the opportunity of winning popularity, and regard this as part of your compensation, at present."

"I am quite satisfied, sir," said Harry, his heart fluttering with joy and triumph. "May I write you some more sketches?"

"I shall be happy to receive and examine them; but you must not be disappointed if from time to time I reject your manuscripts."

"No, sir; I will take it as a hint that they need improving."

"I will revise my friend's stories, sir," said Oscar, humorously, "and give him such hints as my knowledge of the world may suggest."

"No doubt such suggestions from so mature a friend will materially benefit them," said the editor, smiling.

He opened his pocket-book, and, drawing out a two-dollar bill, handed it to Harry.

"I shall hope to pay you often," he said, "for similar contributions."

"Thank you, sir," said Harry.

Feeling that their business was at an end, the boys withdrew. As they reached the foot of the stairs, Oscar took off his cap, and bowed low.

"Mr. Lynn, I congratulate you," he said.

"I can't tell you how glad I feel, Oscar," said Harry, his face radiant.

"Let me suggest that you owe me a commission[6] for impressing upon

---

6) commission : 대리수수료, 구전.

the editor the propriety of paying you."

"How much do you ask?"

"An ice-cream will be satisfactory."

"All right."

"Come round to Copeland's then. We'll celebrate your success in a becoming[7] manner."

---

7) becoming : suitable, proper

CHAPTER XXIX.

MRS. CLINTON's PARTY.

When Oscar and Harry reached home they were met by Maud, who flourished in her hand what appeared to be a note.

"What is it, Maud?" asked Oscar. "A love-letter for me?"

"Don't flatter yourself,[1] Oscar. No girl would be so foolish as to write you a love-letter. It is an invitation to a party on Saturday evening."

"Where?"

"At Mrs. Clinton's."

"I think I will decline," said Oscar. "I wouldn't like to leave Harry alone."

"Oh, he is included too. Mrs. Clinton heard of his being here, and expressly[2] included him in the invitation."

"That alters the case. You'll go, Harry, won't you?"

"I am afraid I shouldn't know how to behave at a fashionable party," said Harry.

"Oh, you've only got to make me your model," said Oscar, "and you'll be all right."

"Did you ever see such conceit, Mr. Walton?" said Maud.

"It reminds me of Fletcher," said Harry.

"Fitz Fletcher? By the way, he will probably be there. His family are acquainted with the Clintons."

"Yes, he is invited," said Maud.

"Good! Then there's promise of fun," said Oscar. "You'll see Fitz with his best company manners[3] on."

"I am afraid he won't enjoy meeting me there," said Harry.

"Probably not."

"I don't see why," said Maud.

"Shall I tell, Harry?"

"Certainly."

---

1) flatter oneself : 자만하다, 편리하게 생각하다.
2) expressly : definitely
3) company manners : 남 앞에서만 차리는 예의범절.

"To begin with, Fletcher regards himself as infinitely superior to Walton here, because his father is rich, and Walton's poor. Again, Harry is a printer, and works for a living, which Fitz considers degrading. Besides all this, Harry was elected President of our Debating Society, — an office which Fitz wanted."

"I hope" said Maud, "that Mr. Fletcher's dislike does not affect your peace of mind, Mr. Walton."

"Not materially,"[4] said Harry, laughing.

"By the way, Maud," said Oscar, "did I ever tell you how Fletcher's pride was mortified at school by our discovering his relationship to a tin-pedler?"

"No, tell me about it."

The story, already familiar to the reader, was graphically told by Oscar, and served to amuse his sister.

"He deserved the mortification," she said. "I shall remember it if he shows any of his arrogance at the party."

"Fletcher rather admires Maud," said Oscar, after his sister had gone out of the room; "but the favor isn't reciprocated. If he undertakes to say anything to her against you, she will take him down, depend upon it."[5]

Saturday evening came, and Harry, with Oscar and his sister, started for the party. Our hero, having confessed his inability to dance, had been diligently instructed in the Lancers[6] by Oscar, so that he felt some confidence in being able to get through without any serious blunder.

"Of course you must dance, Harry," he said. "You don't want to be a wall-flower."[7]

"I may have to be," said Harry. "I shall know none of the young ladies except your sister."

"Maud will dance the first Lancers with you, and I will get you a partner for the second."

"You may dispose of me as you like, Oscar."

"Wisely said. Don't forget that I am your Mentor."

---

4) materially : 크게, 현저히.
5) depend upon it : 반드시, 분명히.
6) the Lancers : 4인조 댄스.
7) a wall-flower : 혼자 있는 사람.

When they entered the brilliantly lighted parlors, they were already half full. Oscar introduced his friend to Mrs. Clinton.

"I am glad to see you here, Mr. Walton," said the hostess, graciously. "Oscar, I depend upon you to introduce your friend to some of the young ladies."

"You forget my diffidence, Mrs. Clinton."

"I didn't know you were troubled in that way.'"

"See how I am misjudged. I am painfully bashful."

"You hide it well," said the hostess, with a smile.

"Escort my sister to a seat, Harry," said Oscar. "By the way, you two will dance in the first Lancers."

"If Miss Maud will accept so awkward a partner," said Harry.

"Oh, yes, Mr. Walton. I'll give you a hint if you are going wrong."

Five minutes later Fletcher touched Oscar on the shoulder.

"Oscar, where is your sister?" he asked.

"There," said Oscar, pointing her out.

Fletcher, who was rather near-sighted, did not at first notice that Harry Walton was sitting beside the young lady.

He advanced, and made a magnificent bow, on which he rather prided himself.

"Good-evening, Miss Vincent," he said.

"Good-evening, Mr. Fletcher."

"I am very glad you have favored the party with your presence."

"Thank you, Mr. Fletcher. Don't turn my head[8] with your compliments."

"May I hope you will favor me with your hand in the first Lancers?"

"I am sorry, Mr. Fletcher, but I am engaged to Mr. Walton. I believe you are acquainted with him."

Fletcher for the first time observed our hero, and his face wore a look of mingled annoyance and scorn.

"I have met the gentleman," he said, haughtily.

"Mr. Fletcher and I have met frequently," said Harry, pleasantly.

"I didn't expect to meet you *here*," said Fletcher with marked emphasis.

"Probably not," said Harry. "My invitation is due to my being a friend

---

8) turn one's head : ~자만하게 하다.

of Oscar's."

"I was not aware that you danced," said Fletcher who was rather curious on the subject.

"I don't—much."

"Where did you learn—in the printing office?"

"No, in the city."

"Ah! Indeed!"

Fletcher thought he had wasted time enough on our hero, and turned again to Maud.

"May I have the pleasure of your hand in the second dance?" he asked.

"I will put you down for[9] that, if you desire it."

"Thank you."

It so happened that when Harry and Maud took the floor,[10] they found Fletcher their *vis-a-vis*. Perhaps it was this that made Harry more emulous to get through without making any blunders. At any rate, he succeeded, and no one in the set suspected that it was his first appearance in public as a dancer.

Fletcher was puzzled. He had hoped that Harry would make himself ridiculous, and throw the set into confusion. But the dance passed off smoothly, and in due time Fletcher led out Maud. If he had known his own interest, he would have kept silent about Harry, but he had little discretion.

"I was rather surprised to see Walton here," he began.

"Didn't you know he was in the city?

"Yes, I met him with Oscar."

"Then why were you surprised?"

"Because his social position does not entitle him to appear in such a company. When I first knew him, he was only a printer's apprentice." Fletcher wanted to say printer's devil, but did not venture to do so in presence of a young lady.

"He will rise higher than that."

"I dare say," said Fletcher, with a sneer, "he will rise in time to be

---

9) put~ down for~ : ~를 ~으로 간주하다.
10) take the floor : 춤에 끼어들다.

a journeyman with a salary of fifteen dollars a week."

"If I am not mistaken in Mr. Walton, he will rise much higher than that. Many of our prominent men have sprung from beginnings like his."

"It must be rather a trial to him to come here. His father is a day-laborer, I believe, and of course he has never been accustomed to any refinement or polish."[11)]

"I don't detect the absence of either," said Maud, quietly.

"Do you believe in throwing down all social distinctions, and meeting the sons of laborers on equal terms?"

"As to that," said Maud, meeting her partner's glance, "I am rather democratic. I could even meet the son of a tin-pedler on equal terms, provided he were a gentleman."

The blood rushed to Fletcher's cheeks.

"A tin-pedler!" he ejaculated.

"Yes! Suppose you were the son, or relation, of a tin-pedler, why should I consider that? It would make you neither better nor worse."

"I have no connection with tin-pedlers," said Fletcher, hastily.

"Who told you I had?"

"I only made a supposition, Mr. Fletcher."

But Fletcher thought otherwise. He was sure that Maud had heard of his mortification at school, and it disturbed him not a little, for, in spite of her assurance, he felt that she believed the story, and it annoyed him so much that he did not venture to make any other reference to Harry.

"Poor Fitz!" said Oscar, when on their way home Maud gave an account of their conversation, "I am afraid he will murder the tin-pedler some time, to get rid of such an odious relationship."

---

11) polish : 품위, 세련.

CHAPTER XXX.

TWO LETTERS FROM THE WEST.

The vacation was over all too soon, yet, brief as it was, Harry looked back upon it with great satisfaction. He had been kindly received in the family of a man who stood high in the profession which he was ambitious to enter; he had gratified his curiosity to see the chief city of New England; and, by no means least, he had secured a position as paid contributor for the "Standard."

"I suppose you will be writing another story soon," said Oscar.

"Yes," said Harry, "I have got the plan of one already."

"If you should write more than you can get into the 'Standard,' you had better send something to the 'Weekly Argus.'"

"I will; but I will wait till the 'Standard' prints my first sketch, so that I can refer to that in writing to the 'Argus.'"

"Perhaps you are right. There's one advantage to not presenting yourself. They won't know you're only a boy."

"Unless they judge so from my style."

"I don't think they would infer it from that. By the way, Harry, suppose my father could find an opening[1)] for you as a reporter on his paper,—would you be willing to accept it?"

"I am not sure whether it would be best for me," said Harry, slowly, "even if I were qualified."

"There is more chance to rise on a city paper."

"I don't know. If I stay here I may before many years control a paper of my own. Then, if I want to go into politics, there would be more chance in the country than in the city."

"Would you like to go into politics?"

"I am rather too young to decide about that; but if I could be of service in that way, I don't see why I should not desire it."

"Well, Harry, I think you are going the right way to work."

"I hope so. I don't want to be promoted till I am fit for it. I am going to work hard for the next two or three years."

---

1) an opening : 공석, 결원, 취직자리.

"I wish I were as industrious as you are, Harry."

"And I wish I knew as much as you do, Oscar."

"Say no more, or we shall be forming a Mutual Admiration Society," said Oscar, laughing.

Harry received a cordial welcome back to the printing office. Mr. Anderson asked him many questions about Mr. Vincent; and our hero felt that his employer regarded him with increased consideration, on account of his acquaintance with the great city editor. This consideration was still farther increased when Mr. Anderson learned our hero's engagement by the "Weekly Standard."

Three weeks later, the "Standard" published Harry's sketch, and accepted another, at the same price. Before this latter was printed, Harry wrote a third sketch, which he called "Phineas Popkin's Engagement." This he inclosed to the "Weekly Argus," with a letter in which he referred to his engagement by the "Standard." In reply he received the following letter:—

"Boston, Jan., 18—,

"MR. FRANK LYNN,—Dear Sir: We enclose three dollars for your sketch,—'Phineas Popkin's Engagement.' We shall be glad to receive other sketches, of similar character and length, and, if accepted, we will pay the same price therefor.

"I. B. FITCH & Co."

This was highly satisfactory to Harry. He was now an accepted contributor to two weekly papers, and the addition to his income would be likely to reach a hundred dollars a year. All this he would be able to lay up, and as much or more from his salary on the "Gazette." He felt on the high road to success. Seeing that his young compositor was meeting with success and appreciation abroad, Mr. Anderson called upon him more frequently to write paragraphs for the "Gazette." Though this work was gratuitous, Harry willingly undertook it. He felt that in this way he was preparing himself for the career to which he steadily looked forward. Present compensation, he justly reasoned, was of small importance, compared with the chance of improvement. In this view, Ferguson, who proved to be a very judicious friend, fully concurred.

Indeed Harry and he became more intimate than before, if that were possible, and they felt that Clapp's departure was by no means to be regretted. They were remarking this one day, when Mr. Anderson, who had been examining his mail, looked up suddenly, and said, "What do you think, Mr. Ferguson? I've got a letter from Clapp."

"A letter from Clapp? Where is he?" inquired Ferguson, with interest.

"This letter is dated at St. Louis. He doesn't appear to be doing very well."

"I thought he was going to California."

"So he represented. But here is the letter." Ferguson took it, and, after reading, handed it to Harry.

It ran thus: —

"St. Louis, April 4, 18—.

"JOTHAM ANDERSON, ESQ., —Dear Sir: Perhaps you will be surprised to hear from me, but I feel as if I would like to hear from Centreville, where I worked so long. The man that induced me and Harrison to come out here left us in the lurch[2] three days after we reached St. Louis. He said he was going on to San Francisco, and he had only money enough to pay his own expenses. As Luke and I were not provided with money, we had a pretty hard time at first, and had to pawn some of our clothes, or we should have starved. Finally I got a job in the 'Democrat' office, and a week after, Luke got something to do, though it didn't pay very well. So we scratched along[3] as well as we could. Part of the time since we have been out of work, and we haven't found 'coming West' all that it was cracked up to be.

"Are Ferguson and Harry Walton still working for you? I should like to come back to the 'Gazette' office, and take my old place; but I haven't got five dollars ahead to pay my travelling expenses. If you will send me out thirty dollars, I will come right on, and work it out after I come back. Hoping for an early reply, I am,

"Yours respectfully,
"HENRY CLAPP."

---

2) leave one in the lurch : 남이 곤경에 취해 있는 것을 내버려두다.
3) scratch along : 이럭저럭 생계를 이어가다.

"Are you going to send out the money, Mr. Anderson?" asked Ferguson.

"Not I. Now that Walton has got well learnt, I don't need another workman. I shall respectfully[4] decline his offer."

Both Harry and Ferguson were glad to hear this, for they felt that Clapp's presence would be far from making the office more agreeable.

"Here's a letter for you, Walton, also post-marked St. Louis," said Mr. Anderson, just afterward.

Harry took it with surprise, and opened it at once.

"It's from Luke Harrison," he said, looking at the signature.

"Does he want you to send him thirty dollars?" asked Ferguson.

"Listen and I will read the letter."

"DEAR HARRY," it commenced, "you will perhaps think it strange that I have written to you; but we used to be good friends. I write to tell you that I don't like this place. I haven't got along well, and I want to get back. Now I am going to ask of you a favor. Will you lend me thirty or forty dollars, to pay my fare home? I will pay you back in a month or two months sure, after I get to work. I will also pay you the few dollars which I borrowed some time ago. I ought to have done it before, but I was thoughtless, and I kept putting it off. Now, Harry, I know you have the money, and you can lend it to me just as well as not, and I'll be sure to pay it back before you need it. Just get a post-office order, and send it to Luke Harrison, 17 R—— Street, St. Louis, and I'll be sure to get it. Give my respects to Mr. Anderson, and also to Mr. Ferguson.

"Your friend,
"LUKE HARRISON."

"There is a chance for a first-class investment, Harry," said Ferguson. "Do you want to join me in it?"

"No, I would rather pay the money to have 'your friend' keep away."

"I don't want to be unkind or disobliging," said Harry, "but I don't feel like giving Luke this money. I know he would never pay me back."

---

4) respectfully : 공손히, 정중하게.

"Say no, then."

"I will. Luke will be mad, but I can't help it."

So both Mr. Anderson and Harry wrote declining to lend. The latter, in return, received a letter from Luke, denouncing him as a "mean, miserly hunks;" but even this did not cause him to regret his decision.

CHAPTER XXXI.

ONE STEP UPWARD.

In real life the incidents that call for notice do not occur daily. Months and years pass, sometimes, where the course of life is quiet and uneventful. So it was with Harry Walton. He went to his daily work with unfailing regularity, devoted a large part of his leisure to reading and study, or writing sketches for the Boston papers, and found himself growing steadily wiser and better informed. His account in the savings-bank grew slowly, but steadily; and on his nineteenth birthday, when we propose to look in upon him again, he was worth five hundred dollars.

Some of my readers who are favored by fortune may regard this as a small sum. It is small in itself, but it was not small for a youth in Harry's position to have saved from his small earnings. But of greater value than the sum itself was the habit of self-denial and saving which our hero had formed. He had started in the right way, and made a beginning which was likely to lead to prosperity in the end. It had not been altogether easy to save this sum. Harry's income had always been small, and he might, without incurring the charge of excessive extravagance, have spent the whole. He had denied himself on many occasions, where most boys of his age would have yielded to the temptation of spending money for pleasure or personal gratification; but he had been rewarded by the thought that he was getting on in the world.[1]

"This is my birthday, Mr. Ferguson," he said, as he entered the printing-office on that particular morning.

"Is it?" asked Ferguson, looking up from his case with interest. "How venerable are you,[2] may I ask?"

"I don't feel very venerable as yet," said Harry, with a smile. "I am nineteen."

"You were sixteen when you entered the office."

"As printer's devil—yes."

"You have learned the business pretty thoroughly. You are as good

---

1) get on in the world : 출세하다, 성공하다.

2) How venerable are you? : How old are you?

a workman as I now, though I am fifteen years older."

"You are too modest, Mr. Ferguson."

"No, it is quite true. You are as rapid and accurate as I am, and you ought to receive as high pay."

"That will come in time. You know I make something by writing for the papers."

"That's extra work. How much did you make in that way last year?"

"I can tell you, because I figured it up last night. It was one hundred and twenty-five dollars, and I put every cent into the savings-bank."

"That is quite an addition to your income."

"I shall make more this year. I am to receive two dollars a column, hereafter, for my sketches."

"I congratulate you, Harry,—the more heartily, because I think you deserve it. Your recent sketches show quite an improvement over those you wrote a year ago."

"Do you really think so?" said Harry, with evident pleasure.

"I have no hesitation in saying so. You write with greater ease than formerly, and your style is less that of a novice."

"So I have hoped and thought; but of course I was prejudiced in my own favor."[3)]

"You may rely upon it. Indeed, your increased pay is proof of it. Did you ask it?"

"The increase? No, the editor of the 'Standard' wrote me voluntarily that he considered my contributions worth the additional amount."

"That must be very pleasant. I tell you what, Harry, I've a great mind to set up opposition to you in the story line."

"Do so," said Harry, smiling.

"I would if I had the slightest particle of imagination; but the fact is, I'm too practical and matter-of-fact. Besides, I never had any talent for writing of any kind. Some time I may become publisher of a village paper like this; but farther than that I don't aspire."

"We are to be partners in that, you know, Ferguson."

"That may be, for a time; but you will rise higher than that, Harry."

"I am afraid you overrate me."

---

3) in one's own favor : ~에게 유리하도록.

"No; I have observed you closely in the time we have been together, and I have long felt that you are destined to rise from the ranks in which I am content to remain. Haven't you ever felt so, yourself, Harry?"

Harry's cheek flushed, and his eye lighted up.

"I won't deny that I have such thoughts sometimes," he said; "but it may end in[4] that."

"It often does end in that; but it is only where ambition is not accompanied by faithful work. Now you are always at work. You are doing what you can to help fortune, and the end will be that fortune will help you."

"I hope so, at any rate," said Harry, thoughtfully. "I should like to fill an honorable position, and do some work by which I might be known in after years."

"Why not? The boys and young men of to-day are hereafter to fill the highest positions in the community and State. Why may not the lot fall to you?"

"I will try, at any rate, to qualify myself. Then if responsibilities come, I will try to discharge them."

The conversation was here interrupted by the entrance of Mr. Anderson, the editor of the "Gazette." He was not as well or strong as when we first made his acquaintance. Then he seemed robust enough, but now he was thinner, and moved with slower gait. It was not easy to say what had undermined his strength, for he had had no severe fit of sickness; but certainly he was in appearance several years older than when Harry entered the office.

"How do you feel this morning, Mr. Anderson?" asked Ferguson.

"I feel weak and languid, and indisposed to[5] exertion of any kind."

"You need some change."

"That is precisely what I have thought myself. The doctor advises change of scene, and this very morning I had a letter from a brother in Wisconsin, asking me to come out and visit him."

"I have no doubt it would do you good."

"So it would. But how can I go? I can't take the paper with me," said Mr. Andersen, rather despondently.

---

4) end in~ : ~으로 끝나다.

5) indisposed to~ : reluctant

"No; but you can leave Harry to edit it in your absence."

"Mr. Ferguson!" exclaimed Harry, startled by the proposition.

"Harry as editor!" repeated Mr. Anderson.

"Yes; why not? He is a practised writer. For more than two years he has written for two Boston papers."

"But he is so young. How old are you, Harry?" asked the editor.

"Nineteen to-day, sir."

"Nineteen. That's very young for an editor."

"Very true; but, after all, it isn't so much the age as the qualifications, is it, Mr. Anderson?"

"True," said the editor, meditatively. "Harry, do you think you could edit the paper for two or three months?"

"I think I could," said Harry, with modest confidence. His heart beat high at the thought of the important position which was likely to be opened to him; and plans of what he would do to make the paper interesting already began to be formed in his mind.

"It never occurred to me before, but I really think you could," said the editor, "and that would remove every obstacle to my going. By the way, Harry, you would have to find a new boarding-place, for Mrs. Anderson would accompany me, and we should shut up the house."

"Perhaps Ferguson would take me in?" said Harry.

"I should be glad to do so; but I don't know that my humble fare would be good enough for an editor."

Harry smiled. "I won't put on airs," he said, "till my commission is made out."[6]

"I am afraid that I can't offer high pay for your services in that capacity," said Mr. Anderson.

"I shall charge nothing, sir," said Harry, "but thank you for the opportunity of entering, if only for a short time, a profession to which it is my ambition to belong."

After a brief consultation with his wife, Mr. Anderson appointed Harry editor pro tem.,[7] and began to make arrangements for his journey. Harry's weekly wages were raised to fifteen dollars, out of which he

---

6) make out : 작성하다, 입증하다.

7) pro tem. : pro tempore, 임시적인, 임시의.

waa to pay Ferguson four dollars a week for board.

So our hero found himself, at nineteen, the editor of an old established paper, which, though published in a country village, was not without its share of influence in the county and State.

CHAPTER XXXII.

THE YOUNG EDITOR.

The next number of the Centreville "Gazette" contained the following notice from the pen of Mr. Anderson:—

"For the first time since our connection with the 'Gazette,' we purpose taking a brief respite from our duties. The state of our health renders a vacation desirable, and an opportune invitation from a brother at the West has been accepted. Our absence may extend to two or three months. In the interim[1] we have committed the editorial management to Mr. Harry Walton, who has been connected with the paper, in a different capacity, for nearly three years. Though Mr. Walton is a very young man, he has already acquired a reputation, as contributor to papers of high standing in Boston, and we feel assured that our subscribers will have no reason to complain of the temporary change in the editorship."

"The old man has given you quite a handsome notice, Harry," said Ferguson.

"I hope I shall deserve it," said Harry; "but I begin now to realize that I am young to assume such responsible duties. It would have seemed more appropriate for you to undertake them."

"I can't write well enough, Harry. I like to read, but I can't produce. In regard to the business management I feel competent to advise."

"I shall certainly be guided by your advice, Ferguson."

As it may interest the reader, we will raise the curtain and show our young hero in the capacity of editor. The time is ten days after Mr. Anderson's absence. Harry was accustomed to do his work as compositor in the forenoon and the early part of the afternoon. From three to five he occupied the editorial chair, read letters, wrote paragraphs, and saw visitors. He had just seated himself, when a man entered the office and looked about him inquisitively.

"I would like to see the editor," he said.

"I am the editor," said Harry, with dignity.

The visitor looked surprised.

---

1) in the interim : 그 사이에, 당분간.

"You are the youngest-looking editor I have met," he said. "Have you filled the office long?"

"Not long," said Harry. "Can I do anything for you?"

"Yes, sir, you can. First let me introduce myself. I am Dr. Theophilus Peabody."

"Will you be seated, Dr. Peabody?"

"You have probably heard of me before," said the visitor.

"I can't say that I have."

"I am surprised at that," said the doctor, rather disgusted to find himself unknown. "You must have heard of Peabody's Unfailing[2] Panacea."

"I am afraid I have not."

"You are young," said Dr. Peabody, compassionately; "that accounts for it. Peabody's Panacea, let me tell you, sir, is the great remedy of the age. It has effected more cures, relieved more pain, soothed more aching bosoms, and done more good, than any other medicine in existence."

"It must be a satisfaction to you to have conferred such a blessing on mankind," said Harry, inclined to laugh at the doctor's magniloquent style.

"It is. I consider myself one of the benefactors of mankind; but, sir, the medicine has not yet been fully introduced. There are thousands, who groan on beds of pain, who are ignorant that for the small sum of fifty cents they could be restored to health and activity."

"That's a pity."

"It is a pity, Mr. ——"

"Walton."

"Mr. Walton,—I have called, sir, to ask you to co-operate with me in making it known to the world, so far as your influence extends."

"Is your medicine a liquid?"

"No, sir; it is in the form of pills, twenty-four in a box. Let me show you."

The doctor opened a wooden box, and displayed a collection of very unwholesome-looking brown pills.

"Try one, sir; it won't do you any harm."

---

2) unfailing : 틀림없는, 확실한.

"Thank you; I would rather not. I don't like pills. What will they cure?"

"What won't they cure? I've got a list of fifty-nine diseases in my circular,[3] all of which are relieved by Peabody's Panacea. They may cure more; in fact, I've been told of a consumptive patient who was considerably relieved by a single box. You won't try one?"

"I would rather not."

"Well, here is my circular, containing accounts of remarkable cures performed. Permit me to present you a box."

"Thank you," said Harry, dubiously.

"You'll probably be sick before long," said the doctor, cheerfully, "and then the pills will come handy."[4]

"Doctor," said Ferguson, gravely, "I find my hair getting thin on top of the head. Do you think the panacea would restore it?"

"Yes," said the doctor, unexpectedly. "I had a case, in Portsmouth, of a gentleman whose head was as smooth as a billiard-ball. He took the pills for another complaint, and was surprised, in the course of three weeks, to find young hair sprouting all over the bald spot. Can't I sell you half-a-dozen boxes? You may have half a dozen for two dollars and a half."

Ferguson, who of course had been in jest,[5] found it hard to forbear laughing, especially when Harry joined the doctor in urging him to purchase.

"Not to-day," he answered. "I can try Mr. Walton's box, and if it helps me I can order some more."

"You may not be able to get it, then," said the doctor, persuasively. "I may not be in Centreville."

"If the panacea is well known, I can surely get it without difficulty."

"Not so cheap as I will sell it."

"I won't take any to-day," said Ferguson, decisively.

"You haven't told me what I can do for you," said Harry, who found the doctor's call rather long.

"I would like you to insert my circular to your paper. It won't take

---

3) circular : 광고삐라.
4) come (in) handy : (여러 가지로) 편리하다.
5) be in jest : 농담으로

more than two columns."

"We shall be happy to insert it at regular advertising rates."

"I thought," said Dr. Peabody, disappointed, "that you might do it gratuitously, as I had given you a box."

"We don't do business on such terms," said Harry. "I think I had better return the box."

"No, keep it," said the doctor. "You will be willing to notice it, doubtless."

Harry rapidly penned this paragraph, and read it aloud:—

"Dr. Theophilus Peabody has left with us a box of his Unfailing Panacea, which he claims will cure a large variety of diseases."

"Couldn't you give a list of the diseases?" insinuated the doctor.

"There are fifty-nine, you said?"

"Yes, sir."

"Then I am afraid we must decline."

Harry resumed his writing, and the doctor took his leave, looking far from satisfied.

"Here, Ferguson," said Harry, after the visitor had retired, "take the pills, and much good may they do you. Better take one now for the growth of your hair."

It was fortunate that Dr. Peabody did not hear the merriment that followed, or he would have given up the editorial staff of the Centreville "Gazette" as maliciously disposed to underrate his favorite medicine.

"Who wouldn't be an editor?" said Harry.

"I notice," said Ferguson, "that pill-tenders and blacking manufacturers are most liberal to the editorial profession. I only wish jewellers and piano manufacturers were as free with their manufactures. I would like a good gold watch, and I shall soon want a piano for my daughter."

"You may depend upon it, Ferguson, when such gifts come in, that I shall claim them as editorial perquisites."

"We won't quarrel about them till they come, Harry."

Our hero here opened a bulky communication.[6)]

"What is that?" asked Ferguson.

"An essay on 'The Immortality of the Soul,'—covers fifteen pages

---

6) communication : 문서

foolscap. What shall I do with it?"

"Publish it in a supplement with Dr. Peabody's circular."

"I am not sure but the circular would be more interesting reading."

"From whom does the essay come?"

"It is signed 'L. S.'"

"Then it is by Lemuel Snodgrass, a retired schoolteacher, who fancies himself a great writer."

"He'll be offended if I don't print it, won't he?"

"I'll tell you how to get over[7] that. Say, in an editorial paragraph, 'We have received a thoughtful essay from 'L. S.', on 'The Immortality of the Soul.' We regret that its length precludes our publishing it in the 'Gazette.' We would suggest to the author to print it in a pamphlet.' That suggestion will be regarded as complimentary, and we may get the job of printing it."

"I see you are shrewd, Ferguson. I will follow your advice."

---

7) get over~ :~을 극복하다.

CHAPTER XXXIII.

AN UNEXPECTED PROPOSAL.

During his temporary editorship, Harry did not feel at liberty to make any decided changes in the character or arrangement of the paper; but he was ambitious to improve it, as far as he was able, in its different departments[1]. Mr. Anderson had become rather indolent in the collection of local news, merely publishing such items as were voluntarily contributed. Harry, after his day's work was over, made a little tour of the village, gathering any news that he thought would be of interest to the public. Moreover he made arrangements to obtain news of a similar nature from neighboring villages, and the result was, that in the course of a month he made the "Gazette" much more readable.

"Really, the 'Gazette' gives a good deal more news than it used to," was a common remark.

It was probably in consequence of this improvement that new subscriptions began to come in, not from Centreville alone, but from towns in the neighborhood. This gratified and encouraged Harry, who now felt that he was on the right tack[2].

There was another department to which he devoted considerable attention. This was a condensed summary of news from all parts of the world, giving the preference and the largest space, of course, to American news. He aimed to supply those who did not take a daily paper with a brief record of events, such as they would not be likely, otherwise, to hear of. Of course all this work added to his labors as compositor; and his occasional sketches for Boston papers absorbed a large share of his time. Indeed, he had very little left at his disposal for rest and recreation.

"I am afraid you are working too hard, Harry," said Ferguson. "You are doing Mr. Anderson's work better than he ever did it, and your own too."

"I enjoy it," said Harry. "I work hard I know, but I feel paid by

---

1) departments : (잡지, 신문 등의) 상설 특별 난.
2) be on the right tack : 방침이 올바른

the satisfaction of finding that my labors are appreciated."

"When Mr. Anderson gets back, he will find it necessary to employ you as assistant editor, for it won't do to let the paper get back to its former dulness."

"I will accept," said Harry, "if he makes the offer. I feel more and more that I must be an editor."

"You are certainly showing yourself competent for the position."

"I have only made a beginning," said our hero, modestly. "In time I think I could make a satisfactory paper."

One day, about two months after Mr. Anderson's departure, Ferguson and Harry were surprised, and not altogether agreeably, by the entrance of John Clapp and Luke Harrison. They looked far from prosperous. In fact, both of them were decidedly seedy. Going West had not effected an improvement in their fortunes.

"Is that you, Clapp?" asked Ferguson. "Where did you come from?"

"From St. Louis."

"Then you didn't feel inclined to stay there?"

"Not I. It's a beastly place. I came near starving."

Clapp would have found any place beastly where a fair day's work was required for fair wages, and my young readers in St. Louis, therefore, need not heed his disparaging remarks.

"How was it with you, Luke?" asked Harry. "Do you like the West no better than Clapp?"

"You don't catch me out[3)] there again," said Luke. "It isn't what it's cracked up to be. We had the hardest work in getting money enough to get us back."

As Luke did not mention the kind of hard work by which the money was obtained, I may state here that an evening's luck at the faro table had supplied them with money enough to pay the fare to Boston by railway; otherwise another year might have found them still in St. Louis.

"Hard work doesn't suit your constitution[4)], does it?" said Ferguson, slyly.

"I can work as well as anybody," said Luke; "but I haven't had the

---

3) catch~ out : ~를 (뜻밖의 장소에서) 만나다

4) constitution : 체격, 체질

luck of some people."

"You were lucky enough to have your fare paid to the West for you."

"Yes, and when we got there, the rascal left us to shift for ourselves.[5) That aint much luck."

"I've always had to shift for myself, and always expect to," was the reply.

"Oh, you're a model!" sneered Clapp. "You always were as sober and steady as a deacon. I wonder they didn't make you one."

"And Walton there is one of the same sort," said Luke. "I say, Harry, it was real mean in you not to send me the money I wrote for. You hadn't it, had you?"

"Yes," said Harry, firmly; "but I worked hard for it, and I didn't feel like giving it away."

"Who asked you to give it away? I only wanted to borrow it."

"That's the same thing—with you. You were not likely to repay it again."

"Do you mean to insult me?" blustered Luke.

"No, I never insult anybody. I only tell the truth. You know, Luke Harrison, whether I have reason for what I say."

"I wouldn't leave a friend to suffer when I had plenty of money in my pocket," said Luke, with an injured air.

"If you had been a different sort of fellow I would have asked you for five dollars to keep me along till I can get work. I've come back with empty pockets."

"I'll lend you five dollars if you need it," said Harry, who judged from Luke's appearance that he told the truth.

"Will you?" said Luke, brightening up. "That's a good fellow. I'll pay you just as soon as I can."

Harry did not place much reliance on this assurance; but he felt that he could afford the loss of five dollars, if loss it should prove, and it might prevent Luke's obtaining the money in a more questionable way.

"Where's Mr. Anderson?" asked Clapp, looking round the office.

"He's been in Michigan for a couple of months."

"You don't say so! Why, who runs the paper?"

---

5) shift for oneself: 자립으로 꾸려가다.

"Ferguson and I," said Harry.

"I mean who edits it?"

"Harry does that," said his fellow-workman.

"Whew!" ejaculated Clapp, in surprise. "Why, but two years ago you was only a printer's devil!"

"He's risen from the ranks," said Ferguson, "and I can say with truth that the 'Gazette' has never been better than since it has been under his charge[6]."

"How much does old Anderson pay you for taking his place?" asked Luke, who was quite as much surprised as Clapp.

"I don't ask anything extra. He pays me fifteen dollars a week as compositor."

"You're doing well," said Luke, enviously. "Got a big pile of money laid up, haven't you?"

"I have something in the bank."

"Harry writes stories for the Boston papers, also," said Ferguson.

"He makes a hundred or two that way."

"Some folks are born to luck," said Clapp, discontentedly. "Here am I, six or eight years older, out of a place, and without a cent to fall back upon. I wish I was one of your lucky ones."

"You might have had a few hundred dollars, at any rate," said Ferguson, "if you hadn't chosen to spend all your money when you were earning good wages."

"A man must have a little enjoyment. We can't drudge all the time."

"It's better to do that than to be where you are now."

But Clapp was not to be convinced that he was himself to blame for his present disagreeable position. He laid the blame on fortune, like thousands of others. He could not see that Harry's good luck was the legitimate consequence of industry and frugality.

After a while the two left the office. They decided to seek their old boarding-house, and remain there for a week, waiting for something to turn up.

The next day Harry received the following letter from Mr. Anderson: —

---

6) under one's charge : ~에게 맡기다.

"DEAR WALTON: My brother urges me to settle permanently at the West. I am offered a partnership in a paper in this vicinity, and my health has much improved here. The West seems the place for me. My only embarrassment is the paper. If I could dispose of the 'Gazette' for two thousand dollars cash, I could see my way clear to remove. Why can't you and Ferguson buy it? The numbers which you have sent me show that you are quite capable of filling the post of editor; and you and Ferguson can do the mechanical part. I think it will be a good chance for you. Write me at once whether there is any likelihood of your purchasing.

"Your friend,
"JOTHAM ANDERSON."

Harry's face flushed eagerly as he read this letter, Nothing would suit him better than to make this arrangement[7], if only he could provide the purchase money. But this was likely to present a difficulty.

---

7) make arrangement : 결말을 짓다.

CHAPTER XXXIV.

A FRIEND IN NEED.

Harry at once showed Ferguson the letter he had received.

"What are you going to do about it?" asked his friend.

"I should like to buy the paper, but I don't see how I can. Mr. Anderson wants two thousand dollars cash."

"How much have you got?"

"Only five hundred."

"I have seven hundred and fifty," said Ferguson, thoughtfully.

Harry's face brightened.

"Why can't we go into partnership?" he asked.

"That is what we spoke of once," said Ferguson, "and it would suit me perfectly; but there is a difficulty. Your money and mine added together will not be enough."

"Perhaps Mr. Anderson would take a mortgage on[1] the establishment for the balance."

"I don't think so. He says expressly that he wants cash."

Harry looked disturbed.

"Do you think any one would lend us the money on the same terms?" he asked, after a while.

"Squire Trevor is the only man in the village likely to have money to lend. There he is in the street now. Run down, Harry, and ask him to step in a minute."

Our hero seized his hat, and did as requested. He returned immediately, followed by Squire Trevor, a stout, puffy little man, reputed shrewd and a capitalist.

"Excuse our calling you in, Squire Trevor," said Ferguson, "but we want to consult you on a matter of business. Harry, just show the squire Mr. Anderson's letter."

The squire read it deliberately.

"Do you want my advice?" he said, looking up from the perusal. "Buy the paper. It is worth what Anderson asks for it."

---

1) take a mortgage on~ : ~을 저당 잡다.

"So I think, but there is a difficulty. Harry and I can only raise twelve hundred dollars or so between us."

"Give a note for the balance. You'll be able to pay it off in two years, if you prosper."

"I am afraid that won't do. Mr. Anderson wants cash. Can't you lend us the money, Squire Trevor?" continued Ferguson, bluntly.

The village capitalist shook his head.

"If you had asked me last week I could have obliged you," he said; "but I was in Boston day before yesterday, and bought some railway stock which is likely to enhance in value. That leaves me short[2)]."

"Then you couldn't manage it?" said Ferguson, soberly.

"Not at present," said the squire, decidedly.

"Then we must write to Mr. Anderson, offering what we have, and a mortgage to secure the rest."

"That will be your best course."

"He may agree to our terms," said Harry, hopefully, after their visitor had left the office.

"We will hope so, at all events."

A letter was at once despatched, and in a week the answer was received.

"I am sorry," Mr. Anderson wrote, "to decline your proposals, but, I have immediate need of the whole sum which I ask for the paper. If I cannot obtain it, I shall come back to Centreville, though I would prefer to remain here."

Upon the receipt of this letter, Ferguson gave up his work for the forenoon, and made a tour of the Village, calling upon all who he thought were likely to have money to lend. He had small expectation of success, but felt that he ought to try everywhere before giving up so good a chance.

While he was absent, Harry had a welcome visitor. It was no other than Professor Henderson, the magician, in whose employ he had spent three months some years before, as related in "Bound to Rise."

"Take a seat, professor," said Harry, cordially. "I am delighted to see you."

"How you have grown, Harry!" said the professor. "Why, I should

---

2) short : 돈이 모자란.

hardly have known you!"

"We haven't met since I left you to enter this office."

"No; it is nearly three years. How do you like the business?"

"Very much indeed."

"Are you doing well?"

"I receive fifteen dollars a week."

"That is good. What are your prospects for the future?"

"They would be excellent if I had a little more capital."

"I don't see how you need capital, as a journeyman printer."

"I have a chance to buy out the paper."

"But who would edit it?"

"I would."

"You!" said the magician, rather incredulously.

"I have been the editor for the last two months."

"You—a boy!"

"I am nineteen, professor."

"I shouldn't have dreamed of editing a paper at nineteen; or, indeed, as old as I am now."

Harry laughed.

"You are too modest, professor. Let me show you our last two issues."

The professor took out his glasses, and sat down, not without considerable curiosity, to read a paper edited by one who only three years before had been his assistant.

"Did you write this article?" he asked, after a pause, pointing to the leader[3] in the last issue of the "Gazette."

"Yes, sir."

"Then, by Jove[4], you can write. Why, it's worthy of a man of twice your age!"

"Thank you, professor," said Harry, gratified.

"Where did you learn to write?"

Harry gave his old employer some account of his literary experiences, mentioning his connection with the two Boston weekly papers.

"You ought to be an editor," said the professor. "If you can do as

---

3) the leader : 주요기사, 사설, 논설.
4) by Jove : (놀람, 찬성을 나타내어) 맹세코, 반드시!

much at nineteen, you have a bright future before you."

"That depends a little on circumstances. If I only could buy this paper, I would try to win reputation as well as money."

"What is your difficulty?"

"The want of money."

"How much do you need?"

"Eight hundred dollars."

"Is that all the price such a paper commands[5]?"

"No. The price is two thousand dollars; but Ferguson and I can raise twelve hundred between us."

"Do you consider it good property?"

"Mr. Anderson made a comfortable living out of it, besides paying for office work. We should have this advantage, that we should be our own compositors."

"That would give you considerable to do, if you were editor also."

"I shouldn't mind," said Harry, "if I only had a paper of my own. I think I should be willing to work night and day."

"What are your chances of raising the sum you need?"

"Very small. Ferguson has gone out at this moment to see if he can find any one willing to lend; but we don't expect success."

"Why don't you apply to me?" asked the professor.

"I didn't know if you had the money to spare."

"I might conjure up some. Presto![6]—change!—you know. We professors of magic can find money anywhere."

"But you need some to work with. I have been behind the scenes[7]," said Harry, smiling.

"But you don't know all my secrets, for all that. In sober earnest, I haven't been practising magic these twenty-five years for nothing. I can lend you the money you want, and I will."

Harry seized his hand, and shook it with delight.

"How can I express my gratitude?" he said.

"By sending me your paper gratis,[8] and paying me seven per cent.

---

5) command : (물건이) ~의 값에 팔리다.
6) Presto! : (요술장이 기합소리) 얏!
7) behind the scenes : 부대 뒤에서, 내막에 밝아서
8) gratis : 무료로, 공짜로

interest on my money."

"Agreed. Anything more?"

"Yes. I am to give an exhibition in the village to-morrow night. You must give me a good puff."

"With the greatest pleasure. I'll write it now."

"Before it takes place? I see you are following the example of some of the city dailies."

"And I'll print you some handbills for nothing."

"Good. When do you want the money? Will next week do?"

"Yes. Mr. Anderson won't expect the money before."

Here Ferguson entered the office. Harry made a signal of silence to the professor, whom he introduced. Then he said:—

"Well, Ferguson, what luck?"

"None at all," answered his fellow-compositor, evidently dispirited. "Nobody seems to have any money. We shall have to give up our plan."

"I don't mean to give it up."

"Then perhaps you'll tell me where to find the money."

"I will."

"You don't mean to say—" began Ferguson, eagerly.

"Yes, I do. I mean to say that the money is found."

"Where?"

"Prof. Henderson has agreed to let us have it."

"Is that true?" said Ferguson, bewildered.

"I believe so," said the professor, smiling. "Harry has juggled the money out of me,—you know he used to be in the business,—and you can make your bargain as soon as you like."

It is hardly necessary to say that Prof. Henderson got an excellent notice in the next number of the Centreville "Gazette;" and it is my opinion that he deserved it.

CHAPTER XXXV.

FLETCHER's OPINION OF HARRY WALTON.

In two weeks all the business arrangements were completed, and Ferguson and Harry became joint proprietors of the "Centreville Gazette," the latter being sole editor. The change was received with favor in the village, as Harry had, as editor pro tem. for two months, shown his competence for the position. It gave him prominence also in town, and, though only nineteen, he already was classed with the minister, the doctor and the lawyer. It helped him also with the weekly papers to which he contributed in Boston, and his pay was once more raised, while his sketches were more frequently printed. Now this was all very pleasant, but it was not long before our hero found himself overburdened with work.

"What is the matter Harry? You look pale," said Ferguson, one morning.

"I have a bad headache, and am feeling out of sorts[1])."

"I don't wonder at it. You are working too hard."

"I don't know about that."

"I do. You do nearly as much as I, as a compositor. Then you do all the editorial work, besides writing sketches for the Boston papers."

"How can I get along with less? The paper must be edited, and I shouldn't like giving up writing for the Boston papers."

"I'll tell you what to do. Take a boy and train him up as a printer. After a while he will relieve you almost wholly, while, by the time he commands good wages, we shall be able to pay them."

"It is a good idea, Ferguson. Do you know of any boy that wants to learn printing?"

"Haven't you got a younger brother?"

"The very thing[2])," said Harry, briskly. "Father wrote to me last week that he should like to get something for ——."

"Better write and offer him a place in the office."

---

1) out of sorts : 건강(기분)이 안 좋은.

2) The very thing : 바로 그거네.

"I will."

The letter was written at once. An immediate answer was received, of a favorable nature. The boy was glad to leave home, and the father was pleased to have him under the charge of his older brother.

After he had become editor, and part proprietor of the "Gazette," Harry wrote to Oscar Vincent to announce his promotion. Though Oscar had been in college now nearly two years, and they seldom met, the two were as warm friends as ever, and from time to time exchanged letters.

This was Oscar's reply:—

"HARVARD COLLEGE, June 10.

"DEAR MR. EDITOR: I suppose that's the proper way to address you now. I congratulate you with all my heart on your brilliant success and rapid advancement. Here you are at nineteen, while I am only a rattle-brained sophomore. I don't mind being called that, by the way, for at least it credits me with the possession of brains. Not that I am doing so very badly. I am probably in the first third of the class, and that implies respectable scholarship here.

"But you—I can hardly realize that you, whom I knew only two or three years since as a printer's apprentice (I won't use Fletcher's word), have lifted yourself to the responsible position of sole editor. Truly you have risen from the ranks!

"Speaking of Fletcher, by the way, you know he is my classmate. He occupies an honorable position somewhere near the foot of the class, where he is likely to stay, unless he receives from the faculty leave of absence[3] for an unlimited period. I met him yesterday, swinging his little cane, and looking as dandified as he used to.

"'Hallo! Fletcher,' said I, 'I've just got a letter from a friend of yours.'

"'Who is it?' he asked.

"'Harry Walton.'

"'He never was a friend of mine,' said Fitz, turning up his delicately chiselled nose,—'the beggarly printer's devil!'

"I hope you won't feel sensitive about the manner in which Fitz spoke

3) leave of absence : 결석허가.

of you.

"'You've made two mistakes,' said I. 'He's neither a beggar nor a printer's devil.'

"'He used to be,' retorted Fitz.

"'The last, not the first. You'll be glad to hear that he's getting on well.'

"'Has he had his wages raised twenty-five cents a week?' sneered Fitz.

"'He has lost his place,' said I.

"Fletcher actually looked happy, but I dashed his happiness by adding, 'but he's got a better one.'

"'What's that?' he snarled.

"'He has bought out the paper of Mr. Anderson, and is now sole editor and part proprietor.'

"'A boy like him buy a paper, without a cent of money and no education!'

"'You are mistaken. He had several hundred dollars, and as a writer he is considerably ahead of either of us.'

"'He'll run the paper into the ground[4],' said Fitz, prophetically.

"'If he does, it'll only be to give it firmer root.'

"'You are crazy about that country lout,' said Fitz. 'It isn't much to edit a little village paper like that, after all.'

"So you see what your friend Fitz thinks about it. As you may be in danger of having your vanity fed by compliments from other sources, I thought I would offset them by the candid opinion of a disinterested and impartial scholar like Fitz.

"I told my father of the step you have taken. 'Oscar,' said he, 'that boy is going to succeed. He shows the right spirit. I would have given him a place on my paper, but very likely he does better to stay where he is.'

"Perhaps you noticed the handsome notice he gave you in his paper yesterday. I really think he has a higher opinion of your talents than of mine; which, of course, shows singular lack of discrimination. However, you're my friend, and I won't make a fuss about[5] it.

---

4) run~ into the ground : ~을 못쓰게 만들다.

"I am cramming for the summer examinations and hot work I find it, I can tell you. This summer I am going to Niagara, and shall return by way of the St. Lawrence and Montreal, seeing the Thousand Islands, the rapids, and so on. I may send you a letter or two for the 'Gazette,' if you will give me a puff in your editorial columns."

These letters were actually written, and, being very lively and readable, Harry felt quite justified in referring to them in a complimentary way. Fletcher's depreciation of him troubled him very little.

"It will make me neither worse nor better," he reflected. "The time will come, I hope, when I shall have risen high enough to be wholly indifferent to such ill-natured sneers."

His brother arrived in due time, and was set to work as Harry himself had been three years before. He was not as smart as Harry, nor was he ever likely to rise as high; but he worked satisfactorily, and made good progress, so that in six months he was able to relieve Harry of half his labors as compositor. This enabled him to give more time to his editorial duties. Both boarded at Ferguson's, where they had a comfortable home and good, plain fare.

Meanwhile, Harry was acknowledged by all to have improved the paper, and the most satisfactory evidence of the popular approval of his efforts came in an increased subscription list, and this, of course, made the paper more profitable. At the end of twelve months, the two partners had paid off the money borrowed from Professor Henderson, and owned the paper without incumbrance.

"A pretty good year's work, Harry," said Ferguson, cheerfully.

"Yes," said Harry; "but we'll do still better next year."

---

5) make a fuss about~ :~ 을 칭찬하다.

CHAPTER XXXVI.

CONCLUSION.

I have thus traced in detail the steps by which Harry Walton ascended from the condition of a poor farmer's son to the influential position of editor of a weekly newspaper. I call to mind now, however, that he is no longer a boy, and his future career will be of less interest to my young readers. Yet I hope they may be interested to hear, though not in detail, by what successive steps he rose still higher in position and influence.

Harry was approaching his twenty-first birthday when he was waited upon by a deputation of citizens from a neighboring town, inviting him to deliver a Fourth of July oration. He was at first disposed, out of modesty, to decline; but, on consultation with Ferguson, decided to accept and do his best. He was ambitious to produce a good impression, and his experience in the Debating Society gave him a moderate degree of confidence and self-reliance. When the time came he fully satisfied public expectation. I do not say that his oration was a model of eloquence, for that could not have been expected of one whose advantages had been limited, and one for whom I have never claimed extraordinary genius. But it certainly was well written and well delivered, and very creditable to the young orator. The favor with which it was received may have had something to do in influencing the people of Centreville to nominate and elect him, to the New Hampshire Legislature a few months later.

He entered that body, the youngest member in it. But his long connection with a Debating Society, and the experience he had gained in parliamentary proceedings[1)], enabled him at once to become a useful working Member. He was successively re-elected for several years, during which he showed such practical ability that he obtained a State reputation. At twenty-eight he received a nomination for Congress[2)], and was elected by a close vote. During all this time he remained in charge

1) parliamentary proceedings : 의회 운영절차.
2) Congress : 국회

of the Centreville "Gazette," but of course had long relinquished the task of a compositor into his brother's hands. He had no foolish ideas about this work being beneath him; but he felt that he could employ his time more profitably in other ways. Under his judicious management, the "Gazette" attained a circulation and influence that it had never before reached. The income derived from it was double that which it yielded in the days of his predecessor; and both he and Ferguson were enabled to lay by a few hundred dollars every year. But Harry had never sought wealth. He was content with a comfortable support and a competence. He liked influence and the popular respect, and he was gratified by the important trusts which he received. He was ambitious, but it was a creditable and honorable ambition. He sought to promote the public welfare, and advance the public interests, both as a speaker and as a writer; and though sometimes misrepresented, the people on the whole did him justice.3)

A few weeks after he had taken his seat in Congress, a young man was ushered into his private room. Looking up, he saw a man of about his own age, dressed with some attempt at style, but on the whole wearing a look of faded gentility.

"Mr. Walton," said the visitor, with some hesitation.

"That is my name. Won't you take a seat?"

The visitor sat down, but appeared ill at ease. He nervously fumbled at his hat, and did not speak.

"Can I do anything for you?" asked Harry, at length.

"I see you don't know me," said the stranger.

"I can't say I recall your features; but then I see a great many persons."

"I went to school at the Prescott Academy, when you were in the office of the Centreville 'Gazette.'"

Harry looked more closely, and exclaimed, in astonished recognition, "Fitzgerald Fletcher!"

"Yes," said the other, flushing with mortification, "I am Fitzgerald Fletcher."

"I am glad to see you," said Harry, cordially, forgetting the old antago-

---

3) do~ justice : ~을 올바르게 평가하다.

nism that had existed between them.

He rose and offered his hand, which Fletcher took with an air of relief, for he had felt uncertain of his reception.

"You have prospered wonderfully," said Fletcher, with a shade of envy.

"Yes," said Harry, smiling. "I was a printer's devil when you knew me; but I never meant to stay in that position. I have risen from the ranks."

"I haven't," said Fletcher, bitterly.

"Have you been unfortunate? Tell me about it, if you don't mind," said Harry, sympathetically.

"My father failed three years ago," said Fletcher, "and I found myself adrift with nothing to do, and no money to fall back upon. I have drifted about since then; but now I am out of employment. I came to you to-day to see if you will exert your influence to get me a government clerkship, even of the lowest class. You may rest assured, Mr. Walton, that I need it."

Was this the proud Fitzgerald Fletcher, suing, for the means of supporting himself, to one whom, as a boy, he had despised and looked down upon? Surely, the world is full of strange changes and mutations of fortune. Here was a chance for Harry to triumph over his old enemy; but he never thought of doing it. Instead, he was filled with sympathy for one who, unlike himself, had gone down in the social scale, and he cordially promised to see what he could do for Fletcher, and that without delay.

On inquiry, he found that Fletcher was qualified to discharge the duties of a clerk, and secured his appointment to a clerkship in the Treasury Department[4], on a salary of twelve hundred dollars a year. It was an income which Fletcher would once have regarded as wholly insufficient for his needs; but adversity had made him humble, and he thankfully accepted it. He holds the position still, discharging the duties satisfactorily. He is glad to claim the Hon[5]. Harry Walton among his acquaintances, and never sneers at him now as a "printer's devil."

---

4) Treasury Department : 재무부

5) Hon. : Honorable, 연방 및 주의회 의원

Oscar Vincent spent several years abroad, after graduation, acting as foreign correspondent of his father's paper. He is now his father's junior partner, and is not only respected for his ability, but a general favorite in society, on account of his sunny disposition and cordial good nature. He keeps up his intimacy with Harry Walton. Indeed, there is good reason for this, since Harry, four years since, married his sister Maud, and the two friends are brothers-in-law.

Harry's parents are still living, no longer weighed down by poverty, as when we first made their acquaintance. The legacy which came so opportunely improved their condition, and provided them with comforts to which they had long been strangers. But their chief satisfaction comes from Harry's unlooked-for success in life. Their past life of poverty and privation is all forgotten in their gratitude for this great happiness.

Essays in Criticism

ROBBER BARONS AND HORATIO ALGER*

Rod W. Horton and Herbert W. Edwards

More spectacular than the rise of the cities but just as tawdry, was the rapid creation of a class of men known admiringly at the time as the "captains of industry" or the "lords of finance." These individuals, most of whom were just entering their twenties when the Civil War broke out, were somehow delivered from the inconveniences of military service without being required to forswear the fruits of military victory. Falling in, at a precociously early age, with the booming opportunities of a war economy, they turned their youthful aggressiveness and natural, God-given brass into fantastic profits; shrewd and animally clever, they learned early when to stalk the tempting quarry of Opportunity, how to seize her by the proverbial forelock, and, perhaps most valuable of all, when to let her go. Charged with the adventurous spirit of the pioneers, they did their pioneering behind desks, in whispered conferences, or in the weltering hysteria of the Stock Exchange; inculcated with the traditional American spirit of individualism, they transmuted this spirit with crude alchemy, through a philosophy of opportunism, into a residuum of ill-gotten gold.

In a way, these financial wizards were merely a logical extension of the spirit of the colonial days. Americans had admired business shrewdness from Puritan times. The Calvinist believed in conducting his practical affairs "with high seriousness as in itself a kind of religion" both as an antidote for satanic temptation and a sign of possible Election, while the spirit of the Enlightenment, particularly as interpreted by Benjamin Franklin, was strongly colored by the ideals of bourgeois industriousness. True, both the Calvinist and the disciple of Franklin stressed honesty and absence of greed in business relationships, but neither had been submitted to the temptations of a war economy. With the booming opportunities of the Sixties and Seventies, it was an easy step to alter eighteenth-century business morality into a philosophy of

---

* Rod W. Horton and Herbert W. Edwards, *Backgrounds of American Literary Thought*, 3rd edition. (New Jersey : Pretence-Hall, INC, 1974), P. 154-160.

driving ambition, lust for power, animal cunning, and the sort of perverted self-reliance that leads one to trample his neighbors to be first to the bargain counterand first to the exit in case of fire.

The story of the rise of these new promoters of industrial enterprise is one of the most fascinating in our history but is, unfortunately, too devious and too laden with financial detail to be summarized here. The slippery, but highly profitable cleverness of Daniel Drew, Jim Fisk, Jay Gould, Cornelius Vanderbilt, Jim Hill, Collis Huntington, and Leland Stanford in railroad speculation, stock watering, and mutual throat-cutting; the hard-boiled methods of the senior Rockefeller; the arrogant power tactics of a Carnegie or a Morgan; the smooth salesmanship of Jay Cooke, whose brokerage firm lured the savings and scrimpings of tens of thousands of trusting persons and whose failure brought the country close to financial ruin; all of these and many more go to make up a tale more lurid and amazing than fiction and one which fittingly supports Mark Twain's designation of the period as a "Gilded Age."

Along with the unhampered financial shenanigans of the wizards of grab developed the unpalatable spectacle of a corrupt political structure. The new millionaires, eager to preserve their hunting rights in Wall Street, were quite willing to share some of their recently won wealth with the local, state, and national lawmakers in return for friendly consideration in the legislatures. Aided by a succession of sympathetic Presidents, beginning with Grant, and well able to purchase the benevolence of senators, mayors, or judges, the lords of the financial universe quickly turned the political scene into an open sewer and made even the office of the Presidency noisome to persons not yet caught in the speculative madness. It cost relatively little to buy a legislator: a few thousand dollars, perhaps, and what was that where millions were to be gained? A few hundred shares of stock in the new corporation was an even better device, for even a senator would sometimes forget public interest when his own property was at stake. Occasionally there would be a scandal, of course, and even a catastrophe: the Jay Cooke failure, Black Friday, the Credit Mobilier, the Panic of '73, the Tweed Ring and other episodes aroused honest journalists to prophetic denunciation and temporary headlines and made decent folks shake their heads in apprehension, but such things passed and recurred with such increasing frequency that eventually even honest people became calloused and apathetic.

The spirit of the Gilded Age was truly medieval, the awkward age of American industry, and it was no idle poetic whim that caused Matthew Josephson to refer to its principal figures as "robber barons." Inspired originally by the Hamiltonian scheme of paternalistic protection for manufactures, the period rode its uninhibited course on the crest of the wave of a booming economy, a moral and ethical holiday proclaimed by an indulgent, well-controlled government. It was a triumph of the Hamiltonian system on a scale Hamilton himself would never have imagined and had an accompanying atmosphere of vulgar chicanery he would never have approved. Unworried by any consideration save the loss of power, the barons continued their high-handed and splendid course, impregnable in their wealth and envied for their grandeur. "What do I care about the law?" Cornelius Vanderbilt once exclaimed. "Hain't I got the money?," and both government and populace weakly concurred with this pungent and characteristic expression of *noblesse oblige*.

But even more significant than the cavortings of the market place was the resultant spirit engendered throughout the entire texture of American society. To the people at large, the whole scale of values underwent a transformation, and an entire nation danced to the tunes of the Pied Pipers of financial success. The Fisks, Goulds, Carnegies, Rockefellers, and Vanderbilts became folk heroes, symbols of the highest potential of individual enterprise in a democratic society. Long forgotten was the Jerffersonian dream of a "happy mediocrity"; the new leaders set forth a type of success that could be counted and displayed, a type of power that had to be respected. Industriousness and self-reliance had long been an admired virtue in the land; what greater proof of these virtues could be had than the spectacle of the poor boy who, like Carnegie or Gould, rose through his own ingenuity to become a millionaire? After many decades of hardship and frontier deprivations, the nation grasped eagerly at the fruits of industry. Those who were clever enough to attain those fruits elicited only respect, and if some of the methods of the successful failed to square with traditional teachings of right and wrong, they could be rationalized by the ingrained American tendency to admire clever horse-trading. After all, this was a new game that was being played and it required new rules. Some of the operations might be a bit dubious, to be sure, but so long as they created wealth they could be sanctioned on the grounds that "when the big fellow makes money, we all make money." The new barons were rough-hewn and more than a trifle vulgar, but they represented to the masses the hardy bluffness of the frontier, the pardonable crudities of the pioneer who was nature's nobleman and whose rough exterior housed a stout heart and a strong will. "We have made the country rich; we have developed the country," boasted Jay Gould at a congressional investigation of his business methods, and the respectful senators were, like the country at large, duly impressed by his reasoning. To Murat Halstead, the deferential biographer of Jay Gould and ardent apologist for the new piracy, the captains of industry were simply the tangible examples of the "American pluck and enterprise and those traits of industry that have built up the greatness of the nation." No wonder that when John D. Rockefeller insisted that his millions had been given him by God Himself nobody laughed.

Thus there arose a great tradition, *a mystique* which inspired many thousands of young men for three generations and which seemed to be cast in the best spirit of democracy. Taught from childhood, immortalized by the avidly read novels of Horatio Alger and his imitators, the tradition exalted the virtues of pluck and luck, of relentless industry, of the boundless ambition and self-reliance which, in a world of ever-increasing opportunity, would carry the worthy from rags to riches, from humble (though never disgraceful) poverty to the peak of wealth, power, and universal acclaim[1]. Naturally, this rise must be accomplished only through the most impeccable honesty, with the accompanying virtues of chastity, temperance, and extreme consideration for children, old ladies, and dumb animals.

Today we are inclined to smile a bit indulgently at this Horatio Alger tradition and to regard its few surviving adherents as naive and anachronistic bores, but in the post Civil War years it had a considerable basis

1) Horatio Alger, Jr. (1834-1899) was a clergyman and philanthropist whose one hundred and sixty novels were eagerly sought after by children and adults alike. Despite the author's use of a monotonously standardized plot formula — the rise of a poor but honest lad to wealth and fame — the novels sold over 20,000,000 copies, most of which were literally read to tatters.

in reality. In those expansive times, it was not at all uncommon for Tattered Tom or Ragged Dick or Phil the Fiddler to become a millionaire through hard work; opportunities were plentiful, and intelligent and industrious youths were marked for great things in our expanding economy. But the tradition was weakened by its own vulgarity and naivete. Its chosen idols, the self-made men, were often shown in congressional investigations and journalistic exposes as having gained their millions through anything but honest dealing, while its too ready tendency to measure a man's success through his accumulation of money alone alienated the more refined and intelligent.

The greatest danger of the tradition, however, lay in its stubborn refusal to die out even after the simple formula of pluck and luck had been rendered obsolete by the settling of American economy into a more and more centralized pattern of large-scale enterprise. In a society of small shopkeepers, the rugged individualist can make his way with ease and security; in the twentieth century world of huge corporations, income taxes, and government regulation, both Tarrered Tom and the old-style robber baron are but memories of a romantic past. And yet it was not until the great crash of 1929 that most Americans were made reluctantly to realize that the old order had changed and that the Horatio Alger formula no longer applied in our present-day impersonal economy. With some, the destroying of the old spirit of pioneer individualism brought about a reciprocal feeling of cynicism and despair, with others it brought about a desire for some radically different form of society. But the more intelligent regarded the change as a sign of national maturity and looked back upon the turbulent days of boom and boodle with the amused indulgence with which one regards a naughty but exciting adolescence.

FINAL APPRAISAL*

Gary Scharnhorst

I. Reputation

When Horatio Alger died in 1899, the writer of his brief obituary in noted that the author "was perhaps better known to the boys of thirty years ago than to the present generation."[1] Available sales statistics tend to substantiate this observation. Certainly the only four best sellers of his long writing career were published between 1868 and 1871,[2] and in 1897 Alger himself estimated his aggregate sales of all volumes at only about 800,000.[3] Sales of the six volumes in the early "Ragged Dick series" contribute a disproportionate share to this total, for Alger also estimated in 1888 that total sales of single books in this series amounted to about 150,000.[4] The reason for his modest popularity in the late nineteenth century would seem to be the charge, leveled frequently by reviewers, parents, ministers, and teachers, that his juvenile fiction was tainted by "sensationalism." For example, a Boston minister in an address at the opening of a branch of the Boston Public Library in 1877 complained about the "endless reams of such drivel poured forth by Horatio Alger, Jr.," and asked "on what principle the managers feel called upon to provide for young and growing minds books which can only weaken and demoralize them."[5] A typical review of an Alger juvenile novel during the Gilded Age indicated that Alger

> is always sure of a public, no matter how bad his rhetoric, how unreal his situations, or how crude his workmanship. His latest book, 'Victor Vane, the Young Secretary,' tells, as usual, of the impossible virtues, triumphs and successes of a boy of seventeen, who becomes private secretary and confidential

---

* Gary Scharnhorst, *Horatio Alger, Jr.*, (Boston: Twayne Publishers, 1980.) p. 140-146.

1) E. S. Martin, "This Busy World," 5 August 1899, p. 761.

2) Frank Luther Mott, (New York, 1947), pp. 309, 321, 322.

3) 1899-1900, ed. John W. Leonard (Chicago, 1899), p. 10. In a letter to Blake (25 March 1897, HH MSS) Alger mentioned the receipt of the information form to be completed for this volume.

4) Horatio Alger, Jr. to R. A. Alger, 2 May 1888, UM MSS.

5) "Literary Rubbish,", II (1878), 299.

> adviser and friend to a Western Congressman, and transacts a large amount of important business in the most experienced fashion. Such stories as this call for little comment. We must recognize the fact that they have taken possession of the mind of the ordinary unreflective boy with a strong hold, and, if possible, supplement this taste for tales of street life with a liking for those that are truly literary.[6)]

Strangely, after the author's death there occurred an Alger revival which lasted nearly two decades. In 1910 Alger's juvenile novels were enjoying an sale of over one million[7)]—that is, more of his books were sold each year during the Progressive era than were sold in total during his life—and his books received more favorable comment from reviewers who could sympathize with their moral content if not their literary style. As a reviewer of one Alger reprint suggested in 1906, "If there are no more heroes in grown-up fiction, at least they still exist in young people's stories. Here, for instance, in 'The Young Musician,' is a boy who always does the right thing at the right moment."[8)] Alger's books remained popular until the early 1920s and sold an estimated total of between seventeen and twenty million in that period.[9)] Thereafter, sales declined rapidly. In 1926, two years before Herbert R. Mayes's debunking biography appeared, the circle of Alger readers had so shrun k[10)] that the leading publisher of his books stopped printing them. By 1932, the centenary of Alger's birth, less than twenty per cent of seven thousand surveyed New York boys recognized Alger's name, and only about fourteen per cent admitted to having read even one of his books.[11)] In the same year he was described in the pages of as "forgotten."[12)] By 1947, a poll of twenty thousand New York children aged eight to fourteen found that ninety-two per cent of those sampled "had never heard of Alger. Less than one per cent had read any of his books."[13)]

---

6) "New Books and New Editions," 29 June 1895, p. 476.
7) Everett T. Tomlinson, "The Perpetual 'Best-Sellers,'", XX (June 1910), p. 13045.
8) "Found: A Hero," 8 December 1906, p. 846.
9) Mott, p. 159.
10) Arthur M. Jordan, (Chapel Hill, NC, 1926), .
11) "The Cynical Youngest Generation,", 17 February 1932, p.186.
12) "A Forgotten Boy's Classic," 30 January 1932, p.20.
13) "Horatio Alger is an Unknown to 92% of Boys and Girls in Seven Clubs in City," 13 January 1947, p. 23, col. 2-3.

Still, it is significant that the period of Alger's greatest popularity occurred during the Progressive period of American history when, as Richard Hofstadter has contended, nostalgia for an imagined time of equal opportunity and equitable business practices was intense.[14] Interestingly, at least one edition of and issued by the New York Book Company during the first decade of the new century has on its cover a picture of President Theodore Roosevelt, although Alger died before the Great Trustbuster assumed the presidency and on no occasion referred to him in his fiction. Alger's most direct successor, Edward Stratemeyer, whose syndicate dominated the juvenile field for over two decades until Stratemeyer's death in 1930, adapted Alger's morality to his own juvenile fiction.[15] Although he changed the formula slightly, as in the Tom Swift series, in general his fiction was a testimony to the endurance of the pattern of moral heroism established by Alger. Two other popular writers of the period who cashed in on the Alger formula, Harold Bell Wright and Gene Stratton-Porter, innovated slightly on the pattern by actually doing what Alger was only accused of doing. Virtuous millionaires and characters who struggle from rags to riches frequent their novels, as in *When a Man's a Man*(1916) and *Michael O'Halloran* (1916). In other words, in their fiction the basic Alger pattern was adopted and slightly modified to suit the materialistic temper of the times, and it seems that Alger, as his own popularity among juveniles waned, was credited with (or blamed for) the innovation. Certainly the cliched phrase "Horatio Alger hero" entered the popular currency only after Alger himself was rarely read. Indeed, the first appearance in print of that phrase may have occurred as late as 1926, in reference to Alger's old friend Frank A. Munsey,[16] even as Alger's publishers were discontinuing the cheap editions of his books and libraries were removing Alger juveniles from the shelves. That Wright, Porter, and Alger all tapped the same wellsprings of popular sentiment seems apparent from the fact that all were popular during the early years of this century and all had lost that popularity by the eve of the Depression.

The distinction between Alger's modest popularity before his death

---

14) Richard Hofstadter, (New York, 1955), pp. 131-73.
15) Russel B. Nye, (New York, 1970), p. 76.
16) "Frank A. Munsey as a Horatio Alger Hero,", 9 January 1926, p. 48.

and his period of greatest popularity after his death suggests that there are in effect two Algers—the first a Harvard-educated moralist who expressed his genteel abhorrence of the mercenary Gilded Age, the second a best-selling writer of juvenile stories about poor boys who make good. The first, historical Alger sought a reputation as a teacher and benefactor; the second, distorted, symbolic Alger came to be considered an apologist for industrial capitalism who genuflected at the altar of Success. What accounts for the transformation? The problem, as Malcolm Cowley has stated it, is this: "What I cannot understand is how [Alger] should come to be regarded as the prophet of business enterprise; nor why the family melodrama that he wrote and rewrote for boys should be confused with the American dream of success."17) While a complete answer to this question—if one is possible—would consume an entire volume of cultural and literary history, three factors instrumental in the transformation can briefly be noted here.

First, the confusion surrounding the publication of the cheap editions of Alger's juveniles early in the twentieth century allowed his moral purpose to be misunderstood. Reprinted in bulk by approximately forty firms between Alger's death and the mid-1920s, the novels consequently were not read in their order of composition during their period of greatest popularity. Indeed, only within the past dozen years, as bibliographers have catalogued Alger's original serializations of the novels and recognized his several pseudonyms, has it been possible to reconstruct the order in which Alger wrote his juvenile books. Because some of Alger's earliest, least mercenary novels were the least reprinted after the turn of the century, a mistaken impression of what Alger did write about was conveyed by the selection of the novels reprinted in cheap editions. And because several of the publishers of cheap Alger juveniles "abridged" some of the books by deleting significant amounts of material, erroneous judgments about the contents of an Alger book were inevitable. The deleted sections often contained descriptions of the hero's charitable activities, never his receipt of his final reward, and thus the moral message of the book was garbled by faulty editing.

A second factor contributing to the distortion of the "first Alger" is

---

17) Malcolm Cowley, "Horatio Alger: Failure," XII (Summer 1970), 65.

that the "second Alger," the mythmaker whose saga of success bears little relation to the books themselves, came into his majority during a period of critical acquiescence. The Alger stories were generally ignored by critics and reviewers even as their popularity soared during the early years of this century. Only the fact of their popularity, not their content, earned the grudging respect of the *literati*. It may be that the success story of the Alger hero was misconstrued during this period at least partly because the modest success of the Alger hero came to be confused with the astounding sales success of the books. If true, this would also account for the persistent, mistaken belief that Horatio Alger was not an author but a character in success stories.

A third factor that contributed to the transformation of Alger into an economic and political symbol was the patriotic fervor of World War II. The process of selective remembering that had begun in the 1920s and 1930s crystallized during the war as Alger became a political shibboleth used in the identification of loyal Americans. The characteristics traditionally (and erroneously) associated with the Horatio Alger hero—the potential greatness of the common man, rugged individualism, economic triumph in a fabled land of opportunity—seemingly summarized the American way of life the war was waged to preserve. In this wartime atmosphere, articles about Alger and his wholesome influence on American youth began appearing for the first time in glossy-paged, mass circulation magazines such as *Esquire, Saturday Review, Time, New Republic,* and the *Atlantic Monthly.* Between November, 1943, and October, 1945, for example, articles about Alger in such mass circulation magazines appeared under the following titles: "A Monument to Free Enterprise," "They Made Me What I Am Today," and "Alger's Vitality."[18] In an apparent attempt to exploit this new interest in Alger during the war, a New York publishing firm in 1945 issued a hardbound reprinting of four Alger novels that had been out of print for a generation, complete with a preface by playwright Russel Crouse. Although the volume was widely reviewed in popular magazines and newspapers, thus reinforcing the popular impression that Alger was enjoying a revival, quite the opposite was the case. Remaindered copies of this 1945 reprinting were available in

18) 1 September 1945, pp. 15-16; , CLXXII (November 1943), 115-17; , 1 October 1945, p. 441.

mint condition as late as 1970, so it would seem that Alger's books were hardly more popular in print than out of print. However, the impression that they were still influential was indelible, and in 1947, soon after the war ended, this Alger-impostor, who was the ideal subject for the publicist, found the best merchandising vehicle for his political and economic wares—the Horatio Alger Awards. Sponsored by the American Schools and Colleges Associations, Inc., which had been "concerned about the trend among young people towards the mind-poisoning belief that equal opportunity was a thing of the past," the Alger Awards Committee has honored such men as Bob Hope, Dwight Eisenhower, Ronald Reagan, Billy Graham, W. Clement Stone, and Ray Kroc for meritorious service to the causes of political and religious conservatism and economic orthodoxy.

II. Literary Influence

Just as the quality of Alger's writing was consistently condemned by critics, the plots of his juvenile novels have been consistently satirized by those authors who have acknowledged it. The critical complaint that Alger was sensational and unrealistic occurred during the same period that two major authors wrote satires of Alger which lampooned his unrealistic "success stories." W. D. Howells, in, *The Minister's Charge, or The Apprenticeship of Lemuel Basker* (1887), satirized the country-boy myth which Alger serviced; at issue in this non-comedic satire was the realism of that myth. Stephen Crane in one of his New York Sketches, "A Self-Made Man: An Example of Success That Anyone Can Follow" (1899), apparently parodied Alger's juvenile novel. Crane attempted to lampoon the solemnity of the Alger story by offering a ridiculous version of one. Believing that Alger was his own parodist, Crane simply exaggerated the defects and unbelievable coincidences of the standard Alger plot.

In the twentieth century Alger has been satirized not as an unrealistic writer of guidebooks for the aspiring entrepreneur so much as a popular symbol of success, a symptom of the cultural malaise which afflicts each succeeding generation. The "second Alger," not the first, has been the target of the satirists in this century. F. Scott Fitzgerald, primarily in three works-his play, or *The Vegetable, or From President to Postman* (1922), the Dan Cody episode in *The Great Gatsby* (1925), and his short story "Forging Ahead"(1929)—parodied Alger the inspiring "mythmaker," the economic symbol. In 1934 Nathanael West parodied Alger in *A Cool Million* by transforming him into a symbol of political repression. More recently, John Seelye in *Dirty Tricks*; or *Nick Noxin's Natural Nobility* (1973) further exploited West's premise to offer a political statement about the presidency of Richard Nixon, and Glendon Swarthout in (1973) chronicled the sexual misadventures of an Algerian anti-hero. William Gaddis in his modernist fiction (1975), in which an eleven-year-old boy operating out of a telephone booth begins by supplying Navy surplus wooden forks to the Army and ends as the head of a multinational corporation, demonstrated the absurd lengths to which the basic Alger plot could be carried. In other words, the longer Alger's books have remained out of print and unread, the more his basic story has been liable to artistic misappropriation.

In his juvenile books Alger not only influenced those parodists who have been inspired by the creaky machinations of his basic plot, but he also influenced a generation of young readers who grew to adulthood early in this century. To be sure, as one familiar only with Alger's undeserved reputation as an apologist for capitalism might expect, many of these readers—such as Benjamin Fairless of U.S. Teel and James A. Farley of Coca-Cola[19]—became real-life counterparts to the fictional heroes. But to consider Alger simply an apologist for capitalism is to distort grossly his humanitarian purpose. John Cawelti has suggested that "there is as much evidence that Alger was an important influence on future reformers as a popular model for incipient robber barons."[20] As one familiar only with Alger's reputation might expect, many writers on the political left—including Theodore Dreiser, Jack London, Upton Sinclair, and Richard Wright[21]—as youngsters read Alger's books and

19) Ralph D. Gardner, "Foreword" to by Horatio Alger, Jr. (Garden City, NY, 1973). p. 12.
20) Cawelti, p. 117.
21) Theodore Dreiser, (New York, 1931), p. 122; Jack London, (New York. 1913), p. 133; Upton Sinclair, (New York, 1962), p. 9; Jay Martin, (New York, 1970), p. 235; Richard Wright, "Alger Revisited, or My Stars! Did We Read That Stuff?" PM, 16 September 1945, magazine

were not stirred to embrace capitalism. It would seem that either Alger was overrated as an economic and political propagandist or-more probably-his books were simply not designed thematically to spread the gospel of orthodox capitalism and convert the readership of *The Masses*.

Instead, his correspondence and the books themselves reveal that Alger wished simply to be a moral teacher of American youth, carefully instructing them in the traditional virtues of filial piety. That he believed he succeeded in this admittedly limited purpose is clear enough from the fact that he reenacted the same domestic melodrama over a hundred times. Still, he hardly believed that he would be long remembered for this slight achievement, much less celebrated as an American success mythmaker. As he wrote to a friend in 1897, "If I could come back 50 years from now probably I should feel bewildered in reading the New York of 1947."[22] He wrote this with a soothsayer's foresight, for one of the items in the news that year that undoubtedly would have bewildered him beyond his wildest flights of fancy reported the inauguration of the annual Horatio Alger Awards. After fifty years, he could not have recognized his progeny.

section, p.13.

22) Alger to Blake, 12 May 1897, HH MSS.

THE FICTIONAL REPUBLIC:

Alger's Appeal to the American Political Imagination*

Carol Nackenoff

> Every fiction is supported by a social jargon, a sociolect, with which it identifies: fiction is that degree of consistency a language attains when it has exceptionally and finds a sacerdotal class (priests, intellectuals, artists) to speak it generally and to circulate it.
>
> . . . each jargon (each fiction) fights for hegemony; if power is on its side, it spreads everywhere in the general and daily occurrences of social life, it becomes *doxa*, nature: this is the supposedly apolitical jargon of politicians, of agents of the State, of the media, of conversation; but even out of power, even when power is against it, the rivalry is reborn, the jargons split and struggle among themselves. A ruthless rules the life of language; language always comes from some place, it is a warrior.
>
> Roland Barthes, *The Pleasure of the Text*[1)]

Alger's fiction is replete with tension between industrialization and community, between glitter and substance, between self-interested men and those who recognize duty, and between those who attempt to make something out of nothing and those who make something of real value. These works act out economic, moral, social and political struggles of the period. The spectrum of reponses to disruption of lived experiences and understandings of the world—in these stories and in other narratives—blend reactionary and potentially progressive critiques. Some responses are mobilized into politics, others are not; since classes are made, not found, it is not obvious in advance where apparently reactionary responses to industrialization may lead. E. P. Thomson discovers the sense of lost status and community, memories of a "golden age," value placed on independence, and social egalitarianism that shaped the worldview of radical leaders among the weavers in early nineteenth-century

---

* Carol Nackenoff. *The Fictional Republic: Horatio Alger and American Political Discourse* (New York: Oxford University Press. 1994.), pp. 261-271.

1) Roland Barthes, Translated by Richard Miller. (New York: Hill and Wang,1975), pp. 27-28.

England.[2)]

Classes and class fractions "remembering" traditional rights and values may use this language of tradition in forging a new oppositional perspective. For Thomson, one of the chief factors mobilizing remembrances into radical, political expressions of a new working class was the segregation of workers into separate communities—a system of apartheid and alienation of classes.[3)] In the United States, many genteel moralists fought to retain these people who threatened to become a class apart. If some attempted to build bridges by lecturing to mechanics' societies or building libraries, writing religious tracts or leading revival movements, Alger built bridges with fiction.

The battle for the Republic had two domestic fronts in the Gilded Age. On one front was a struggle over culture, social distance, difference, and the grounds of discourse. Those who did not choose exit struggled over the terms on which common discourse could be maintained—terms on which all who wished could be part of the Republic. The other front crosscut the first. It was about the terms of participation in the emerging industrial order. The struggle, with a continuum of responses from accommodation to resistance, pitted independence and potency against dependence and powerlessness. Definitions of manliness were at stake.

As Alger and his contemporaries struggled to define and contain the terms on which these battles for the Republic would take place, they fought the politics of class in the language of virtue. And the arena of production, the discourse, still morally charged, turned to power and gender.

Change, in the form of difference and distance, hierarchy and inequality, was addressed in at least four ways in the Gilded Age: by insulation and segregation, compulsory conformity, moral reform, and levelling. Some simply sought to isolate themselves into communities apart; we were not one estate.

In hands other than Alger's, the insistence that class distinctions of taste, habit, and culture be rendered meaningless could and would become an imperative—"Americanism."[4)] Conformity to the standards of

---

2) E. P. Thompson, (New York: Vintage, 1963), p. 295.

3) Thomson, pp. 57, 139, 177, 831-32.

4) See Hartz, p. 206, where "the new Whiggery was able to attach to the Horatio Alger

genteel culture, and to its morality, was required of an American. As industrial development helped shape the *unrecognizability* of some classes of citizens, those demanding conformity demanded that these classes make themselves recognizable—or alternately, they would simply not exist.

Alger, too, yearned for the world in which classes occupied the same theater and engaged in the same discourse. But his particular vision of unity brought the theater closer to ordinary lives. The discourse should have the moral tone of the Cambridge elite, but the voice and fire of Edwin Forrest.

Although the effort to negate class and cultural distance through moral reform was a significant piece in Alger's repertoire, it was not staged alone. Respectable culture—redefined and broadened—was accessible to nonelites. The Republic would have to give up any aristocratic pretense. Those who would engage in affectation, class markers, make money the measure of the man, and demand deference from others would yield the stage to Ragged Dick. Here spoke a kind of resistance to class differentiation, to crass materialism, to the growing gap between rich and poor, and to the breakdown of community. Here was an author who brought down the mighty, challenged power and social hierarchy, performed miracles of levelling, and insisted that nature could triumph over artifice.

Alger resisted surrender of power by the individual, and by the Republic. This fiction could potentially speak to class fractions threatened by the changes industrialization and urbanization were bringing to the United States. Some were increasingly becoming differentiated as classes apart and losers in the development of capitalism.

There was something in Alger for genteel boys from Boston, as there was for those who read the penny papers. And, in a nation where difference poses a threat to identity, a story that can be embraced by different classes is, itself, taken as a kind of vindication that we are of one estate. There are not too many of these myths of unity left.

While this Gilded Age narrative was one kind reconciliation of fact

---

cosmos the grand and glorious label of 'Americanism."

and fiction, it was not *non*sense. But why should American audiences continue to find this particular set of symbols constitutive of reasonable discourse?

For most scholars who use "Alger" as a construct—as shorthand for a set of beliefs in American political culture—Alger is a set of propositions about self-help and individualism, hard work, defense of property, and permeability of economic and social structure. American political stories, language, myths, symbols and metaphors pay homage to Alger despite massive social and economic changes in the century since Alger died. Understandings of how the political economy "works" appear highly static, and conflate aspiration and economic explanation. Self-evident truths look like myths, or false consciousness.

Were it reasonable to "read" Alger as an apologist for capitalism, it would be a serious mistake to treat Alger's stories, as most scholars have, as mere tools of the capitalist class, selling promise of riches and obtaining the complicity of subordinate classes in the race for wealth. In Louis Hartz'a reading of the wedding of Horatio Alger to the liberal Lockean creed, the Whig-Hamiltonian-capitalists were allowed to "throw a set of chains around" the American democrat in a blend of Hamilton and Jefferson, peasant and proletariat. By latching onto equality of opportunity, the American Whigs sold the American democrat a bill of goods—an ideological straightjacket.[5)]

In this view, we are all simply hoodwinked by the Whigs, who woo us with equality of opportunity while themselves winning the race. Political discourse as a product of relations among social classes (Hartz), myth invocation, and false consciousness look identical. Such readings neither do justice to Alger nor to people who use language to think with.

Confronted with an Alger-centered discourse in late twentieth century America, and the prevailing ways in which this has been explained, it is tempting to borrow from Clifford Geertz a very different sort of claim: that ideologies are most prevalently expressed when things don't work—when they don't make sense. Ideological formulations are adduced when the world is changing, and no longer corresponds to one's expectations.[6)]

---

5) Hartz, especially pp. 62-63, 203-5.

6) Clifford Geertz, "Ideology as a Cultureal system," pp. 193-233 in (New York: Basic Books, 1973). Geertz seems to lack a theory of ideological change; it is exogenous.

Alger wrote in—and for—an era experiencing disruptions and changes in lived experience. Could not old doxologies simply be dragged out during other such times? In this functionalist view, the discourse need not maintain material groundings.

But this study suggests some material connection. The greatest similarities between the world of the Alger heroes and that of the latter day believers lie at the level of economic fears and dislocations inherent in a capitalist economy—an economy in which the creation of new wealth and new consumption capacities for some take place alongside deindustrialization, unemployment, poverty, and non-European immigrations. In a society where stations are not fixed by birth and where a dynamic economy has brought massive change if not always improvement in well-being, the Alger formula counsels patience, preparation, and optimism. A set of ostensibly timeless propositions is built upon the *rejection* of stasis and decline in economy and society.

The tension between the belief that individuals could produce their own economic security or well-being and the phenomena of poverty and mass unemployment may have emerged in particularly stark form for the first time during the Gilded Age, but it was repeated during twentieth century recessions and depressions.

Reagan and Bush paeans to the formulas associated with Alger re-emerge during the era of deindustrialization and massive change in where and how people work. The argument that struggling manfully against adversity "pays off" materially is a hard times message. After all, who needs success stories in an economy that vindicates the model? In this view, success stories are most useful when extensive social mobility is—not when it is widespread. The narratives are about how to *avoid* filling the undesirable positions in the economic order. Alger heroes succeed because they avoid economic marginality, starvation, and depersonalized work environments. No one needs formulas to attain the lot that will otherwise fall to them by default.

In an era of erosion of real wages, fiscal retrenchment, a debt that makes a lie of independence, and uncertainty about the meaning of America, the narratives continue. In an economically interdependent and increasingly integrated world, the hope of independence and self-reliance—and of stable, fulfilling work with rising wages—may be all the more seductive.

Structuralist historical materialists have claimed that ideologies must "make sense" of the system in which classes participate, directing them to places to be occupied in that system if the system is to be reproduced. Classes must have some means of understanding and legitimating their role in the social structure to perform these roles. In this view, if there are mismatches between rules and values, on the one hand, and conditions of lived experience on the other, either these rules and values will change or the system will cease to exist.[7] But a notion of "correspondences," while better than invocations of "false consciousness," still requires better conceptualization and exploration of the relationship between words and deeds—or between worldviews and politics to make sense of the American case.

If an Alger-based discourse tends to reproduce the social relations of corporate capitalism, it is no *explanation* of how and why this grammar of American politics is affirmed and reproduced. People are not merely passive bearers of structure; they construct worldviews and meanings that make sense to them. Social contextualiztion is essential.

Fictions, myths, and stories are forms of discourse about tensions in the society in question. These scripts offer a variety of texts and subtexts, but they remain historically grounded. For Levi-Strauss, narratives are myths seeking to resolve conceptual contradictions in a particular society; narratives have a social function.[8] Frederic Jameson elaborates: One can examine "the various semantic tokens, the various mechanism *for* the production of meaning, or as they are currently known, the various binary oppositions, out of which the narrative is constructed." Oppositions can be constructed and characters "read" in the context of codes. The narratives serve as "a representation. . . of a struggle going on in the real world of history itself."[9] Stories may address—and even resolve—contradictions that, in life, remain unresolved.

7) Louis Althusser and Étienne Balibar, (London: New Left Books, 1970); see also the work of Adam Przeworski.

8) Claude Levi-Strauss, Chapter 11, "Structural study of Myth," in (New York: Basic Books, 1963).

9) Jameson, "Ideology, Narrative Analysis, and Popular Culture," 549, 555.

It is sometimes possible to see beyond traditional debates when we free up our language. This study proposes that political discourse participates in the realm of texts. In discourse, as in texts, there are reconciliations of fact and fiction. Fact and fiction must be woven together to construct a narrative. Discourse is the product and progress of struggle; there are struggling forces within amy text. "On the stage of the text, no footlights: there is not, behind the text, someone active (the writer) and out front someone passive (the reader.)"[10)]

As we transcend dualisms such as actor-recipient, it is no longer acceptable to suggest that the readers and public were sold a bill of goods and were coopted by Alger (or by other romances, tales, and promises). It does not advance our understanding of the persistence of Alger to claim an author merely misread his surroundings; it is a mistake to pronounce readers readers. Locating Alger amid the tensions and anxieties produced by the rapid industrialization of America, we see that the narrative is neither simply pro- nor anticapitalist. Alger was a creature the emergence of nineteenth century American capitalism. He could not possibly stand outside it. Expressing both fears and desires that emerge from the logic of capitalism, Alger was embedded in a system of representation;". . . that, producing objects of approval and disapproval both, is more important than any attitude one might imagine oneself to have toward it [capitalism]."[11)]

The Alger symbols may be frequently woven into a specific class dialect—a doxology — but there are others. People appropriate texts— political and literary—to their own uses. Just as the historical Alger was appropriated differently by various audiences and critics, there is a continual struggle over meaning and symbol in language.

Just as readers constitute texts, they confer meaning on the symbols they use. The Alger hero is for appropriation by different communities. The enduring appeal of this formula is explained in part because the

---

10) Roland Barthes, p. 16. " means ; but whereas hitherto we have always taken this tissue as a product, a ready-made veil, behind which lies, more or less hidden, meaning (truth), we are now emphasizing, in the tissue, the generative idea that the text is made, is worked out in a perpetual interweaving; lost in this tissue- his texture- the subject unmakes himself, like a spider dissolving in the constructive secretions of its web" (p.64).

11) Michaels, p. 19.

meaning of the foils and juxtapositions is to a variety of American political and cultural conflicts. While the narrative conveys different meanings to different users, "the differences in the meanings we attribute to the symbols tend to go unrecognized, and the myth of their common meaning is preserved." To understand the power of political symbols, one must discover "how they become the focal points of diverse meaning and commonly salient objects condensing and indexing different experiences. fears, apprehensions, hopes, and interests.[12] The social variability of meaning gives symbols their peculiar potency.

Is the Alger hero a symbol about equal opportunity under capitalism, or is it a symbol about bringing justice to the market? Is it a symbol of laissez-faire individualism or of the triumph of community and character over impersonality, selfishness, and corruption? Does it celebrate economic growth or flight a rear-guard action against differentiation of economic fortunes and of habits, taste, and culture? It can incorporate all of these.

These formulas became identified with a predominant grammar of American politics because they managed to accomplish several things that successful worldviews do. Political discourse does not merely reflect conditions of material life, but mediates these conditions. Just as ideology never works when it is a complete or accurate representation of the changed world, the Alger amalgam of fact and fiction found continuities between traditional values and understandings of the world and new environments. Political language creates national stories about our experience, and in so doing, helps constitute future experiences.[13]

Alger's selective portrait of the transformations of the political economy wrought by the Gilded Age manages the scope and pace of change in such a way as to mediate disorder, uncertainty and transition. There is accommodation to the new order; travel and adventure, hope, and new opportunities appear. Heroes improve their standard of living and generally acquire business-related careers. The centrality of private property and of market relations were underscored, but so, too, were values and virtues of the past as the Alger story turned away from capitalism's less attractive features. Neglected or denied are certain troubling or unin-

---

12) Charles D. Elder and Roger W. Cobb, (New York: Longman, 1983), p. 35.
13) See Lance Bennett, (New York: St. Martin's, 1992).

telligible activities; others are named and defined out of community-sustaining behavior. Foils are lighting rods for a variety of populist and anticapitalist discontents. This particular articulation of the transforming economic environment framed industrial age problems and solutions in a potentially compelling manner.

The formula also succeeds by narrating its ambivalence toward capitalism, much as does a political discourse stressing individual opportunity, mistrust of big business, and divisions between haves and have-nots. By making justice pay in dollars, Alger acknowledges the importance that materialism has come to have. Generally, however, the wild dreams entertained in these stories are, as in the case of Darnton's seventeenth century peasants who fantasize about a full belly, about attaining stable, salaried positions, with cordial personal relations with an employer. His reconciliations of price and value leave tradition and modernity in uneasy tension.

The author who rights the scales of justice and restores the equation of price and value as Alger does exhibits loyalty to the system. Constant interventions in the market demonstrate that this version of market justice was fundamentally at odds with science—or economic science. But instead of concluding that the market exists in disharmony from the values he would promote, Alger draws a different lesson. Change and tradition are reconcilable; character, virtue, power, independence, and individual agency can triumph in the age of capital. Not only can community be rescued in the face of the economic and social dislocations occasioned by capitalism, but the individual can remain the locus of responsibility, morality, and activity. Stories can have happy endings. Alger may have diffused frustration; since the formulas can be used to participate in the modern capitalist era, they may have played a role in demobilizing and depoliticizing resistance to the emerging order.

But the melodrama and symbols he created, incorporating ambivalence, accommodation, criticism, and resistance to the new order, generate space for some incendiary meanings. Had these been either simple morality tales or simple celebrations of the new order, they would have been far less serviceable as the components of political grammar.

Political formulations, as representations, are always in some sense "fictions." But they remain ways of connecting the past, present, and future. But when political discourse loses the capacity to connect experience and symbols, it loses its capacity to persuade. Fiction pure and simple loses its power to integrate, just as when politicians are perceived as liars, the public perceives the gap between words and deeds.

Another aspect of American experience permits the Alger story to weave this version of a past, present, and future into a plausible narrative. Many scholars have found a fusion of sacred and secular meanings to be characteristic American political discourse—a peculiarity in the language and rhetoric of American politics. Religious meanings may be inseparable from the very language and style of political exhortation we use.[14] Emphasis is on community, purpose, and virtue; a fused religious and secular compact pervaded language as it pervaded politics.[15] Garry Wills found this strain in the Nixon-Wallace backlash, and in the morality of the market.[16] Michael Kammen found it to be part of America's "contrapuntal civilization."[17]

The close linkage between religious thought and American political discourse points, for Sacvan Bercovitch, to the Puritan heritage. Puritan theology originated a special American telos, which he calls the myth of America. Puritans expected their community, the New Jerusalem set apart physically from the sins of Europe, to be the locus of the final confrontation with God. Collective covenant fulfilling was essential in order to reap the rewards God promised (as he had promised the Hebrews): Material rewards, worldly protection, power and privilege.[18] The idea of a "city on a hill" captured the sense of collective mission and helped foster the sense, in 1787, that "the eyes of the world are

---

14) For Kenneth Burke, this is not peculiar to discourse in the United States, since religious systems can be deduced (in form and content) from the very structure of language as a symbol system (Berkeley, Calif.: University of California Press, 1970).

15) See Sacvan Bercovitch, (Madision, Wis.: University of Wisconsin Press, 1978) and (New Haven, Conn.: Yale University Press, 1975); Wilson Carey McWilliams, (Berkeley, Clalif.: University of California Press, 1973); and Robert Bellah, (New York: Harper & Row, 1976).

16) This moralism could be seen in reactions to the New Deal. The Nixon-Wallace backlash was also something other than "Lockeanism gone underground" (Hartz) or the "irrational moods of mass Lockeanism" (Rogin). Wills, too, sees a thread running from this sense of moralism to the notion of the morality of the market, a notion betrayed by Nixon in Garry Wills, (New York: New American Library, 1970).

17) Michael Kammen, (New York: vintage, 1972).

18) Bercovitch, p. 81 and passim. See also T .

upon us".

In this Puritan narrative, there is a collective obligation to prosper — an obligation to perform this, and not some altered contract. And so, in a nation founded on the rhetoric of social contract and the right to revolution, there was a peculiar fear of change.19) Change could take the form of republican reform and restoration, but popular pressures for change threaten the very "truth" of the revolution — that God approved of our design, or even created it. Guarding American liberty entailed a relationship with the natural and divine order. The public interest takes on a meaning in which there can be no fundamental conflict of interest.20) Failure was a matter of personal culpability and collective treason.21)

America was a promise and a destiny as well as a place; past, present and future were fused as secular heroes were invested with sacred purpose.22) The historical was not merely man-mad but part of the natural(God-given) order of things. As the American Jeremiad evolved as a political form, language reflected this fusion.

Alger's fiction merges mid-nineteenth century Unitarian tenets concerning character and lived ethics with secular success stories. The "art" of this sacred-secular fusion is that it is *less* transparently materialistic than a Conwell "Acres of Diamonds" sermon or Carnegie's "Gospel of Wealth,"

---

19) Religion in America and Americanism as religion have been held to help explain a peculiar resistance to socialist ideas. For a good discussion of these themes, see John H. M. Laslett and Seymour Martin Lipset, eds. (Garden City: New York: Anchor / Doubleday, 1974), especially contributions by Leon Samson, Mark Karson, and Philip Foner.

20) Belief in collective striving — "we can" as well as "I can" (Kammen, pp. 115-16) is both conducive to a positive role for the state and to acceptance of hegemonic logic: Rather than playing zero-sum games, we play a game where we think everyone can win.

21) For Bercovitch, there is a linkage between Emerson and Thoreau's reinterpretation of the search for the perfect community (for Thoreau, individual self-reliance is the economic model of the only true American) and Horatio Alger, who extolled conformity as an act of supreme individualism(p. 185). The American evidence on clerical exhortations to economic activity, self-help and the secular search for salvation has been marshalled by I. G. Wyllie in I have greatly profited from conversation with J. David Greenstone on the individualist collectivist (or communal) duality in American thought. The idea that there are losers produced (in fact, the whole concept of structure) is dissonant and unintelligible when the rhetoric of individual and collective success are conflated.

22) Communism, unlike almost all other possible beliefs, posed a simultaneous threat to sacred and secular missions. For, it is judged "godless" and "atheistic" at the same time that it challenges private appropriation of property — or rather, property in the means of production

and yet secular than religious fiction and the Oliver Optic stories of the period that so often involved a stronger dose of religious education. And yet, the proposition that rewards come to those who persevere and who make themselves "men" is a religious—not finally an economic—one. If those who heard the message that justice pays confused earthly and heavenly rewards, Alger had invited them to.

Conflating sacred and secular rewards, merging fact and fiction, history and telos, and individual and republican stories, a key to Alger's success lay in devising a formula better-suited to those who wanted to have the new world without losing anything in the process.

Alger's story about the youth's rite of passage served as an allegory of the adolescent Republic, in which individual and collective pilgrimages, sacred and secular meanings were indistinguishable. However, Alger's republic is not the same as the New Jerusalem, and the product of these fusions is not merely another jeremiad.

In contrast to overtones of declension and apocalypse in the jeremiads of the period, Alger told a far more optimistic story and exhibited more faith in democracy. The optimism and good cheer of Alger's adolescent hero are never seriously shaken by adversity—a real moral for the Republic under siege or experiencing identity crisis.

Is the Alger hero, then, another Candide? Does he continue to believe, with Pangloss, that everything is for the best in the best of all possible worlds? Alger's heroes, like Candide, constantly faced challenges to their view of the universe and its belief in progress, design, intelligibility, and goodness. Candidie's experiences are disconfirming; he finally settles down and reaps a share of happiness with his entourage in a spot rather far removed—even untouched by—the ravages of the age of reason. The Alger hero's optimism fares a little better. The dangers, greed, hardship, cupidity, and selfishness encountered never shake his philosophy. Happiness remains possible. If it is not the best of all possible worlds, there are still many good people in it. Despite—or even through—travails, the basic order of the universe is confirmed.

The Alger hero leaves the Garden of Eden (which no longer supports him and thus is no more) and goes to Sodom and Gomorrah, where he will almost invariably remain. There, he replicates the community that has been lost. If he cannot return to the garden, he can have the next best thing. If Adam and Eve receive knowledge, then Alger heroes receive manhood—self-sufficiency in the marketplace. Leaving behind lost innocence and economic autonomy, man as citizen may become an intelligent and moral being; he becomes free and a member of a community. This is more Rousseau than Voltaire.

Alger's fiction does not exhibit the disenchantment of Beecher and others about the direction of historical change in the nineteenth century. If Henry Ward Beecher would remark in *Norwood* that "The steps of decline are melancholy and instructive." Alger would have none of it.[23] Vice was deplorable and created many innocent victims, but it was not allowed to become the undoing of the Republic. He was not party to Calvinist assumptions about human depravity, and, whatever his apprehensions about the future, he did not believe in the likelihood or inevitability of decline. True to his Harvard Unitarian heritage, Alger displayed an optimism about human nature and was more inclined to think the human personality perfectable.[24]

Jeremiads recall the nation to its original principles, from which it has diverged. The alternative is self-destruction. Less certain that disaster waits in the wings, Alger is more forward-looking, allowing the nation to grow and mature. Nations that struggle with adversity acquire power, independence, and virtue.

It is almost as if America could evolve toward near-universal morality. Out of chaos comes order. Almost all the characters whom the hero touches are improved by the time we leave them—even villains are often poorer but wiser. If the universe is not evolving toward economic, political, and moral improvement, neither is it backsliding into ruin. There is plenty of room for virtue to flourish.

Alger created a fictional republic. In it, there were no classes. all decent citizens spoke the same language and recognized the same values. Men produced themselves; they were not controlled by others. Proletarianization was escapable, and character was universal currency. The story of the fictional adolescent in the Republic and the narrative of the adolescent Republic were made one.

---

23) Henry Ward Beecher, (NewYork: Charles Scribner & Company, 1868), p. 452. He is discoursing on Thanksgiving as a fast day.

24) Howe, p. 6.

With such a combination of religious and secular formulations, of affirmation of tradition and stepping forth with courage into the unknown and dangerous waters of the industrial era, Alger may have inspired readers of the late nineteenth and early twentieth centuries. But he also seems to have stumbled upon a formula that works well as a political grammar. With this set of tools and symbols, we reaffirm something essential about who we think we are, face the unknown, and prepare to remake the unknown to fit our prior experiences. As we do so, we reconstitute both our prior and our current experience—our "truths" about the order of things.

Horatio Alger, Jr. unwittingly derived a formula to deal with hopes and anxieties in a rapidly changing world. He captured a form of discourse that not only spoke to many in the era in which he wrote but could still be spoken by later generations. The story, "fiction" by the time the ink was on the page, touched something vital. The narrative about our future and our past—and the relation between these—constitutes political identity. In it, Jeffersonian virtues meet the industrial era and survive. The country meets the city, and both win: Virtue and economic opportunity are wedded. The American jeremiad exhorts its audience to stand true to its principles and meet the forces threatening to undo the grand experiment. And the Republic of the creator, emerging from its rite of passage, triumphs.

Conclusion*

CATHY BIRKENSTEIN-GRAFF

The most remarkable thing to me about the American Dream of rags-to-riches success is the extent to which most people think they already understand it. The idea that America is a fair, open society that rewards merit (regardless of one's gender, race, or class background), and that individuals control their own economic fate is so pervasive that, like the air we breathe, it can easily be taken for granted. Even critics who expose the idea of individual responsibility as a lie or a myth-as an instance of propaganda that unfairly blames the poor for their poverty and legitimates wealth, and that thwarts the development of collective political action—usually assume that they are dealing with a set, already known entity. My goal in this dissertation, however, has been to defamiliarize this deeply familiar story and show that, in many (though not all) of its formulations, the American rags-to-riches story contains unexpected complexities and divisions that, largely because of their unexpectedness, have been widely overlooked.

But before reviewing these overlooked complexities it might be helpful to sketch in just how pervasive this idea of individual self-uplift has been. Ever since the ideal of self-made success was first articulated in the revolutionary era by writers like Benjamin Franklin, Thomas Jefferson, and Mason Locke Weems, it has been central to Americans' self-definition and self-image. At that time, the ideal of self-made success served as a critique of the Old World's rigid class structures. Whereas the individual in Europe and England, it was said, was doomed to the social station into which he was born, that same individual, in America, it was said, could rise as far and as high as his (though at this time almost never "her") talents would take him. And whereas the governing class in Europe and England was said to have been based on birth and wealth (as in the case of the "artificial aristocracies" about which Jefferson so

---

* Cathy Birkenstein-Graff, *Rereading the American Rags-to-Riches Story: Conflict and contradiction in the works of Horatio Alger, Booker T. Washington, and Willa Cather.* (Chicago: Loyola University, 2003), pp. 154-164.

often worried), America's ruling class was (or, as Jefferson saw it, should be) what Jefferson called a "natural" or "true aristocracy" based not on family lineage but on the individual's innate talents and virtues.

But it was Benjamin Franklin who hit on the recipe for upward mobility that had the deepest influence on the American national imaginary, and on the way average citizens think about such intimate matters as their bodies, desires, and feelings. In his own rags-to-riches autobiography, Franklin focused not just on his rise from poverty to wealth, but on what have come to be known as the Protestant, bourgeois virtues which ostensibly propelled that rise, and which have at their core a strict regime of bodily control and discipline. The prototypical self-uplift story, Franklin's autobiography shows him arriving penniless on the shores of Philadelphia and, because America is an apparently fair, meritocratic society, rising up the class hierarchy not only as a talented printer, scientist, and philosopher, but as a respected ambassador and politician. Yet those parts of the autobiography that have the most far-reaching consequences for my own dissertation are those that address Franklin's ongoing determination not simply to acquire money and status, but, in do doing, to conquer his body's aberrant emotions and impulses—to be industrious, temperate, orderly, frugal, chaste, and humble, to name just a few of the items in Franklin's list of 13 virtues. The term "work ethic" fails to capture the full depth of Franklin's program, which has at its core new ways of not only thinking about class mobility, but about the body and desire.

As it was first articulated in the eighteenth century, then, the self-uplift ideal ushered in a distinctly American sense of class fluidity, and what Lauren Berlant and Michael Warner have identified as a distinctly American compulsion toward emotional and physical effacement. It was a new type of world where individuals, by gaining systematic control over their ostensibly erratic bodies, also gained control over their socio-economic standing.

In the following century and a half, particularly between the Civil War and World War I, the period I focus on in this study, the ideal of individual, upward mobility was adapted to meet the nation's changing economic and cultural needs. When the Civil War ended, the family-run homesteads and small, agrarian communities that Jefferson envisioned for the nation gave way to large-scale industry, the proletarianization of labor, and to urban centralization and overcrowding. In addition, with the rise of mass industry, the intimate, small-scale apprenticeship system in which Franklin had trained as a printer was rendered obsolete. In this new, rapidly changing context, as I have shown, a special type of urban moral reformer emerged with the intention of simultaneously taming and disciplining the masses' potentially dissident energies and, by and large, of demonstrating the need to join, rather than fight against, the industrial, capitalist system. As I read them, the industrial self-uplift stories of the sort that I have focused on by Horatio Alger, Booker T. Washington, and Willa Cather were propagated in large measure to help fill this pressing void. The story, with its emphasis on becoming a self-reliant capitalist (or, in Washington's case, an independent farmer or small business-person) through such Franklinesque virtues as orderliness, sobriety, and self-restraint, fit well with the new crusaders' goal of channeling potentially dissident energies in ways that the bourgeois order could support.

For instance, in the novels of Horatio Alger, who modeled himself as a moral reformer through his work at the Children's Aid Society and the YMCA, we are presented with virtuous, self-reliant boys who climb the ladder of success by virtue of their self-control and discipline. In Alger's popular Ragged Dick series, for instance, the hero, Ragged Dick, only begins to climb the nation's meritocratic class hierarchy when, early in the first novel, he learns to stop squandering his money on immediate consumer pleasures like cigars, bawdy theatre, and expensive dinners, and to channel his efforts instead toward his future self-improvement. In the process, Dick defeats several dirty, shifty-eyed, downwardly mobile villains who devote themselves to gratifying their immediate impulses through various criminal, get-quick-rich schemes, and, in the case of some of Alger's more colorful villains, to a homosexually-coded form of image-conscious posturing and display. On Alger's view, then, it is in the individuals' own interest (rather than the interest of the state or of the rising capitalist-industrialist order), to behave in a respectable, disciplined manner. Respectable self-discipline leads to upward mobility, while vulgarly acting on impulse leads, as in the villains' case, to downward mobility and poverty.

These same lessons about the benefits of self-control can also be found in Booker T. Washington's autobiography, *Up From Slavery* and Willa Cather's *O Pioneers!*. In his autobiography, we saw, Washington shows himself rising up from slavery to freedom, and from poverty to middle-class respectability not just by working hard and setting his sights high, but also by learning to eat at regular hours, bathe on a regular basis, make his bed each morning, and so forth. In so doing, Washington claims that the Jim-Crow South is a fair, meritocratic society that seeks out talented, disciplined blacks and rewards them accordingly. In Cather's novel, which translates this theme of merit rewarded to the case of a female pioneer-farmer, the degree of bodily discipline is even more extreme. The novel's heroine, we saw, overcomes poverty and misogyny by virtue of her ability not only to manipulate the land as an abstract, capitalist commodity, but to gain control over her physical body. Besides sublimating her powerful sexuality into her entrepreneurial career, Alexandra Bergson berates herself and douses her body with cold water whenever she has what she considers to be a shameful sexual fantasy.

With the mass influx of immigrants into the nation at the turn of the last century, the ideal of individual self-uplift became a central feature of the immigrant experience. Lured by images of endless opportunity, these new immigrants not only sought out economic gain, but were "burning," as the Polish Jewish author, Anzia Yezierska, puts it, "to get calm and sensible like the born Americans"—to comport themselves in a certain type of controlled, disembodied way (110). Today, despite the massive changes in the American economy and the rise of consumer culture, the rhetoric of self-reliance and rags-to-riches success remains pervasive. In addition to being exported both to other nations with the spread of global capitalism, the rhetoric is still central to the American economy, the nation's dwindling welfare state, and mainstream American political discourse.

Regardless of their actual class backgrounds, political candidates continue to insist upon their humble, unpretentious roots—on a Tennessee farm for Al Gore, in an impoverished Austrian village for Arnold Schwartzenager, in a quasi-dysfunctional, "white-trash" family for Bill Clinton, and in small-town Midland, Texas for George W. Bush. Bush is a particularly interesting case, not only because, in his autobiography,

A Charge to Keep, he tells several rags-to-riches stories about successful Mexican immigrants, but also because he presents his own life itself, however improbably, as a rags-to-riches story. Andover, Yale, the Texas National Guard, the oil industry, the Texas Rangers, and his Texas governorship are all presented not as the instances of the unearned privilege and nepotism that they appear in fact to have been, but as proving grounds for self-reliance in which Bush learns, in his own words, that "I could make . . . my way, no matter where I found myself in my life"(22). The book's back cover shows a Charles Wesley painting of a rugged horseman making his way up a steep, jagged terrain—as if Bush's own life were a similarly difficult, upward struggle.

It is important to get the rags-to-riches narrative right, then, because it has had and continues to have an immensely powerful impact not only on mainstream politics and economics, but also on the way, at an extremely intimate level, we carry ourselves and experience desire. Indeed, in part because of its far-reaching impact, the rags-to-riches story has traditionally been treated by academics as a done deal—in effect, as a species of one-dimensional, sub-literary popular culture if not outright propaganda that, being already understood, requires little further investigation. In recent years, with the rise of popular culture studies, some of this dismissive attitude toward the uplift narrative has waned, and interesting new work has been done on what the narrative says about heterosexual masculinity and homosexuality, corporate capitalism, and the twentieth century welfare state[2)]. But even this new work, to my mind, has not gone far enough in challenging our standard picture of the rags-to-riches story, as I have tried to do in this dissertation. Whether they defend or critique the uplift story, most commentators overlook the ways that the story often contradicts and critiques itself.

The two groups of scholars that I have focused on in this dissertation see the rags-to-riches story whitewashing American life—even if they cannot agree on whether this whitewashing works to society's betterment or detriment. One the one hand, we have seen, many leftist academics

2) See Michael Moon for an analysis of homosocial bonding and its relationship to corporate capitalism in Horatio Alger's novels. See Bruce Robbins's as-yet-unpublished manuscript for an analysis of economic collectivism and the welfare state in the rags-to-riches narrative in general.

treat the narrative as a cruel hoax or myth that evades the nation's injustices and inequalities. On this view the narrative is a dangerous ideological construct that blames capitalism's victims for their victimization and masks the fact that wealth and privilege are often seized or inherited rather than earned through hard work. On the other hand, we have seen, other scholars who defend the uplift narrative, while conceding that it idealizes and sanitizes American life, claim that the narrative has to do so in order to offer a reformist, utopian vision of what, in the Jeffersian tradition, the nation should or ought to be. According to these defenders, the uplift narrative does evades the nation's brutal, harsh realities, but it does so not to legitimate those realities, but to encourage Americans to even the playing field and make opportunity equally available to everyone. But whether they critique the genre or defend it, scholars tend to see the genre as one that, for good or ill, romanticizes American life and ignores its oppressive underside. Whether they like it or loathe it, most scholars see the rags-to-riches story as a one-dimensional celebration of American meritocracy.

My goal in this dissertation, however, has been to show that, though many rags-to-riches stories are indeed one-sided romanticizations, many others are what Mihail Bakhtin would call dialogical (or multi-sided, multi-voiced) works that stage ultimately unresolved conflicts over their own meritocratic ideology. Through my analysis of Alger, Washington, and Cather, I show that works long considered one-dimensional and sometimes even child-like and simplistic are in fact permeated by unexpected conflicts over industrial, bourgeois capitalism and its allied ideals of corporeal discipline.

In Alger's novels, we saw, these oppositional voices emerge through what I identified as Alger's Caliban-style villains. Given the facts of the narrative that Alger himself presents, several of Alger's villains, rather than being definitively discredited, are accorded some of the most persuasive lines in Alger's oeuvre. Although readers are clearly supposed to side with Alger's sober, clean-cut heroes, several of the villains (many of whom are subtly associated with sexual deviance, and thus with Alger's recently discovered pederasty) express convincing critiques of industrial capitalism and the hero's respectable, middle-class manners and codes. Very often, when the hero has a success and moves a notch further up the class hierarchy, he is confronted by some angry villain who charges not only that the nation's free-enterprise system is rigged and unfair, but that the hero, in rising to success, is abandoning his working-class peers, or masking his ambitious will-to-power with a hypocritical veneer of respectable, bourgeois modesty.

The villains' accusations that society is rigged, we saw, directly challenge Alger's implied claim that it is open and fair. In addition, we saw that the villains' accusations that the hero's modesty is a ruse and that he is really abandoning his peers directly challenge Alger's persistent claim that his heroes—and, by extension, the American rags-to-riches ideology that Alger is championing—are "thorough[ly] democrat[ic]" (Alger, *Ragged Dick* 64). After all, what Alger celebrates in his novels are not only individuals who rise to success, but who on achieving it comport themselves in a humble, modest, and ostensibly democratic, egalitarian way that connects them to their humble roots. In effect, the successful, self-made man says to the nation's struggling masses (of which he had once been a part): "Yes, I may be successful, but as a truly democratic American I know deep down that I'm just like you and no better than anyone else." Hence, when the villains insist that the hero, in rising up the class hierarchy, is "puttin' on airs," that he is abandoning his working-class peers and aggressively trying to outshine them, they do more than offer superficial, surface-level critiques of the hero's personal disposition. Instead, they expose a fault line that Alger seems anxiously aware of in America's self-uplift ideology between its democratic and elitist, egalitarian and hierarchical impulses. While Alger assures readers that his heroes are "thorough democrats" who have "no desire to outshine [their] associates," he also repeatedly shows and insists on his heroes' profound "ambition": their unending desire to rise above their former associates and outdo them through a Darwinian form of free-market competition (Alger, Ragged Dick 64).

As a result, there is good reason to believe that Alger's villains are right. Were the hero not ambitious, and not intent on outshining his peers, he would have no motivation for rising up the class hierarchy, but instead would remain, as in the Old World ostensibly, in the impoverished station into which he was born. Although readers are encouraged to dismiss the villains' critiques as the whining complaints of capitalism's sore losers, these critiques are, if anything, borne out by details of the narratives themselves—and by Alger's anxious interventions as a narrator in his own texts. As a result, a gap opens up between the sanitized, celebratory way that Alger asks us to read his stories and the often convincing counter-viwes that his Caliban-villains offer.

Similar counter-views, we have seen, can also be found in Washington's *Up From Slavery*. But whereas the critical counter-views in Alger's novels emerge through Alger's angry villains, these counter-views enter Washington's text through stories and anecdotes highlighting the racial injustices that Washington otherwise plays down. No sooner does Washington proclaim that the post-bellum South gives the Negro "a man's chance in the commercial world" than he turns around and describes blacks being barred from various commercial establishments, sometimes under threat of white-mob violence (100). No sooner does Washington proclaim slavery a "school" that helped train and discipline black labor than he turns around and tells several stories of slave duplicity, and of slavery undermining blacks' vocational skills. In these ways and others, we saw, Washington undermines his own celebratory view of blacks pulling themselves up, as it were, by their bootstraps.

As in Agler's novels, then, there is a division in Washington's autobiography between what it proclaims and what it shows: between the didactic, accommodationist generalizations that Washington imposes on his text and several of the concrete stories that he tells. In other words (and this is perhaps explained by the prohibitions on black speech in Washington's Jim-Crow context), a gap opens up between what Washington claims about the South, and what his body and emotions recall: between his abstract claims celebrating American openness to black aspirations and his frightening recollection of being stared at by a group of white men on a segregated Southern train; between his abstract generalizations about blacks being "the most . . . faithful, law-abiding . . . people that the world has seen" and his tender, early-childhood memory of being awakened by his mother to be fed stolen chickens, an image that blends economic transgression with tender, maternal bonding.

And finally, in Cather's novel, we have seen, a similar split exists between the abstract and the concrete, capital and labor, and the disembodied lure of Enlightenment rationality and the downward pull of the body. Although Alexandra Bergson appears to triumph over poverty and over her misogynist brothers, her success is in fact marred when the son-like brother charged with carrying on her upward trajectory is murdered by an enraged, radical populist farmer. In addition, although Alexandra appears to triumph over her own sexuality by becoming what Cather presents as a brainy, head-centered entrepreneur, this triumph is compromised when her brother succumbs to his lust for a married woman. Hence, Cather's story of a woman's self-uplift is filled with divisions and complications that, perhaps because they are buried in the novel's complex, soap-opera like subplot, critics have failed to fully appreciate. Cather's novel is not only about the ascendance of capital over labor and the mind over the body, as critics have argued, but also about the apparently superseded forces of labor and the body rising up and, as in Raymond Williams's scheme, refusing to be domesticated and relegated to the residual, outmoded past.

Let me conclude by suggesting why I think it is important to notice these sorts of critical eruptions in the American uplift story. It is important, I think, because of what appears to be the increasingly widespread consensus in American culture and among many students not simply that the ideology of individual responsibility is true, but that it has no alternatives. Even my most counter-cultural looking students who come to class with nose rings and purple hair usually agree with their more conventional peers that America is a free and open society, that race (and gender) are no longer barriers to success, and that individuals, rather than being controlled by large social structures, are responsible for their own fate. With the decline of the Soviet Bloc, the rise of global capitalism, and the consolidation of media ownership, social critics often argue, alternatives to this ideology of individual responsibility are increasingly hard to find.

To read the story as I read it, however, with attention to its unacknowledged critiques and internal divisions, could help open up a space for a very different vision of American culture. In other words, by reading American Dream stories against the grain for their unnoticed divisions and counter-critiques, readers could see that, rather than being an immutable fact of nature, the American Dream ideology is one among many competing ideologies—an ideology that, by its own account, like any ideology, has its own passionate detractors and critics. It is often complained that, since the 1960s, American culture has been increasingly dominated by conservative, pro-market voices that allow for no opposition. Although I sympathize with this complaint, I have tried to show in this dissertation is that oppositional voices can be found buried all around us in the most unlikely of places: in our culture's most widely circulated, all-American discourses and stories.

편저자_박거용

서강대학교 영문학과를 졸업하고 동대학원에서 문학석사 학위를 취득했다. 캐나다 앨버타대학교에 방문 교수로 다녀왔고, 민주화를 위한 전국교수협의회 공동 의장 등을 역임하였으며, 현재 한국대학교육연구소 소장과 상명대학교 영어교육과 교수로 재직중이다.

『한국대학의 현실』 등을 집필하였고, 『러시아 형식주의』, 『미국문화 사상의 배경』, 『자신을 거부하는 문학』, 『보르헤스, 문학을 말하다』, 『역지사지 미국사』, 『문화유물론의 이론적 전개』와 『대학과 자본주의 국가』 등을 번역하였다.

RISEN FROM THE RANKS, OR HARRY WALTON'S SUCCESS.
개천에서 용났다: 해리 월튼 출세기

1판 1쇄 찍음 • 2011년 2월 15일
1판 1쇄 펴냄 • 2011년 2월 20일

편저자 • 박 거 용
발행인 • 정 현 걸
발　행 • 신 아 사
인　쇄 • 예지인쇄

출판등록 • 1956년 1월 5일 (제9-52호)
서울특별시 은평구 녹번동 28-36번지 2F
전화 (02)382-6411 • 팩스 (02)382-6401
홈페이지 • www.shinasa.co.kr
이메일 • shinasa@chol.com
ISBN 978-89-8396-726-8 (93840)

정가 **13,000** 원